Mothers and Daughters

Mothers and Daughters: The First Three Years offers a new perspective on female development and the origins of mother-daughter relationship pleasures and stresses.

In addition to emotional development and the impact of mothers' childhood memories on mother-daughter interactions, this book explores the enmeshment of personal and cultural themes about being female. Filled with mothers' intimate and surprising insights about the links between their own childhood memories and current interactions with their daughters that lead to solutions to typical mother-daughter conflicts, this book demonstrates the influence a little girl can have on her mother to discover new aspects of herself. In a changing world, where women are gaining more social, economic, and political power, this book illustrates how remnants of the past live on in the present.

Through the lens of female empowerment, mothers' memories are integrated with societal changes to shed new light on supporting the next generation of women.

Ilene S. Lefcourt established the Sackler Lefcourt Center for Child Development in 1982, was the director, led the mother-baby-toddler groups, and taught child psychiatry residents and psychoanalytic parent-infant psychotherapy trainees about her work for over 35 years. She is a faculty member at the Columbia University Center for Psychoanalytic Training and Research and is currently in private practice. Ms. Lefcourt is the author of *Parenting and Childhood Memories: A Psychoanalytic Approach to Reverberating Ghosts and Magic* (2021), *Mother-Baby Toddler Group Guide: A Psychodynamic Approach* (2022), and *When Mothers Talk: Magical Moments and Everyday Challenges from Birth to Three Years* (2024), Routledge.

"Ilene Lefcourt draws on over 35 years of a changing culture for women, while running parenting groups for mothers and their infants and toddlers. This is a well-spring of knowledge in the creation of optimal daughter-mother engagements that may help 'promote a little girl developing a strong, clear voice and becoming a woman who knows her own mind and expects her voice to be heard.' This book is an antidote to eons of female demure silence, fostered in the name of a 'femininity' that is destructive to the ability of women to hold their own in a patriarchal society.

The text is lively and available, with informative, emotionally telling vignettes of pitfalls and successes. It shows how women help each other in the groups, fostered by the author. The growth and responsiveness of these (lucky) children form the cherished centerpiece.

The book should be read by all mental health workers – not only child and family workers, but also therapists with mothers in their practices, and psychoanalysts, who hear sorrowful adult daughters rejecting being 'like my own mother.' The more we learn from the observations of fine practitioners like Ms. Lefcourt, the more we can appreciate the psychic complexities and range of mother-daughter bonding and their surrounding networks of internalized family figures. No longer are female-to-female dynamics unworthy of such detailed study, as in the past. Little girls can be helped toward a sturdier psychic future."

Rosemary H. Balsam, M.D., *Associate Clin. Professor of Psychiatry, Yale Medical School; Training and Supervising Analyst, Western New England Institute for Psychoanalysis; author, Women's Bodies in Psychoanalysis; editor of two volumes on the work of Hans Loewald, 2024; The Sigourney Award for psychoanalytic excellence, 2018.*

"*Mothers and Daughters: The First Three Years* is a treasure trove of wisdom that evokes childhood memories and leads to personal reflections that enrich the valuable information, and a deep attunement to a little girl's developing mind. This book invites mothers to claim their own minds and voices at a time when a baby's enormous needs can eclipse their own.

Drawing on 35 years of experience as the director of an early childhood center in New York City, Ilene Lefcourt generously shares her remarkable knowledge and her cogent understanding of the minds of mothers, babies, and toddlers in these crucial and formative early years of life. Ms. Lefcourt has a deep understanding of how intergenerational issues, when not reflected upon, can readily take up residence in the nursery. It is rare to read a book about early development that can have such a profound impact and be equally valuable to mothers and professionals."

Susan Coates, Ph.D., *Clinical Professor of Clinical Psychology, Columbia University Medical Center; Faculty, Columbia University Center for Psychoanalytic Training and Research. 2016, Can Babies Remember Trauma, Journal of the American Psychoanalytic Association. 8: 115–148. 2003, September 11 Trauma and Human Bonds. Routledge, London, New York. 1998, "Having a Mind of One's Own and Holding the Other in Mind."*

"Writing in a clear, articulate style, Lefcourt brings a sophisticated psychoanalytic perspective to early development without ever losing the immediacy of her subject – the everyday experience of mothers and daughters and how that experience is woven into the daughter's emerging sense of herself. Grounded in vivid descriptions drawn from her 35 years leading mother-baby groups, Lefcourt illuminates the role played by the mother's feelings and ideas about being female in her responses to her little daughter's behavior. She smoothly balances her accounts of struggles with those of successes, of conflicts with those of resolutions, offering gentle guidance to mothers who read the book. In addition to mothers of daughters, teachers, students of child development, and all of us who are daughters, will learn a great deal from this wonderful book. In addition to the powerful content – my passion these days is to bring psychoanalytic knowledge to front-line caregivers. Lefcourt does this beautifully."

Alexandra Harrison, M.D., *Training and Supervising Analyst, Boston Psychoanalytic Society and Institute; Assistant Professor of Psychiatry, Harvard Medical School; Founder, Supporting Childcare Givers – Infant-Parent Mental Health Training Nonprofit Throughout the World*

"*Mothers and Daughters: The First Three Years* is Ilene Lefcourt's most recent contribution to the literature on the early development of the parent-child relationship. This rich volume completes a quartet of books that draw upon Ms. Lefcourt's vast experience running a center for parents and their very young children. The book incorporates an enormous amount of literature and knowledge relating to the first three years of life, as well as being written in simple and elegant prose that makes complex ideas lucidly understandable.

Ms. Lefcourt reveals with clinical acuity, how aspects of a mother's history and her own unconscious representations can affect her relationship with her daughter. As in the best writing, this is always done through the technique of 'show, don't tell.' Ms. Lefcourt illustrates her book with moving vignettes: beautifully written composites which demonstrate how readily the mother-daughter relationship can activate a mother's unconscious and lead to troublesome repetitions of the past in the present. Given the greater likelihood of identification (or dis-identification) with a child of the same sex, it is no exaggeration to say that Ms. Lefcourt is easily one of the most informed insiders to report back from this domain. It is perhaps not surprising that this latest volume would focus specifically on the development of the mother-daughter relationship.

Ms. Lefcourt is a master at illuminating, in her vivid examples, which are always skillfully interpolated with developmental theory, how the past can become the present if a mother is not given the space to reflect upon the ways her daughter's very existence can trigger unconscious reverberations of the past. The fortunate mothers in her groups benefited not only from Ms. Lefcourt's astute observations as the leader of the group, but also from their own identifications with other mothers and daughters, and were able to develop the crucial tool of reflective function. Sensitively spotlighting the personal and cultural prism of gender to refract aspects of development, Ms. Lefcourt's latest book is actually a handbook that should be required reading for any and all mothers who are raising young daughters. It has depth, practicality, and most of all, it makes riveting reading."

Susan Scheftel, Ph.D., *Assistant Clinical Professor of Medical Psychology in Psychiatry Columbia Psychoanalytic Center for Training and Research; Former Program Chair Association for Psychoanalytic Medicine; Vice President, Margaret Mahler Foundation for Child Development, Author, Psychoanalytic Study of the Child, Papers on Childhood and Creativity*

"As a researcher who has been studying and following families at high risk for depression across generations for 40 years, it is absolutely refreshing to read Ilene Lefcourt's book about mothers and daughters. The detailed clinical stories are fascinating as they provide insights into the mechanisms, that is, how disturbances in mother-daughter relationships can begin. Most importantly, this book provides helpful directions on how relationships can be repaired and how the damage may have happened in the first place. Mothers with daughters of any age will recognize the origins of current interactions with their daughters and will benefit from their insights. In addition to being a useful parenting book, *Mothers and Daughters: The First Three Years* is an important enrichment to research studies."

Myrna M. Weissman, Ph.D., *Diane Goldman Kemper Family Professor of Epidemiology and Psychiatry. Columbia University Vagelos College of Physicians and Surgeons. Inventor of Interpersonal Psychotherapy. Weissman M. and Mootz, 2024. Interpersonal Psychotherapy: A Global Reach. Oxford Press*

Mothers and Daughters

The First Three Years

Ilene S. Lefcourt

Routledge
Taylor & Francis Group

LONDON AND NEW YORK

First published 2026
by Routledge
4 Park Square, Milton Park, Abingdon, Oxon OX14 4RN

and by Routledge
605 Third Avenue, New York, NY 10158

Routledge is an imprint of the Taylor & Francis Group, an informa business

© 2026 Ilene S. Lefcourt

For Product Safety Concerns and Information please contact our EU representative GPSR@taylorandfrancis.com. Taylor & Francis Verlag GmbH, Kaufingerstraße 24, 80331 München, Germany.

British Library Cataloguing-in-Publication Data
A catalogue record for this book is available from the British Library

ISBN: 978-1-041-17040-2 (hbk)
ISBN: 978-1-041-17039-6 (pbk)
ISBN: 978-1-003-68760-3 (ebk)

DOI: 10.4324/9781003687603

Typeset in Times New Roman
by KnowledgeWorks Global Ltd.

Contents

About the Author

Ilene S. Lefcourt brings her unique experience with mothers and daughters during the earliest years of their relationship to understanding female development. Ms. Lefcourt established the Sackler Lefcourt Center for Child Development in New York City in 1982. She was the director, led the mother-baby-toddler groups, and provided developmental consultation to parents for over 35 years. She taught child psychiatry residents and psychoanalytic parent-infant psychotherapy trainees about her work. Within a changing culture where women have more economic, political, and social power, Ms. Lefcourt explores the intimate, true stories about mothers' childhood memories and their current interactions with their baby and toddler girls.

Ms. Lefcourt is a faculty member at the Columbia University Center for Psychoanalytic Training and Research Parent-Infant Program. She is currently in private practice. She is the author of *Parenting and Childhood Memories: A Psychoanalytic Approach to Reverberating Ghosts and Magic* (2021), *Mother-Baby Toddler Group Guide: A Psychodynamic Approach* (2023), and *When Mothers Talk: Magical Moments and Everyday Challenges from Birth to Three Years* (2024). Website: ilenelefcourt.com

Acknowledgments

As the mother-daughter attachment relationship is central to a girl's development, so too are my professional attachment relationships central to my work. Selma Fraiberg's historic paper, "Ghosts in the Nursery," is a landmark for me, and her book *The Magic Years* is an essential perspective on a child's developing mind. *The Reproduction of Mothering* by Nancy Chodorow set the psychoanalytic discussion of motherhood in a sociological context – a major contribution. A special thank you to Rosemary Balsam and Myrna Weissman, whose expertise is not in early development, but each an expert in her field for believing that there is broad value in *Mothers and Daughters: The First Three Years*. Myrna Weissman's years of intergenerational depression research, her astute mind, numerous publications, and comments on multiple drafts, in addition to her everlasting support have been invaluable. I also wish to thank my infant mental health colleagues and friends, who gave generously of their knowledge and wisdom. They not only contributed to my thinking about the ideas at the core of this project, but to me personally. They shared their intimate stories and professional experiences. When uncertain, they reassured me. Their thoughtful comments on manuscript drafts at various points in the writing process were invaluable. Susan Coates' cogent ideas about childhood trauma and gender are integral to this book. Her thoughtful readings of several manuscript drafts helped to sculpt many details. I thank Alexandra Harrison for her indefatigable, international, intercultural work with mothers, babies, and community health-care providers. Her broad perspective and continuing collaborations help to clarify my thinking. Emily Jane Goodman's judicial and women's rights perspective informs my thinking. Her ongoing support and manuscript comments always encourage me. I frequently returned to Alicia Lieberman's classics (2018), "Angels in the Nursery" and *The Emotional Life of a Toddler* for her wisdom and inspiration. I relied heavily on Robert Michels' breadth of knowledge and intellectual acumen. Patricia Nachman's developmental and clinical clarity guided me throughout. Wendy Olesker's observations of early child development and male-female differences were an essential compass. Meriamne Singer's careful consideration of the ideas that I struggled with provided needed coherence and precision. I also wish to thank: Gail Davis, Toby Golick, Edith Gould, Judy Levitan, Robert Horn, Janice Leiberman, and Alanna Levine. Their thoughtful, and always helpful critiques of multiple drafts of *Mothers and Daughters* refined my thinking and honed the final text.

I thank the mothers and daughters who participated in my mother-baby-toddler groups over the many years. This book would not have been possible without them.

In addition, I thank Aline Dasilva, Tania Fulgencio, Joelle Lerouxelle, and Remy Montgomery for their international and cross-cultural perspectives.

I wish to acknowledge the extraordinary Margaret Mahler Child Development Board of Directors, whose outstanding work is aimed at increasing understanding of a child's psychological and emotional development during the first three years of life – the separation-individuation process.

I thank Betsy Lynn for her organizing, administrative assistance, and Kate Hawes, Zoe Meyer, Ayushi Awasthi, and the entire Routledge team for their commitment to publishing books about early child development and motherhood. A special thank you to Maria Fahey for her thorough editorial comments.

With deepest love and affection, I thank my daughter, daughter-in-law, and granddaughters for the precious mother-daughter times we have shared. I also thank my son, grandson, and son-in-law; they have helped to shape my ideas about mothers and daughters.

Introduction

The moment a woman hears "It's a girl!" her ideas about what being a girl means are set in motion. During the first three years of her daughter's life, a mother's own childhood experiences are reawakened and new ideas crystallize. She contemplates some ideas explicitly while others occupy her mind subliminally with the potential to emerge into conscious awareness. A mother's own activated childhood memories that mingle with current cultural themes contribute to her aspirations for her daughter. Historically, when girls did not have the opportunities that they have today and women could not achieve what they do today, being a "good girl," which meant obediently complying with prescribed gender roles, was overvalued. Today, in contrast, a girl knowing what she thinks, how she feels and the significance of how she feels, and believing that she is able to attain what she wants are clearly valued. A girl's first relationships create the foundation for achieving these goals. Early mother-daughter interactions can create enduring bedrock.

This book is about the earliest mother-daughter relationship. It is about the ways in which a mother's feelings and ideas about being female – both her reawakened little girl feelings and her adult woman feelings – are deliberately and inadvertently communicated to her daughter during the first three years of life. The clashes between mothers' goals for their daughters and the ubiquitous aspects of early child development that create conflict in mother-baby and mother-toddler interactions are discussed. Although universal aspects of early child development create the same typical parent-child conflicts with both girls and boys, with mothers and fathers (Lefcourt, I. 2021), the conflicts may have different meanings and outcomes. This book focuses on mothers and daughters. The child development theories presented offer an approach to the typical conflicts that emerge between mothers and daughters. The goal is to promote a little girl developing a strong, clear voice, and growing into a woman who knows her own mind and expects her voice to be heard. The inevitable mother-daughter conflicts that arise and the ways in which they can be resolved are described in an effort to promote sturdy development leading to success in the world and happiness in relationships.

For over 35 years at a neighborhood program in New York City, I led discussion groups for mothers with their babies and toddlers (Lefcourt, I. 2023). About 500 of the children were girls. The women were well-educated; some had jobs, some were on maternity leave, and others were uncertain about their future careers. Women

DOI: 10.4324/9781003687603-1

joined the groups with their first-born and later born babies and toddlers to learn more about child development, to meet other mothers, and for their children to be in a playgroup. Groups met once or twice weekly for an hour, for one to three years. Discussions focused on the underlying meanings of both the children's and the mothers' behavior and on the impact of the mothers' own childhood memories on interactions with their babies and toddlers. The mothers' childhood memories that emerged illustrated the ways in which the mothers' experiences as little girls were reactivated in interactions with their daughters. Mothers' memories and insights revealed solutions to everyday difficulties with their daughters. The mothers' reflections illustrated the impact little girls have on their mothers to see the world through their daughters' eyes.

In order to maintain confidentiality, all examples are disguised, fictionalized composites of the participating mothers and daughters in my groups. While each mother and her daughter are unique and their histories and current life circumstances are specific, the examples presented illustrate universals about mothering and being a little girl. In addition, scenes from movies and books are used to provide a framework to discuss how personal and cultural themes are enmeshed. Furthermore, while it is evident that the father-daughter relationship has a profound influence on a little girl's development, and in every family where there are two parents each relationship influences the others, and when there are siblings, grandparents, and other caregivers they also influence early development, this book focuses on the mother-daughter relationship.

Between 1982 and 2020, the years in which I led mothers' discussion groups, the voice of feminism grew louder. Legal and political battles about equal rights for women were fought; many were won and others continue. Women's Studies programs at universities expanded. The idea of date-rape was introduced and legally recognized. The "Me Too" movement enabled women to report sexual harassment and rape that had often gone unacknowledged and unpunished. Guidelines about sexual consent were debated; some were established. Women gained more political, legal, and economic power. These changes influenced mother-daughter interactions; little girls had more potential, and this was communicated to them.

As I began to write about my work with mothers and their little girls, the 1958 movie *Gigi* came to mind. When I was a young girl, the opening scene in 1900 Paris painted a vivid picture of a girl's value. At the time I had been enchanted, (as were the women who participated in an informal survey), but now realize that the surface pretty picture concealed a disturbing subtext. While girls frolicked with abandon, the song "Thank Heaven for Little Girls" seemed adoring, as might be imagined from the title. In sharp contrast, the next words of the song are devaluing but went unnoticed: "Thank heaven for little girls … so helpless and appealing … without them what would little boys do." Today, what jumps out about these words is the idea that little girls appearing helpless are appealing, and that their purpose and value is the pleasure that they provide for boys. For many girls without awareness, the diminishing words were absorbed as a prescription. For some women, the unacknowledged words were part of their belittled identity that they wanted to shed. Yet, *Gigi* won nine Oscars and in 1991 was selected by the Library of

Congress to be preserved in the United States National Film Registry. Many of the ideas about being a girl that are dramatized in the movie have also been preserved in our cultural unconscious and passed from one generation to the next. As illustrated throughout this book, even ideas that mothers reject intellectually can remain emotionally active and be communicated to their daughters.

During interactions with their daughters, without awareness, rejected ideas that are embedded in a mother's personal history and the current culture can emerge. Feelings connected to rejected ideas can erupt. Today when watching *Gigi*, Maurice Chevalier singing "Thank Heaven for Little Girls" may evoke disturbing feelings. He may be seen as a predator: a dapper wolf preying on little girls and women. In fact he brags about his romantic conquests and sneers with contempt at unmarried women. In the past his swagger may have been appealing and imply protection of the girls in the background excitedly giggling while they play. His contempt for unmarried women may have been shared by the viewing public so it went unnoticed. When Gigi skips past him and drops her books at his feet, he rescues them. She pauses cautiously, but compliantly. Her story unravels. Gigi is being raised to be the kept mistress of a wealthy man. She is surrounded by lovers, but denies any desire of her own. At first she defiantly rejects the mistress arrangement proposed by an eligible man and he walks away. Gigi then accepts the role which moves him to surrender and offer marriage to her. Marriage is portrayed in the film as a path to dignity. Although Gigi wins marriage and respect, she sacrifices her own vitality; she assumes a stiff, haughty posture.

Decades later, a variation of these themes was depicted in the 1990 film *Pretty Woman*. The heroine is a street prostitute in present-day California who finds true love with her wealthy, confirmed bachelor client who dresses her elegantly, introduces her to opera, polo, and fancy French restaurants, and offers her financial security. When she ultimately rejects his offer to be his mistress, he proposes marriage and dramatizes rescuing her. She declares, "I will rescue you right back." In both movies, produced more than thirty years apart, in settings almost a hundred years apart, marriage is portrayed as a measure of a women's self-worth and is cloaked in fantasies of happily-ever-after.

In 2020 the song "One Margarita" was released. More than half a century after *Gigi* it is in many ways a new version of Gigi's song "The Night They Invented Champagne." As Gigi enjoys her first sips of champagne, her sexual passion is awakened and revealed in a naïve, childlike manner. Although the sexually explicit lines that quickly went viral "Gimme one margarita, I'ma open my legs; gimme two margaritas, I'ma give you some head…" are more sexually graphic, than those that Gigi sings, both songs depict alcohol dissolving barriers for girls to pursue sex. The changes in popular culture, including more explicit sexual content in songs, films, and books, the clothes of young girls that expose bare shoulders, midriffs, and legs, and sexually evocative teen videos on Tik Tok, may conceal the fact that while many things have changed some old ideas about what it means to be female remain.

In 2023, the film *Barbie* captured the imagination of four generations of daughters: grandmothers, mothers, teenagers, and little girls. The millions of viewers, billions of dollars generated, and popular and scholarly commentary were stagger-ing. Why did a movie about a doll for girls get so much attention? One answer is that the little girl in a woman lives on in her memories and continues to influence her.

The courtships dramatized in the movies *Gigi* and *Pretty Woman* may be cari-catures of dating rituals and gender roles from the past that persist transformed superficially. Similarly, remnants of the past are intertwined in mother-daughter interactions. Awareness of the seemingly paradoxical aspect of memories, an inter-weaving of past and present, can promote self-understanding and a greater under-standing of a little girl and early mother-daughter interactions.

This book discusses the ways in which ideas about being female – those that are embraced, those that are rejected, and those that are embedded in childhood memories – are handed down from mother to daughter, often without awareness, during the first three years of life. It explores the process by which a baby girl be-gins to self-identify as female. This book is also about the ways in which having a baby girl influences a woman's evolving ideas about herself and what it means to be female.

Contemporary picture books for babies and toddlers tell the women's libera-tion story and praise its leaders. Scholarly and inspirational books about women's achievements include the social and cultural changes that have occurred. Filled with mothers' insights about the links between their own childhood memories and current interactions with their daughters, this book illuminates the influence that little girls can have on their mothers to see the world and themselves differently and lead to solutions to typical mother-daughter conflicts that empower their daughters.

1 Mother-Daughter Relationship Themes

Novels, memoirs, and films about mothers and daughters that enchant and inspire, or terrify and horrify, capture our imagination because they portray something real about mother-daughter relationships. *Mommie Dearest*, a memoir written by the renowned actress Joan Crawford's daughter, Christine Crawford, is a good example: few mothers actually try to strangle their young daughters, but many daughters feel emotionally strangled by their mothers (Crawford, C. 1978). Many films and books about mothers and their daughters embody the ongoing complexities of the mother-daughter relationship.

There are four entwined themes that can help us to understand mother-daughter interactions: (1) Being the Same and Being Different, (2) Attachment Needs and Autonomy Strivings, (3) Identifying with and Individuating from, and (4) Pleasing Oneself and Pleasing Others. These themes also help to understand the multiple meanings of mothers' childhood memories that get activated and influence mother-baby and mother-toddler interactions. Although the themes are conceptualized in terms of opposites, and the interpersonal and intrapsychic dynamics that they describe have variable concrete and abstract components, they co-exist and simultaneously influence the behavior of both the mother and the child. The themes help to understand the typical mother-daughter conflicts that arise during the first three years and ways to resolve them that promote sturdy emotional development and fulfilling motherhood.

Being The Same and Being Different

Being identified as female is the first documented designation of a baby being the same as her mother. A mother's reactions to having a baby girl are influenced by what being female means to her and by what being female means in her family and in the larger world. Furthermore, a mother's reactions to having a daughter may be influenced by what it means to the mother that her baby is the same sex as she is. With and without the mother's awareness, being the same sex can have a profound impact on their interactions. For the mother, the sex of her baby may be the fulfillment of a wish, a disappointment, or may elicit feelings that neutralize a prior preference. In other words, in response to her actual baby, a mother's wished-for baby can fade as her actual baby becomes claimed by her as "my baby."

DOI: 10.4324/9781003687603-2

Being the same as someone else is often valued; it can be validating. Adolescent girls play being the same; for example, dressing alike or speaking a secret language to create an exclusive private universe of two. Often friendships and romances are kindled by shared interests, preferences, and philosophies. Similarities can be attractive, but they can also intensify rivalry. Kaitlin explained during a mothers' group:

"I always thought I had beautiful hair. It is still my best feature. Fiona is only two and a half, but already she has beautiful, long, thick hair just like mine. People are always admiring her hair. No one even notices my hair anymore. I can't believe I feel competitive with my own daughter. I remember when I was a teenager my mother always complained, "Men used to look at me, but when we are together they only look at you." I guess I feel the same way my mother did."

Maya added to the discussion:

"Yvette is 3 years old and has beautiful long blond, wavy hair with natural highlights like her dad. I wish I had her hair. I have short, mousy, brown straggly hair, but it doesn't matter to Yvette. Yesterday she told me that she does not like her hair and wants her hair to look like mine. Maybe she knows how envious I am. I hope she will enjoy her beautiful hair when she is older, but I can't help that I wish I had her hair."

For Kaitlin, her daughter having hair that is admired diminishes the positive feelings that she has about her own hair, fuels her rivalry with her daughter, and reminds her of her mother's similar feelings about losing the attention of men. Maya's daughter's hair is "beautiful," but her daughter wants the same kind of hair that her mother has, "short, brown, straggly hair." She wants to be the same as Mommy. Maya feels guilty that she envies her daughter and worries that her envy is contributing to Yvette wanting the same kind of hair that she has, "straggly hair." Maya wants to do what she can to help Yvette enjoy something beautiful about herself.

Though a mother and daughter are alike in that they are both female, they have different traits. The ways in which the differences are assimilated into the mother-daughter relationship can be a complex process. A mother can feel enhanced by her daughter having a desirable trait that she does not have. The appealing trait that her daughter has can contribute to the mother's expanding positive sense of self. However, a coveted trait that her daughter has can also evoke painful feelings of inadequacy and envy. The attention that a mother craves and that her cute baby gets from the world can be vicariously enjoyed by the mother, but can also trigger life-long feelings of not being seen. Mothers and daughters both being female is a significant sameness in the context of multiple differences.

Being the same sex can intensify reactions to differences and make it difficult for a mother to imagine her daughter's different perspective. Dawn had long, slim legs; she had a dancer's body. When she was a little girl, she was always chosen to be in the front line during ballet performances. Her three-year-old daughter's body type was different: it was like her father's – short and stocky. Dawn described her reaction:

"Lyra likes to twirl around in her pink tutu, but it just makes her look fat. I feel so guilty. I don't criticize her, but I do have a strong negative reaction. I cringe every time she eats a cookie. My husband thinks she looks adorable and says, 'she may not be a ballerina, but why is that so painful for you? She's having so much fun. She may never have a beautiful figure like you have and her life may be very different from yours. Maybe she will be the CEO of a major corporation.' In my world, a girl having a beautiful figure is essential; if I had a son, maybe I would feel differently. If he was not tall and thin, I wouldn't care. I'm glad my husband sees the world and Lyra differently than I do. Maybe she won't go nuts like I do every time she gains a pound."

The body differences between Dawn and her daughter activated Dawn's painful feelings about her own body "imperfections." In addition, Dawn was struggling to imagine Lyra's life being satisfying while being so different from her own life.

Mother and daughter, both being female, can intensify reactions to differences and sometimes create feelings of emotional distance. However, mother-daughter differences can also become part of a mother's expanding positive sense of self and contribute to seeing herself and the world differently.

During a lively mothers' group discussion about the words for genitals that mothers choose to teach their daughters, Marina described related childhood memories:

"Arial is only 11 months. I know many mothers from the beginning teach their daughters the word vagina. My mother only said the words, 'down there' and 'private parts.' It was a long time ago and things were different for women. Maybe if my mother used other words I would feel differently about many things. She never even talked to me about getting my period. I never wanted to learn all the specific words for 'down there' until Arial was born. Now I've learned all the words, but I still don't know what words to teach her. I think it's important that we can talk about her body more specifically than 'down there' or 'private parts.' What she is touching is her vulva. It's a part of her body that she has noticed and likes to touch, but I don't feel comfortable saying that word. Vulva seems too sexy. Labia is too medical. Vagina is incorrect. No word feels right. I want Arial to feel comfortable with all the parts of her body. I don't want her to have the same problems that I have. I'm amazed that I am talking about this at all. I don't usually talk about things like this."

This example highlights aspects of the mother's expanding sense of self that include: a change in her wanting to learn words for female genitals that she had never wanted to learn before her daughter was born, talking about things that she had never wanted to talk about before, new reflections about interactions that she had and did not have with her own mother, the ways in which she was envisioning what she and her daughter could talk about as being different from what she and her mother had talked about, and her goals for her daughter to be different in some ways than she is. In addition, Marina noted that cultural changes had led to mothers referring to female genitals as vagina instead of "down there" or "private parts," but her childhood experiences with her own mother were still influencing her. She could not decide what words to teach her daughter.

While family members may talk about body similarities and differences, including eye color, hair color, and right or left-handedness, and they may identify specific traits like dimples and freckles, and note differences in size, they tend to talk less about their feelings about the similarities and differences. Some comparisons that trigger intense feelings may not be talked about at all. A mother's growing love for her daughter gradually deepens her self-reflection and insight about her reactions to all of the ways in which she is similar to and different from her daughter. Understanding how her little girl feels about the similarities and differences may be important and be revealed.

A mother may wonder how she can influence her daughter's developing awareness of and attitudes toward the traits that describe her – those traits that are different and those that are similar to her own. The first step in helping her child is the mother's awareness of her own feelings about the traits and her related childhood memories. Among the most surprising and difficult mother-daughter differences for a mother to assimilate into her relationship with her daughter may be the ways in which her baby or toddler girl is different from the one that she had wished for or had imagined.

Attachment Needs and Autonomy Strivings

Mother-baby and mother-toddler relationships have been studied extensively in terms of attachment – a needed emotional bond. Feelings of safety are the core of a baby's attachment to her mother, and feelings of self-worth emanate from it. Researchers have investigated the details of a baby's attachment to her mother, whether maternal care is primary, shared, or delegated. Attachment research has focused on mother-baby interactions, the baby's interaction strategies for satisfying attachment needs, and the ways in which a mother's thoughts about her own history of attachment relationships influence her interactions with her baby (Bowlby J. 1958; Ainsworth, M., Blehard, M., and Waters, E. 1978; Main, M., Kaplan, N., and Cassidy, J. 1989). The ways in which a mother thinks about her own satisfactions and hardships in relationships influence her interactions with her baby and thereby her baby's attachment. A mother's sensitive caretaking has been found to promote her child's security of attachment.

Mother-baby and mother-toddler attachment relationships have behavioral and psychological elements. The internal emotional bond that a mother and her daughter feel can be seen in the details of their ongoing interactions that include proximity seeking, mutual smiles that evoke delight, tender touching, the mother providing safety and comfort and the child feeling safe and being comforted, stress reactions to separation, and well-being when reunited. A baby's ongoing expectations of care – including protection, comfort, understanding, and love – lead to attachment behavior. Mother-baby attachment is ubiquitous, but the specific interactions are unique for each mother-baby pair. During the first three years of life, the interaction details of this robust system evolve.

As maturation unfolds, the mother-baby attachment relationship becomes increasingly complex. We can imagine the complexity in a baby's mind: '*I am safe, but sometimes I get hurt. I am loved, but sometimes Mommy disapproves of my behavior. I have so much to learn from Mommy, but sometimes I hate learning to do what Mommy wants and do what I want to do. Mommy and I love each other, but sometimes we feel angry; but after we get angry, we get un-angry. I have things I want to do away from Mommy; then I want to be close to Mommy. When Mommy and I are not together, Mommy thinks about me and I think about Mommy. This is one way to feel close.*' A baby's growing attachment to her mother is a synthesis of the baby's expectations to be protected when frightened, comforted when distressed, and her thoughts, feelings, and desires to be understood. She expects to be able to share her pleasures with her mother and derive feelings of self-worth from their interactions. However, the mother-baby attachment relationship is further complicated by a baby's autonomy strivings, which sometimes support attachment interactions, but other times create conflict.

Babies and toddlers have physical, cognitive, and emotional needs outside the attachment matrix. A baby's physical abilities rapidly develop; she vigorously pursues her maturational urges to roll over, sit, crawl, and walk. When her diaper is being changed, she twists and squirms to be free of constraint while her mother wrestles to contain the overflowing poop. Pleasurable play with Mommy that gratifies her attachment needs while her diaper is being changed can momentarily temper her autonomous activities. An interesting toy to explore during diaper changes can support her autonomy and, at the same time, engage her cooperation. Autonomy strivings and attachment needs can conflict, can co-exist, and can be supported simultaneously.

Babies and toddlers are curious to explore the world around them, to figure out how things work, and to test their discoveries. As they venture further away physically from their mothers, they stay emotionally connected through both a developing internal sense of Mommy and ongoing interactions with Mommy called "secure base re-fueling" and "social referencing" (Mahler, M., Pine, F., and Bergman, A. 1955). While playing at a slight distance, a return to cuddle with her mother, a glance across the room, or a mother-baby mutual gaze that communicates their ongoing awareness of each other and refuels their internal bond enables the child's explorative play to continue. Such ongoing mother-daughter interactions communicate and reinforce holding each other in mind and support both autonomy strivings and attachment needs (Coates, S. 1998).

Baby and toddler behavior can also be understood in terms of co-existing attachment needs and autonomy strivings that conflict and create both interpersonal conflict and internal intrapsychic conflict. Babies and toddlers have strong likes, dislikes, and intentions that are not always aligned with those of their mothers.

Throughout early development their autonomy increases, their access to the world around them broadens, their curious explorations intensify, and their intelligence and world knowledge expand. Their investigations may include filling a cup and spilling and splashing its contents. Water is water, but a puddle on the floor and splashed water look different from a cup full of water. Their gravity experiments may include throwing food and plates on the floor and the discovery that everything falls, but food lands softly and plates crash. For both mothers and toddlers, new pleasures and new challenges arise.

A baby girl crawls, walks, and then runs away from her mother, and at the same time, her attachment to her mother intensifies. Although the determination and creativity with which a baby pursues her autonomous wishes and at the same time maintains her attachment to her mother serve her well, at times her behavior may seem contradictory and create conflict with her mother. In one moment she appears independent, and in the next, clingy. Looking at behavior and mother-child interactions through the lens of girl empowerment can be useful. For example, when a baby crawls toward an object that is not to be touched, such as an electric socket, stops and gets her mother's attention, smiles, and then accelerates toward the socket, she is signaling an intention to touch the socket. Although signaling an intention to touch a socket might look like defiance, it elicits protection, an attachment response, and indicates that she is letting her mother know that she is learning the rule. The baby's complex communication can create a mother-baby joint focus of attention on the baby's autonomous thoughts about touching the socket and simultaneously about learning not to do so. The baby's signal includes her memory of her mother's rule, a smile to make the interaction playful, and the expectation of being stopped that is revealed when she increases her speed toward the socket after she gets her mother's attention. A baby signaling an intention to do something that her mother has prohibited indicates that the mother's prohibition is becoming the baby's own self-prohibition. The interaction also reflects the baby's internal conflict and creative compromise between her wish to please Mommy – an aspect of attachment – and wishes to assert autonomy and please herself. The mother-baby interaction provides an opportunity for the mother to reinforce the rule, validate that her baby is learning the rule, and support her baby's autonomy with words such as: "I see you remember, there is no touching the socket. I will help you to stop yourself." In this way, both autonomy strivings and attachment needs are supported.

During the first three years, as attachment needs and autonomy strivings coalesce, they also clash. Babies and toddlers need to feel loved, approved of, and protected by their mothers, and at the same time, they strive to feel autonomous and self-reliant. In one moment they push their mothers away, and in the next seemingly cannot get close enough. In one moment they defy their mothers, and in the next they seek their mother's approval. Internal conflict emerges and mother-daughter conflicts escalate. Recognizing the attachment needs and autonomy strivings that contribute to mother-daughter interactions can help to resolve both the internal and the interpersonal conflicts in ways that promote both a little girl's security of attachment and her autonomy.

Identifying With and Individuating From

The process by which a baby girl develops a unique personality includes both identifying with and individuating from her mother. Her developing personality and sense of self are an integration of both. In other words, a little girl takes some of her mother's thoughts, feelings, and behaviors that make up her mother's personality and are expressed in their interactions to be part of herself, and simultaneously becomes a distinct individual with her own thoughts, feelings, and ways of being. In these ways she remains close to her mother and at the same time distances herself. She both identifies with her mother and individuates from her mother.

A useful way to think about the early process of a girl's identifying with and individuating from her mother is by further exploring the details sketched above about learning codes of behavior. During the first three years, a baby learns many do's and don'ts of everyday life. A primary motivation to learn the codes of behavior that her mother teaches is to earn her mother's approval – an aspect of attachment. Gradually, a little girl learns most of the things that her mother explicitly teaches her, such as no hitting, consideration for others, no throwing food on the floor, and, as described above, no touching electric sockets. Because babies and toddlers want and need their mothers' approval they become more self-observant and self-reflective. This process is part of a baby's identifying with her mother; just as her mother notices when her daughter throws food, her baby starts to notice her own intention to throw food. She is thinking about her own thoughts – a major achievement. When a baby signals an intention to do something that she knows her mother disapproves of, such as throwing food on the floor, she expects that her mother will stop her. Signaling her mother indicates that she wants her mother's help to stop herself, otherwise, she might not signal her mother before she does it. Importantly, a baby signaling her intention to do something that has been prohibited indicates that her mother's prohibition is becoming the baby's own self-prohibition and can be reinforced by her mother, "I see you remember, no throwing food on the floor."

When a baby signals an intention to do something that she knows will be disapproved of, she reveals the tensions between her attachment needs and autonomy strivings, and between identifying with and individuating from her mother. Elements of each can be supported by saying such things as, "I see you are learning to stop yourself from throwing food. I know you like to throw, here is a ball to throw." Even while a behavior is being disapproved of, the love and approval that are an ongoing part of the mother-baby relationship support the baby's feelings of self-worth. Said another way, while a little girl individuates, she also identifies with her mother's supportive and empathic responsiveness, which becomes part of her own ongoing positive sense of self.

A little girl's developing sense of self is a synthesis of her individuating from and identifying with her mother and includes, *I am a girl.* Being seen as a girl starts at the beginning of a girl's life. She is told in a multitude of implicit and explicit ways that she is a girl, and she begins to self-identify as a girl. During the first three years, she also learns a great deal about what it means to be a girl; much of which she learns from her mother. Some of her experiences are: *I am a girl and*

Mommy is a woman. Only mommies can be pregnant and feed their babies milk from their breasts. When I grow up, I will be a woman. These ideas relate to a little girl's dawning awareness of the power of a woman's body to conceive a baby, be pregnant, give birth, and make milk to feed her baby. A little girl's response to this information may be anywhere between amazing and an everyday fact of life. Another experience a little girl has is: *Mommy and I wear dresses. When I wear a dress, everyone says that I look pretty. Only girls wear dresses.* A dress becomes a symbol of femininity that is frequently invoked by mothers, fathers, grandparents, society at large, and little girls. While the attention little girls get when they are wearing dresses focuses on surface appearance and may bring attention to the importance of being pretty, the specific meaning of each interaction may be different, and can have elements of: I adore you. You are wonderful. Being a girl is great.

At the same time a baby girl is identifying with her mother, she is individuating and discovering their separateness of minds. A baby's explorations of their separateness of minds often cause the conflicts that are typical during the first three years. A baby's interactions with her mother that assert and substantiate their separateness of minds and the inevitable conflicts that arise are part of individuating. For example, it is story time and an 11-month-old baby points to the bookcase indicating a book choice. Her mother gets the book, but the baby rejects it and points again. Her mother gets the book she believes her baby is pointing to now and the baby rejects this book also. This interaction is repeated several times until the baby accepts a book. Mothers often experience this frequent mother-baby interaction as their baby's deliberate attempt to annoy them, or their own inability to understand their baby. However, another way to understand the baby's behavior is that she is asserting what is in her mind, practicing having something in mind, changing what is in her mind, demonstrating that what is in her mind can be different from what is in her mother's mind, and her mother cannot know what is in her mind until she lets her mother know. The baby has created an interaction that asserts and substantiates the separateness of their minds. In the moment that the baby accepts the book that her mother offers, the baby may experience her mother giving her exactly what she is imagining: *Yes, I want this one.* Moments of heightened awareness of their separateness of minds, combined with actively getting exactly what she is imagining, promotes both attachment and individuation.

Baby and toddler girls both identify with their mothers and individuate from them. Mothers and daughters both being female influences both the identifying and the individuating processes and can intensify the tensions between them.

Pleasing Oneself and Pleasing Others

Narcissism and masochism are prominent themes in our culture. To use everyday language, being "self-centered" and being a "push-over" are both criticized. Bullying others to control them for one's own satisfaction or benefit is censured. Being a sucker is criticized; however, generosity toward others, even to one's own disadvantage, is sometimes idealized and at times may be considered heroic. What is an optimal balance between pleasing oneself and pleasing others? How is that balance achieved between mothers and their daughters during the first three years?

Motherhood has long been discussed in the context of pleasing oneself and pleasing others. Impassioned arguments about the merits and flaws of the children's book, *The Giving Tree*, by Shel Silverstein (which has sold over 14 million copies), exemplify polarized positions about pleasing oneself and pleasing others. In the book, the tree nurtures the boy throughout his life with shade, apples, and branches. The boy leaves the tree, builds his life, and returns when he needs something from the tree. At the end of the story the boy is a weary old man and the tree that gave her apples and limbs to the boy, is now a stump. The old man rests on the stump; the tree is happy. This story has been portrayed by some as a depiction of the universal life process, by others as an abusive mother-child relationship, and by others as a metaphor for mother-child secure attachment. Mother-child interactions, similar to the boy and the tree, include giving to and taking from each other.

Arianna was nine months old and liked to feed bites of her cookie to her mother rather than eat them all herself; she wanted to share her cookie with her mother. Her mother Julieta felt that eating the cookie crumbs Arianna offered to her was submitting to her daughter. Deciding whether to please her daughter by eating the cookie pieces or to reject the cookie was difficult for Julieta. Childhood memories that were triggered helped to resolve her conflict. Julieta recounted:

> "I have a younger brother. When we were little my mother always made me do what he wanted. She said it was because he was a baby, but I always thought it was because he was a boy. My mother always does what my father wants. I always struggle to do what I want, but often defer to my husband. When I don't eat the cookies, I feel like I'm rejecting her. Maybe it's good for Arianna to please herself by feeding me. Maybe she wants to please me the same way I please her. I do like the cookies. I really wouldn't be submitting to her if I ate the cookies."

Upon reflection, Julieta was able to differentiate current interactions with her baby from childhood memories of feeling compelled to submit to her baby brother. She decided to eat the cookies; her daughter was gratified to be like Mommy.

Whining is sometimes a toddler's compromise between two opposing wishes: the wish to please her mother by renouncing a wish and the wish to demand something to please herself. Gretchen, 26 months old, asked for more cookies. Her mother Sybil said, "Gretchen, I've told you no more cookies; don't ask me again." Gretchen whined for more cookies. Gretchen's wish to please herself by continuing to want and furthermore to demand another cookie conflicted with her wish to please her mother by not asking for or even wanting another cookie. Her internal conflict was revealed by her using a whining voice, rather than her regular assertive voice. Sybil was also conflicted; she preferred that Gretchen not want another cookie. If Gretchen did not want another cookie, she would not ask for one and Sybil would not need to say "No" to her daughter. Sybil wanted to please her daughter: "I don't like to say no to her, but she had enough." Sybil's internal conflict between pleasing her daughter or saying "No" was embedded in her statement, "Don't ask me again." Furthermore, Sybil wanted her daughter to be assertive in the world, but not assertive with her. Both Sybil's and Gretchen's internal conflicts about whom to please were being negotiated interpersonally. Sybil became aware of her own conflicts and acknowledged Gretchen's:

> "I know you really want another cookie. You are asking in your squeaky voice instead of your strong voice because I said, 'Don't ask me again.' I should not have said that. You really like these cookies. I always want to know what you like, what you want, and what you think. You can always tell me. Tomorrow, you can have another cookie."

These may seem like subtle and complex distinctions for a two year old, but having them in the mother's mind was useful to resolve the conflict between mother and daughter about more cookies. The mother acknowledged and validated her toddler wanting more cookies, supported her daughter knowing her own mind as well as her self-assertiveness, addressed the whining, and reaffirmed the limit – no more cookies.

Jenny and her mother also negotiated a conflict between pleasing oneself and pleasing the other. Jenny was 18 months old. Her cousin wanted to hug her, but Jenny did not want to be hugged, pushed him away, and ran to her mother. Family members watching this interaction were critical of Jenny for rejecting her cousin. They accused her of hurting his feelings and being just like her mother. Jenny's mother wanted to support Jenny, was offended by the accusations, and did not want her daughter to be viewed as "a cold fish." Nevertheless she decided it was important to support Jenny's decision to please herself and not be hugged.

Everyday mother-baby and mother-toddler interactions include both the mother's and the child's decisions about pleasing oneself and pleasing the other. A child's wishes to please her mother may conflict with her wishes to please herself. A mother may be in conflict about pleasing herself or pleasing her daughter. As a mother makes decisions in the moment about what she wants to teach her daughter about pleasing others and pleasing herself, the demands of her culture, and her personal history influence her decisions. Mother-baby interactions about pleasing oneself and pleasing others extend to other family members, and when toddler interactions with peers increase, decisions about pleasing oneself and pleasing others extend further. A mother's personal style of pleasing herself and pleasing others in romantic, platonic, and work relationships influences what she teaches her daughter. Cultural biases about a girl pleasing herself or pleasing others may also have an impact on mother-daughter interactions. A mother's own childhood memories can provide an additional perspective. Genevieve remembered:

> "One important lesson my mother taught me, and I want to teach to my daughter is: sometimes it's okay to do something that is important to you even if it makes someone else sad. My older sister always wanted to wear my clothes. Usually it was okay with me, but for my 14th birthday my father

bought me a new purse that I loved and my sister wanted to use it. I didn't want her to, but I never would have said "No" to her. My mother said, 'Your purse was a special gift to you from Daddy. You don't need to let her use it, even if it makes her sad or angry.' There is so much pressure on girls to be nice, I think they need to know it's okay to satisfy themselves. I often remember my mother's words."

Genevieve's mother's words reverberated throughout her life and were frequently recalled by the other mothers who heard about her memory. Childhood memories, including both their disturbing and satisfying elements, can provide important information to understand current mother-baby and mother-toddler interactions and can help mothers to make decisions about pleasing oneself or pleasing others.

The mother-daughter relationship themes that are prominent throughout life – being the same and being different, attachment needs and autonomy strivings, identifying with and individuating from, and pleasing oneself and pleasing others are especially useful to understand mother-daughter interactions during the first three years.

2   Becoming a Mother

When does becoming a mother start? Is it when a little girl plays with her baby-dolls, when she realizes with pride that when she grows up to be a woman, she may be a mommy, when she is captivated by the family dog's pregnancy and care of her puppies, or when she is intrigued by monkey mothers and their babies at the zoo? Does the psychological process of becoming a mother start when a girl begins to reflect on her interactions with her own mother and on the things she wants to do the same and the things she wants to do differently when she becomes a mother? Does becoming a mother begin when a woman creates a frozen embryo? Is it when a woman becomes pregnant, her baby is born, or she adopts a child? The evidence is compelling that the psychological process of becoming a mother includes all of these experiences, as well as the significant changes that occur in a woman as she cares for her baby and their unique relationship evolves.

From the moment a girl gets her first period, she has physical evidence of her potential fertility. The first image of her blood-stained panties may be easily called to mind. A girl's first period may have been an eagerly awaited event, an alarming surprise, or both. Years and decades later, a woman may remember where she was and whom she told. She may remember the congratulations and the warnings that emphasized her fertility possibilities. A personal body experience became public and may have aroused a jumble of feelings; some may have been linked to shame, others to pride. The cramps and bloody inconvenience that needed to be managed may have accompanied the excitement of growing up, the possibility of motherhood, and the power of a woman's body. Or a girl's feelings may have triggered a decision to never be pregnant. As the years pass, a girl's experiences with menstruation evolve; some linger and leave an impression.

A woman's ideas about being pregnant, giving birth, and being a mother originate in childhood. Although some aspects are universal, each girl has her own unique experience becoming a mother. The trajectory for each girl is influenced by the stories her mother tells, the birth of younger siblings, scenes from movies, and scenarios in books. A woman's pregnancies, miscarriages, abortions, and fertility complications influence her path to becoming a mother. Her career and romances

DOI: 10.4324/9781003687603-3

influence her plans for motherhood. A woman's relationship with her own mother plays a role. Her imagination fills in the gaps.

Becoming a mother occurs in a specific cultural context in addition to a personal one. Some aspects of caring for babies and toddlers are idealized, and others are socially, politically, and economically devalued. The fairy godmother is a familiar idealized mother image. A witch epitomizes the mean, scary mother. These images of good and evil mothers emerge and are sustained because they resonate, though disguised, with childhood memories of actual mothers, wished for mothers, and feared mothers. Most adults have memories of their own mothers being loving and angry, gratifying and frustrating, protective and frightening, idealized and devalued: the ghosts and angels of experience that inhabit our minds (Fraiberg, S. 1975; Lieberman, A. 2005). Integrating good and bad mother images into one person with strengths and weaknesses can be a challenge.

For some women, being a mother became a goal when they were little girls and continued throughout development. Other women rarely or never thought about having a baby and therefore have had fewer plans or expectations. For some women, the loving mother-baby relationship they envision having is a replacement for the painful relationship they had or continue to have with their own mothers. For other women, pleasurable mother-daughter relationship memories predominate. Some pregnancies are planned and easy, some are a total surprise, and some include medical complications and arduous undertakings, including in vitro fertilization, donor egg, and donor sperm. Some wished-for pregnancies never happen, and the evolving recognition of that fact may trigger an onslaught of feelings and a variety of adaptations, including adoption or surrogacy. The specifics of each baby's conception, gestation, and delivery may continue to influence mother-baby and mother-toddler interactions. A mother's own conception history may also have an impact. For example, Dallas was adopted at birth. She had never wanted information about her birth mother nor to search for her until she gave birth to her daughter. Dallas explained:

> "My adoptive parents are great. From the time I was very little I knew I was adopted. It was just a fact on paper. My mother was my mother. But when Katharine was born, and I saw the cleft on her chin just like mine, I wanted to see my biological mother. My son did not have a cleft."

Dallas' reaction the first time she saw her baby daughter's cleft chin, an inherited biological trait that they shared, triggered an interest in her own biological roots. The traits that she shared with her son, including blue eyes, did not trigger a desire to see her biological mother. A cleft chin may be more striking and unusual than blue eyes, but for Dallas, having a daughter with a cleft chin was the trigger.

Since every child and every relationship are unique, a mother reacts differently to each of her children. In addition to the innate factors and life experiences that contribute to the differences among children, birth order plays a role (Sulloway, F. J. 1997). While studies about the influence of birth order on development, personality, and life successes are controversial, outcomes suggest that, within a family, the sex of the children and age-spacing between the children influence the impact of birth order. Furthermore, whether a mother is an only child, first-born, or later born will play a role in her response to each of her children's birth order position in the family. In many ways and for many reasons, including birth order, a mother is different with each of her children, which means that each child in the family has a different family environment.

Courtney was pregnant with her fourth child – a girl. She had had significant postpartum depression with her first three babies, who were boys, and was concerned it would happen again. When she was in the middle of her ninth month of pregnancy with the fourth baby, she fell and broke her leg in several places. The baby was delivered by emergency C-section; Courtney had surgery on her leg and, in a few days, went home with her baby. The cast on her leg extended from the tip of her toes to her hip. Unlike when her other babies were born and the demands of her life with her husband and the other children took her away from the baby, this time she was confined to bed. Courtney attended the weekly mothers' group on the phone, with her baby in her arms. All day and much of the night, her newborn stayed in bed with her. She nursed the baby on and off all day and cared for her as much as she was physically able. During the day when they were not in school, the older children gathered around Courtney and the baby in bed. Courtney did not suffer any postpartum depression with this baby. Although there is less of a risk of postpartum depression after the birth of a baby girl, Courtney believed that staying close to her baby was what helped her.

Unlike Courtney, who had an accident, a mother may choose to do things that she did with her first-born differently with her second-born. She has more experience and may believe that some things she did with her first caused problems that she wants to avoid with the second. In addition to difficulties, a mother's decision about how many children to have is influenced by many factors. The sex of her children and the number of children in her family of origin seem to have a significant influence.

Marsha was pregnant with her second child. She had continued to work after her first baby was born, but believed that her job and two children under three years of age would deprive both of her children of the attention that they needed. Therefore, Marsha decided to take a three-year "leave of absence" from work after the birth of her second baby, even though it meant that she might be unable to return to her job. Women gain a wealth of experience being mothers with each of their children, and they change in many ways. Nevertheless, a common discovery of many mothers is the innate uniqueness of each of her children and the specifics of each mother-child relationship.

A Baby Is Born

When a baby is born, the mother's world changes: her body, what she does, and what she thinks about. Her mental landscape is transformed. Some changes emerge slowly, and some instantaneously. A woman's primary intergenerational relationship identity shifts from "I am my mother's daughter" to "I am the mother of my baby." Having a baby has an impact on other important relationships. A mother has new fears and wishes. Her priorities change. Many years ago, a compelling television Public Service announcement, "It's 10:00pm, do you know where your children are?" triggered an emotional reaction in mothers with babies, teenagers, and adult children. The words trigger familiar worries in all mothers. Whether she is monitoring her infant's breathing or her teenager's social life, being a mother changes a woman forever. Within this whirlwind of change, each mother-baby love relationship develops.

Mother-Baby Attachment

The mother-baby falling in love and being in love experience is unique for each mother and baby. It can feel extraordinarily pleasurable and at times stressful, it can emerge immediately or gradually, be exquisitely subtle, breathtakingly intense, and everything in between. The mother-baby love relationship has been studied primarily in terms of attachment. Mother-baby attachment and mother-baby love overlap and merge; they are the same in some ways and different in others. A baby's physical proximity-seeking and readiness for feelings of an intense emotional connection with her mother are part of this robust mother-baby attachment system. It is not only the baby who is nourished by and thrives in the attachment relationship; mother-baby love and attachment also lead to the mother's expanding sense of self.

Good Enough Mothers

The wish to be a "good mother" is shared by women in a multitude of settings with a variety of backgrounds, and becomes more urgent once her baby is born. However, "a good mother" is difficult to define. A good mother in one culture may not be good in another. A protective mother in one family may be overprotective in another. Strict can be viewed as mean, empathic as over-indulgent, and permissive as reckless. A good mother for one child may not be good for another, even in the same family. Furthermore, personal definitions of a good mother may change over time.

For some women, the mother they want to be is unattainable because it is an over-idealized, wished-for fantasy left over from childhood, or a fantasy promoted in popular culture. The over-idealized mother is a version of the fairytale mother who is always gratifying and never gets angry, tired, overwhelmed, bored, or busy with things other than her child. She never makes mistakes. She protects her child from all physical and emotional pain. Her child never gets angry at her. An over-idealized fantasy mother can never be an actual mother. And while idealizations may be intellectually recognized as such and rejected, they may still be emotionally real.

Fairytale witches embody the bad mother who is mean and frightening. Sometimes, childhood memories of an actual mother exude danger or even evil, the essence of a witch. Fear or hate may accompany these memories. Memories of one's own "bad mother" can fuel the desire to be a "good mother" or can be used to maintain "good mother" self-feelings. A mother's dread about being or appearing to be a witch-mother can silently hover and at times intrude into conscious aware-ness. When a crying baby is difficult to comfort, or a toddler has a temper tantrum in public, especially in a confined space like an airplane, the fear of being seen as a "bad mother," another version of feeling like a "bad mother," can escalate.

A woman who self-identifies as an "unnatural mother" may believe she does not inherently have needed maternal traits, or she may be rejecting the attributes that are designated "natural." A woman who feels like an "unnatural" mother may be warding off memories of her own mother, whom she does not want to be like.

In some ways, for all mothers, the personal good-mother-self/bad-mother-self pendulum swings. Integrating the image of the good mother she wishes to be with the mother she thinks she is is an ongoing process. This process includes recog-nizing and accepting that she will be a mother who, at times, she views as being her best, and at other times, she views as being her worst. The notion of a "good enough mother" becomes a useful concept (Winnicott, D. W. 1990). The good enough mother provides a sufficient amount of sensitive maternal care so that the inevitable failures are buffered. Although a standard for what constitutes a sufficient amount does not exist, an important element is that the inevitable ruptures in loving interactions are repaired and loving interactions return, predominate, and promote development. A woman who had been in a mother-baby group 12 years earlier with her first baby explained her feelings about being a good-enough mother:

"I now have three children and often fondly remember what a truly unnatural mother I thought I was. I was exhausted and at times overwhelmed. I got angry, impatient, and bored. And yet I felt assured, even with my first baby, that I was okay and my baby was okay. And we were!"

Expanding Sense of Self

When her baby is born, a mother's expanding sense of self begins to unfold. Her capacity for ongoing self-reflection and insight increases (Lefcourt, 2023). Her growing ability to identify and empathize with her baby is part of her expanding sense of self and is sometimes experienced as a blurring of oneness with and sepa-rateness from her baby. During a new mother-baby group, as we gathered in a small circle on the floor, the mothers described this experience, Ingrid mused:

"Sometimes I don't know for sure if what I am feeling is my own feeling or my baby's feeling. If I feel hot is my baby hot? If I feel cold, is my baby cold? If I feel angry, is my baby angry."

Kaylene, who had gone for a walk without her four-week-old baby for the first time added:

"Each time I came to the end of the sidewalk and waited for the green light I began to slightly sway. I finally realized that swaying was a body memory of rocking the baby carriage. Mentally, my baby was with me."

Raquel's baby was six weeks old, and Raquel had been waking each morning with a swollen upper lip. She explained:

"My baby had developed the typical sucking blister that breastfeeding babies often get. I finally realized that I had been sucking my own lip in the middle of the night, just like my baby. That's why it was swollen."

Angelina confided:

"From the moment my baby was born, I never had my mind to myself. My baby was always there."

These reflections reveal aspects of a mother's developing attachment to her baby and expanding sense of self. A mother's feelings of oneness with and separateness from her baby slip and slide. Her thoughts ricochet between the past, present, and future. Feelings of love, anger, and anxiety can be surprisingly intense. These experiences are all part of a mother's expanding sense of self.

Childhood Memories

Mothers gain a new perspective on memories of their own childhood, and the new meanings that a mother attributes to her childhood memories become part of her expanding sense of self. Self-reflection and new insights help a mother to understand her daughter's developing mind and thereby minimize the inevitable stresses and uncertainties during her baby's first three years of life. Amara recalled:

"I always thought that my sister was a cry-baby and I was strong and independent. She cried whenever my mother went out. She always cried at sleepaway camp. I was proud that I didn't cry. That changed when Calypso was born. I didn't know what to do when she cried until I realized that I had been crying silently for my mother my whole life. I now know how Calypso feels when she cries. She's crying for me and needs me. I realize that I won't spoil her by responding and comforting her."

For Amara, becoming a mother and hearing her baby's cries triggered her insight about her lifelong childhood memory of her sister being a "cry-baby" and her dawning awareness of her own "crying silently." Amara's insight, while painful, changed the meaning of her childhood memory and enabled her to respond empathically to Calypso's cries.

A mother's childhood memories hold some of the answers to the many questions and concerns that typically arise during early motherhood. In addition, memories can enable mothers to reexperience the enchantment of early childhood, recognize early needs that are not structured in language, and discover the deep satisfactions of motherhood. A mother's childhood memories contain the building blocks to create moments of mother-baby shared delight that can nurture development.

Memories are activated during mother-child interactions and sometimes take mothers by surprise. A mother can gain a new perspective on her pleasurable and painful memories and how they influence current interactions with her daughter. Deidre frequently said things that she thought were mean to her 16-month-old daughter, Mandie, and she did not know why she kept doing it:

> "The mean words just spill out of my mouth. My mother says very mean things to me, she always has; I try to keep my distance from her. I remember when I was 12 years old. I was wearing a new party dress and as we were leaving the apartment she said, 'You look ridiculous! What's wrong with you?' I couldn't believe it, but yesterday when Mandie spilled her juice I said, 'What's wrong with you?' I don't know why I say mean things to Mandie. I don't want to."

Deidre's comment about keeping a distance from her own mother helped to identify specific memories and their link to her current interactions with Mandie. Deidre recognized that speaking in her mother's voice by saying mean things was a way to feel close to her mother:

> "Lately, I've been pushing my mother away more than usual. I want to feel close to her even though I am so angry at her and keep my distance. Maybe being mean to Mandie, like my mother is mean to me, is a way to feel close to my mother while I push her away."

This new way of thinking about being the same as her mother in order to feel close helped Deidra to be the kind of mother she wanted to be, not mean.

A mother's understanding of the multiple meanings of her memories and how they are being relived with her daughter is integral to a mother's expanding sense of self. Such insights help to maximize the magical moments of love and the emotional bonds of attachment when a mother's kiss can make everything feel right.

The Mother, Her Baby Girl, and The Grandmother

The mother, her baby girl, and the grandmother trio come alive in the mother's mind when her baby is born. Historically and cross-culturally, before, during, and after childbirth, women gather around a new mother to provide hands-on help, emotional support, and advice. A baby shower and a sex-reveal party are present-day additions. During pregnancy and early motherhood, a stranger's knowing smile or a friend's extra care resonates with a woman's reactivated wishes for tender maternal sensitivity. In a sense, a mother with her newborn is surrounded by and surrounds herself with surrogate mothers. A woman with a new baby also turns internally toward her mother. With and without awareness, both pleasurable and painful elements of her own early relationship with her mother are activated. Memory traces and associated feelings are stimulated. This is the prism through which she navigates early motherhood (Stern, D. N., 1995).

Many grandmothers temporarily move in to assist their daughters after the birth of a baby. For mothers and daughters who have a harmonious relationship, this arrangement is welcomed and deepens their bond. Other mothers may want their mothers physically close, but life circumstances, logistics, or feelings complicate having them close, and such arrangements are avoided. The potential for adult mother-daughter relationship damage repair and a new beginning seems tempting, but may be too stressful to actualize. When a woman has a baby, her reactivated needs for her own mother are primitive. She may need her mother in ways that she has not needed her in years. Her body is sore from either a vaginal delivery or a C-section. A mother's needs for sleep, food, and water compete with the enormous care her newborn baby needs for survival. New mothers are learning new tasks while sleep deprived. A competent woman at work and in the world, she now fumbles with uncertainties, but has no time or bandwidth to feel or to be inadequate. Only in retrospect will she describe the first few weeks of motherhood as overwhelming and fill in the details of the kaleidoscopic blur it was. While she is living it, she gets everything done. Her baby is fed, bathed, and comforted. She gets the help she needs.

I am highlighting a new mother's relationship, both in her mind and in actual interactions, with her own mother. Her baby's other parent, if present, plays a significant role during this phase. Couples may have co-parenting arrangements that have been explicitly or implicitly agreed upon. Some logistical and emotional needs that arise after the baby is born may be surprising and need to be negotiated.

The future of a new mother's relationship with her own mother is filled with promising potential and is vulnerable to conflict. New grandmothers are confronted with reactivated feelings of their own early maternal pleasures and failures. There are baby-care generational differences that can contribute to disagreements between the mother and the grandmother. The new mother is in charge of her baby; the grandmother is experienced. The new mother needs her mother; the grandmother wants a relationship with her granddaughter, and in many ways is dependent on her daughter for contact with her granddaughter. There are many elements ripe for adult mother-daughter conflict. Both the mother and the grandmother are vulnerable to conflict with each other because of activated underlying themes: the mother's revived needs for emotional support and physical help, the grandmother's reawakened feelings of her own inadequacies as a mother, reawakened memories of her own mother, and her own lost pleasures of caring for a baby.

Some women believe they will never themselves be as good a mother as their own mother. This belief can occur for different reasons and play out in different ways. Viewing her own mother as the better mother may protect her from acknowledging her mother's deficits. An idealization of her mother may seem to be needed to preserve a valued adult mother-daughter relationship. Some grandmothers contribute to this dynamic and implicitly demand the status of "best mother." Other mothers are dedicated to being better mothers than their own. For some grandmothers, this adds to their own self-criticism, and results in increased conflict.

Awareness of these dynamics and the difficulties that they create can prevent the potential damage they can cause. Self-reflection and self-awareness can enable the new mother and her mother, who is now the grandmother, to enjoy the new pleasures that this phase of their relationship can provide for them both.

Friendships With Other Mothers

After the initial newborn phase, the ongoing demands of infant care remain demanding. Stresses for mothers include a multitude of new tasks and the enormous responsibility of a baby's survival, which can result in feelings of being a competent woman dissolving into feelings of inadequacy. Caring for a newborn can be overwhelming. Caring for two children can strain feelings of loyalty to each child. Petra described her experience:

> "My life plan was always to have two children. I was so excited throughout my second pregnancy. My labor was progressing easily and I was leaving to go to the hospital. Standing at the door, saying goodbye to my 3-year-old, all of a sudden I became teary and thought, why did I do this? My sense of loss in the moment was so intense – I would never again be just Noah's Mommy. A few hours later Noah visited me at the hospital. His dad and I introduced him to Quimby. It was an extraordinary moment."

Petra's experience captures the extreme ups and downs of early motherhood.

Juggling a career while caring for a baby can be challenging. Demands on a mother's time can feel impossible to satisfy, and conflict about choices can be difficult to resolve. During the middle of the night feedings, isolated windows lit across the street or across the city may capture a mother's attention and imagination: "I am not alone; other mothers with their babies are near." An affinity with mothers and their babies passing in the park or standing close on a supermarket line may rush to the front of her mind. Babies' photographs shown at work that evoke shared joy with other mothers, and personal longings may trigger wishes for a mommy-friend. For many mothers, sharing the pleasures with a friend can be enriching, and sharing the stresses can feel lifesaving (Lefcourt, 2024). Some mothers are eager to meet other mothers, whereas others are less interested or less able. Work schedules may interfere, and lifestyle or other relationships may make having a mommy-friend more difficult or less needed.

When navigating the emotional rollercoaster of early motherhood and the activation of childhood memories, the acceptance and support mommy-friends give to each other can help mothers be less self-critical and more self-forgiving. Mothers can enjoy vicarious feelings of safety and comfort. Doreen, a new mother, told this story:

> "I was 10 years old. My parents got divorced, my father left, and my mother and I moved to New York City. My mother was depressed, and I had no friends; I felt so alone. I lived across the street from a small playground filled with mothers, babies, and little children. It looked like a happy place that I frequently walked past on my way home from school. Sometimes I went in

and sat for a while. It always helped me feel better. When I was 24 years old, Lara was born. She was great, and I was so happy to have a baby. But it was a long, lonely winter. I wanted to meet other mothers and babies. On sunny days, even when it was freezing cold we went to the same playground. But week after week, even when the sun was shining bright, the playground remained cold and empty. I was with my baby, but felt so alone. In April, the playground became the warm, gathering place I was waiting for. I met my first mommy-friend; we formed a mothers' group. Everything felt better."

Doreen's childhood loneliness was reactivated when her baby was born. The winter playground bleakness she describes not only reflects the stresses of new motherhood, but also her deep, reactivated feelings of childhood loneliness. Doreen created a family of mommy-friends.

Early motherhood both reactivates childhood experiences and provides the opportunity for enriching new experiences. Some of the new experiences can heal old wounds. Friendships with other mothers are a cherished and often long-remembered part of this process.

3 Mothers' Childhood Memories

Memory is fundamental to mental life. Pleasurable and painful memories fill our mental landscape. The details of a memory, including those that seem incidental, can have important meanings. Something enjoyable can disguise something emotionally distressing; a delicious, sugar doughnut that seems central to a memory can be an attempt to sugar-coat the painful elements. Memories are ways of coping with stressful events and savoring pleasurable ones. They can help to make sense of our lives and to make decisions. Feelings, ideas, and intentions expressed by someone else in a memory can represent those of the person whose memory it is. A mother's childhood memories are awakened during interactions with her daughter and can help her to understand her daughter's developing mind, ease the inevitable stresses of caring for her baby and toddler, and resolve typical developmental difficulties during the first three years of life. A mother's memories contain her life-long wishes and fears.

Hidden Voices of Little Girls

The voice of a little girl can be heard in every mother's childhood memories; the inner child of a woman can be discovered. Notably, the voices of children and women have been linked throughout history. When the proverb, "Children should be seen and not heard," was coined by the clergyman John Mirk, over 600 years ago, it applied an existing idea about women to children – women should be seen and not heard. The meaning of the proverb is: children should be well behaved, look adorable, and not make trouble for adults; especially men. However, in the late 19th century, a woman's right to vote – to have a voice to be heard – toppled the sentiment and became a national movement in Great Britain, Wales, Scotland, and the United States. Around the same time, the Girl Scouts of America was established and still exists today, with its mission of "… redefining what's possible for girls." In 1920, women in the United States were heard and got the vote. Child labor laws were enacted around the same time. The connection between women's rights, the recognition of children's developmental needs, and the discovery of babies' and toddlers' mental capacities is striking. Historically, the voices of mothers and children are connected. The shared history of women and the childhood memories of each woman are also connected.

DOI: 10.4324/9781003687603-4

The meaning of childhood and the value of children have changed in many ways throughout history, but the vestiges of some old and even ancient ideas remain. According to records since 1500, children have always played. There is evidence that games of hide and seek, games that today we understand to be about a child's way to cope with the stress of separation, have existed in a multitude of cultures throughout history (James, M. 2018). However, it was not until 1952 that parent visitation was allowed when children were hospitalized and has since become general practice. Perhaps traumatic separations were one of the enduring remnants of "Children should be seen and not heard." The inner world of children was not recognized or even considered. However, beginning in the 1940s, research about the emotional life of children exploded, and advice to parents, although sometimes misguided with unintended consequences, followed.

Discovery of the inner world of children is dramatically portrayed in the 1964 movie *Mary Poppins* (Stevenson,1964). In 1910 London, after a suffrage rally attended by the children's mother, the father seeks to hire an authoritarian nanny who will be "firm," "give commands like a general," and replace the "inadequate" nanny who quit. Significantly, this scene about ignoring his children and controlling them is in the context of his wife marching for women's right to vote. The children want a nanny who will meet their emotional needs, which they express clearly in words and behavior. Their mother wants her children to be heard, but defers to her husband, who will not listen. Mary Poppins rescues the entire family: the children whose inner needs are desperate to be heard, the father – including his disavowed inner little boy – and the mother whose wish for her children to be heard represents her own wishes to be heard. Dramatically illustrated in the film is an example of a woman's expressed wishes for her children that reveal wishes that she has for herself, but is less able to voice. A mother's childhood memories are a window into the origins of her wishes.

Confident and assertive, Mary Poppins takes the nanny job on her own terms. When the children watch Mary Poppins unpack what appears to be her empty carpetbag and she removes her many treasured items from it, she demonstrates to the children that she is interested in their inner world and there are precious things about them to be discovered that are not readily seen. Just as a small carpetbag that appears empty can contain an assortment of items that reflect a rich history of the self, a large mirror, and a bright light to see oneself clearly, so too can the contents of a little girl's mind and the meanings of a mother's childhood memories be discovered. In the same way that Mary Poppins unpacks her carpetbag that appears to be empty and amazes the children, a mother discovers her daughter's developing inner world and new facets of her own mind as she relives the enchantment of early childhood with her daughter. This is my vision of the movie and the story of child development and early motherhood that it can tell.

From birth, a girl has a rapidly unfolding inner world with a readiness for social interaction and an interest to make sense out of all that she perceives: to understand explicit communications, to decipher implicit ones, and to process her own complex, and at times conflicted thoughts, feelings, wishes, and intentions. A mother's own childhood memories are an extraordinary guide throughout this process.

Explicit, Implicit, and Relived Memories

Explicit Memories

Explicit memories, sometimes called declarative memories, are constructed narratives about past events (Segal, D. and Hartzell, M. 2005). The following are examples of women's explicit memories about the birth of a sibling. The memory details are different, but the memories of each woman share several similarities. Their memories about the first time they saw their baby brother or sister reveal various ways of coping with the birth of a sibling and reactions to boy-girl differences. For women who are the eldest children in their family, the importance of being first is represented in different ways such as standing on the top step and being "number one." When the baby sibling is a boy, a woman's memory narrative often includes an image of the flatness of the floor or ground surface, which may represent looking down at the flatness of her own naked body as a little girl.

Childhood Memories about the Birth of a Sibling

Kinsley told this memory:

> "I was 5 years old and went with my father to pick-up my mother and baby brother from the hospital. My father was happy he now had a son. When we entered, down two steps, far across the flat lobby floor, I could see my mother holding the baby. The image of the flat floor and me on the top step are vivid. My dad always calls me his number one. I'm not sure if number one means first-born or favorite; maybe both. I took care of my baby brother all the time. I remember pretending that I was his mother."

In Kinsley's memory, standing on the top step, being "number one" even though the baby was a prized boy, and seeing her mother holding the baby far across the "flat lobby floor" were references to birth-order, sibling rivalry, and being female. These meanings of her memory, in addition to representing positive feelings about being a girl who could become a mother, are consistent with her comment, "I remember pretending that I was his mother."

Carrie was four years old when her sister was born; she remembered:

> "I went with my father and aunt to pick them up from the hospital. I was walking towards the hospital and when I got to the top step, I could see a nurse holding the baby. My mother was holding a life-size baby-doll for me. I don't know where my mother got the idea of having a doll for me. I don't know if this was usual or something special for me. I think it was special for me. When we got into the car, my mother and father sat in the front seat, my aunt and I sat in the back; I held my baby sister across my lap. She was precious."

While telling her memory, Carrie emphasized positions or status: top step, front and back car seats, and the pleasure of a special "life-size baby-doll" just for her. As we talked about her memory, Carrie, who was the first-born in her family, added, "My father always calls me his number one." Her mother sat with her father in the front seat and the baby was "precious," but Carrie was "number one." Position, related to sibling rivalry and maybe rivalry with her mother, is important in the details of her memory.

Hannah remembered:

"I was 7 years old when my second brother was born; I went to the hospital with my father to visit my mother. The rule was children could not go into the hospital. Standing outside on the sidewalk that was very flat and looking up, I could see my mother through a window on a high floor holding the baby. It was very strange seeing her but not being able to touch her because that was the rule. When my brother came home, I took care of him all the time. I loved being with him. I took him to the pediatrician for check-ups and loved seeing all the babies. It was very interesting; they were all different. I was especially interested in the black babies. They looked the best; I'm not sure why. I had two brothers so I didn't care about the boy-girl differences."

Seven-year-old Hannah was white, had two brothers, and denied an interest in girl-boy differences; however, she was at an age when male-female differences are usually of interest. Hanna's interest in skin color differences and her comment that "the black babies looked the best but I'm not sure why" can be understood as a disguised reference to sex differences. She may have focused on skin color to distract herself from attention to boy-girl genital differences. Hannah's comments about "looking down at the flat sidewalk," "looking up at my mother," and "It was very strange seeing her but unable to touch her" may have reflected her childhood experiences of looking down at her own naked body, looking up at her mother's naked body, and not being allowed to touch. It is understandable that a little girl's childhood memories about her own naked body and her mother's naked body would be activated in this context. At seven years old, she knew something about conception and childbirth.

Anise remembered:

"When my brother came home from the hospital, my mother, father, older brother, and I were all standing in the very small entry hall. The most important part of my memory is how small and crowded the hall was. I guess I was wondering if there was enough room for me."

Anise attributed sibling rivalry meaning to her memory. Her worry about there being "enough room" for her is consistent with the typical concerns that children have when a sibling is born. Her concerns about "enough room" may also represent a little girl's worries about childbirth.

Another first-born, Bryn, recalled when her sister was born:

"I was 4 years old and the only thing I remember when my sister was born is that I wanted to be the first one to see her, and I was."

For Bryn, being first is central to her memory – being first-born is implicit and the first to see the baby is explicit. Being first helps Bryn cope with her rivalry with her sister. Importantly, in her memory, Bryn asserts her ability to get what she wants.

Some childhood memories about the birth of a sibling reveal attempts to incorporate one's own unacceptable feelings into a positive sense of self and a coherent autobiographical history. Such incorporation can be represented in memory by attributing a disturbing or unacceptable intention to someone else. Chrissy remembered:

> "My baby sister was born and was coming home from the hospital. I was 4 years old and my parents left me alone in the hospital lobby to hold her while they went to get the car. I always protected my sister, but how could they have done that? I could have dropped her. I know my parents would have never really done that; in fact, I recently told them this memory and they said it never happened, but that is what I remember."

Chrissy's memory that includes her assertion about always protecting her sister, her acknowledgement that she could have dropped her, yet at the same time attributing the negligence to her parents, may be a way to feel better about any hostile feelings she had and may continue to have toward her sister.

The above memories about the birth of a sibling illustrate how memories help to cope with stress and maintain positive feelings about the self. They include reactions to male-female differences, wishes to be a mother, and pretending to be a mother by caring for a sibling. The image of surface flatness in memories about the birth of a brother may be a reference to a little girl's experience of looking down at the flatness of her naked body and female-male genital differences. Childhood memories about the birth of a sibling are ways to understand a little girl's experiences of the world she encounters and the ways in which they are represented in memories.

The Meaning of a Memory Can Change

An experience that was difficult or impossible to make sense of as a child can be remembered in a phantasmagorical way. The new perspective of being a mother can change the meaning of such a life-long childhood memory. During an excited mothers' group discussion about parents' sex lives when they have young children, Claudia recounted a fanciful childhood memory:

> "When I was about 8 years old, I was alone in the kitchen and there was a knock on the screen door. As I approached the door, I could see the Easter Bunny through the screen. He was standing up on two legs, much taller than I was. He was holding a basket with two shiny eggs in a nest of brown grass. I know this sounds impossible, but my memory is clear; it feels like it really happened. I ran upstairs to my parents who were still in bed and told them about this amazing thing that I saw."

The women in the group offered possible rational explanations, "A grown-up may have been dressed in a bunny costume. It could have been a toy bunny." Claudia insisted, "It was real, it was alive. I know it sounds impossible, but my memory feels real." Claudia had repeated this memory to others many times and was always told, "It never happened." Being told it never happened, and believing herself that it sounded unrealistic, had never changed her feelings about the memory being real, because her memory reflected her real feelings of amazement and incredulity. That is, Claudia's memory had narrative truth and personal meaning.

Our lively group discussion continued about whether parents close the bedroom door when they have sex, have sex when their child is sleeping in bed with them, or is in the room. Claudia chimed in:

"I never thought of this before. My parents always told me that I once walked in on them when they were having sex but I never remembered it. Maybe the unrealistic Easter Bunny was my way of remembering the unimaginable, incomprehensible sight of my parents having sex."

The excitement Claudia felt during the mothers' group discussion about parents, children, and sex evoked her recurring Easter Bunny memory. Claudia mentioned that the Easter Bunny knocked on the screen door; she described how she looked through the screen to see the bunny. The screen door was a meaningful symbol for Claudia. Claudia was a psychologist and was familiar with the idea of screen memories: memories, or a part of a memory, that have symbolic meaning and provide a screen that obscures other meanings (Freud, S. 1899).

Claudia's experience of being a mother of a daughter created a new context for the emergence of the new meaning that she attributed to her memory: seeing her parents having sex. Specific images in Claudia's memory supported her sexual interpretation of her memory. The basket filled with brown grass and two eggs that the bunny was holding at genital height are vivid details of her memory that may represent pubic hair and breasts. Her parents being in bed when she tells them about the Easter Bunny may have been a reference to the experience of having seen them having sex in bed. These details of Claudia's memory were consistent with her new sexual interpretation of her memory. In addition, Claudia remembered that when she was about eight years old, the same age as in her memory of the Easter Bunny, she had learned about how babies were conceived. Claudia decided to close the door when she and her husband were having sex and explained her decision:

"My mother always talked about sex in a positive open way when I was a little girl. But in a way she involved me in her sex too much. I think by leaving the door open when I had sex, I was doing the same thing with my daughter."

Implicit Memories

Whereas explicit or declarative memories are narrated stories about past events, implicit or procedural memories are not narrated (Segal, D. 2005). Implicit memories can be emotions or bodily sensations. Implicit memories also include procedural body actions such as riding a bike or spinning a hula hoop. Ways of being with others, what has been called relational knowing, including shared smiles, turn-taking rhythms in conversation, patterns of mutual gaze, gaze averting, and hugging, can also be implicit memories. Tastes, scents, and sounds – shivers, quivers, and swoons can be memories. Sometimes music or terms of endearment are part of an implicit memory. For example, a mother recalled:

> "From the time Elizabeth was born I called her sweetie. She's now almost 2 and I just realized that my mother always calls me sweetie. I have a warm feeling all over whenever I say sweetie."

Relived Memories

Feelings activated during a mother's interactions with her baby or toddler may be memories. Said another way, the feelings can be a re-experiencing or reliving of the past without consciously remembering. Interactions can awaken feelings of love and tenderness or anger, fear, disgust, and helplessness. When a memory is being relived emotionally, its "pastness" fades.

A baby's innate sucking instinct – whether for nourishment, comfort, or the pleasure of mouthing objects to explore the world – can evoke strong reactions in mothers. During a mothers' group discussion, Jacqueline, the mother of 10-month-old Chloe, had this insight:

> "Chloe puts everything in her mouth. Everything she touches gets all slimy. It's actually disgusting. I often stop her. It just reminded me, that's the way my mother always kissed me; she got my face and belly all wet. I don't know why she kissed me like that. I always avoid kissing my mother. In fact I avoid kissing; I don't even kiss Chloe."

Jacqueline's new ways of thinking about the links between her childhood memory, her current interactions with her daughter, and her wish for Chloe to enjoy kissing led to further self-reflection and a change. Jacqueline explained:

> "I didn't realize that my strong reaction to Chloe drooling all over her toys was related to my childhood memories about wet kisses from my mother. I knew that I avoided kissing, but I didn't know why. Most people like to kiss. I didn't realize what I might be teaching Chloe about kissing. I want Chloe to like kissing."

A mother can relive memories of childhood helplessness with her own daughter. Nellie described 14-month-old Lindsay's hitting:

> "All of a sudden out of nowhere Lindsay hits me. You wouldn't believe it because she never hits me in front of other people, she only hits me at home when we are alone. No matter what I do, she won't stop."

As Nellie spoke these words, a childhood memory came to mind:

"My mother always spanked me; I always tried to be a good girl but all of a sudden she got so angry and spanked me. She only spanked me at home, never anywhere else. Never in front of anyone. I was so helpless. My father didn't believe me. There was nothing I could do to stop the spankings."

As a child, Nellie was helpless to stop the spankings and to be heard. Recognizing her current feelings of helplessness as a reactivated childhood memory not a current actuality, being believed in the mothers' group, and realizing that her daughter Lindsay was helpless to stop herself from hitting, enabled Nellie to stop Lindsay from hitting her. She began to recognize Lindsay's feelings that triggered her hitting and put them into words, "You are so angry that I said, 'No more cookies.' You can feel angry, but I am not going to let you hit me." With her new insight about the memory of her own childhood experience of being spanked, Nellie was able to help Lindsay stop hitting her.

Belinda had a childhood memory that was activated during interactions with one-year-old Cindy and was related to calling her "a big flirt":

"When I was in second grade, I sat in front of a boy who played with my hair every day. It was wonderful. I liked it, but I think I told him to stop. My mother didn't want me to have boyfriends, but I always did."

The meaning of Belinda's uncertainty about whether she told the boy to stop playing with her hair and what her uncertainty means about her relationship with her own mother is unclear. Belinda's memory raises a number of questions: Did Belinda say stop to the boy, or did she think she should say "stop"? If she said stop, did she want him to stop, or was she doing what she thought her mother wanted her to do? Why did Belinda think her mother did not want her to have boyfriends? How did Belinda's memory influence other aspects of her life, and in what ways does her memory influence interactions with her daughter? Belinda noticed that she frequently called Cindy, "A big flirt" and wondered:

"My mother always accused me of being, 'Boy crazy.' Maybe that's why I call Cindy 'A big flirt.' She's only 1-year-old and I'm accusing her of doing something wrong when she's having fun with her father, uncles, and little boys. In a way I'm reliving my past. Calling Cindy a 'Big flirt' is the same kind of accusation as my mother calling me 'Boy crazy.'"

Felicia added to the discussion:

"I always call Alanna a big flirt also, but it means something different to me. I think it's great that she engages boys and men and I want to support her. I was always good at flirting and felt sorry for the girls that didn't know how."

Both Belinda and Felicia call their daughters "a big flirt" but the words have different meanings to each mother and different related childhood memories.

Childhood memories that are activated and relived during mother-baby and mother-toddler interactions can deepen a mother's understanding of interactions with her daughter and provide a way to resolve everyday difficulties while at the same time promote a little girl's developing positive sense of self. Mothers' childhood memories will be discussed further in chapters by age.

4   Moments of Intersubjectivity

Intersubjectivity includes human interactions when one is aware of or imagines the subjective experience of the other, and the other is simultaneously aware of her own subjective experience (Beebe, B. 2020). The emotional connection between mother and daughter that is experienced during moments of intersubjectivity comes from feeling deeply seen or known and simultaneously recognizing the inner experience of the other. Shared moments of intersubjectivity, imagining and knowing more about her baby's mental world of thoughts and feelings, activate a mother's sense of "we" – a sense of a you, a me, and an us. In other words, interactions that create moments of intersubjectivity are relationship-building blocks. Importantly, moments of intersubjectivity also build a foundation on which a baby can begin to discover her own mind.

As a baby's thoughts and feelings are known, validated, and reflected upon by her mother, a little girl becomes aware of her own inner experiences and aware that she can be deeply known by another (Schechter, D. S. 2017). This experience of emotional connection becomes integrated into her sense of self, other, and sense of self-with-other. Moments of intersubjectivity set in motion a lifelong capacity for emotional intimacy and the satisfactions that come with it. A mother's mutual gaze with her newborn baby can feel like a moment of intersubjectivity to the mother.

Mother-baby interactions with heightened potential for moments of intersubjectivity include first smiles, pointing, communicating intentions – pointing to the future, creating shared memory narratives – pointing to the past, and language acquisition. These everyday mother-daughter interactions create feelings of emotional connectedness derived from a sense of knowing what is in each other's minds and how it feels – an intersubjective meeting of minds.

First Smiles

A smile is an outward sign of an inner experience, and a baby's first smiles invite her mother to imagine the inner experience of her baby. Early smiles can activate a mother's awareness of her baby's dawning consciousness of interpersonal,

DOI: 10.4324/9781003687603-5

relational pleasure. Babies' smiles quickly become communications: *I feel good with you.* During mother-baby mutual smiling, the internal subjective experience of each is communicated to the other, and is sensed by the other. The smile of each influences the smile of the other. We can imagine what this reciprocal interaction with a joint focus of attention to a shared inner experience contributes to a baby's developing sense of self and self-with-other: *We are both smiling. Smiling with each other feels good to both of us. We delight each other. I am loveable.*

Pointing

Mother-baby interactions initiated by a baby pointing to an object and her mother sharing her attention to the object are typical and endlessly repeated. The baby's sense of agency in these moments is powerful. For example, a baby points to a ceiling light. Her mother, excited by the invitation, looks at the light and says some version of, "Yes, I see the light." Mother and baby know that they are both looking at the same thing. They have the same thing in mind. Their certainty is unquestioned. The interaction is compelling because of the inner experience of a meeting of minds: a shared awareness of their joint focus of attention and perception. Such experiences of a meeting of minds that promote an intersubjective sense of self-with-other continue throughout life and may be related to the certainty of feeling understood. So much is happening emotionally, mentally, and interpersonally in this brief interaction triggered by a baby's pointing.

Communicating Intentions – Pointing to the Future

As described earlier, babies discover that intentions can be communicated. Signaling an intention is pointing to the future without the finger gesture, and indicates the baby's awareness of her own intention before she acts. In other words, signaling an intention illustrates her ability to think about thinking. This enormous leap in development is called reflective functioning (Fonagy, P., and Target, M. 1991).

While babies and toddlers seek their mothers' approval and are highly motivated by their approval, sometimes they signal an intention that they know will get disapproval. A child's signal of an intention to do something that she knows her mother disapproves of is an assertion of autonomy and a confirmation that she remembers the rule. In addition, a child signaling an intention to do something that her mother has prohibited creates an opportunity for her mother to help her baby or toddler to stop, and thereby to get her mother's approval. Lally, when 16 months old, was eating yogurt when she signaled her intention to her mother to throw the spoon on the floor. The signal, including raising the spoon full of yogurt with a mischievous twinkle in her eyes, and smiling in mutual gaze with her mother, enabled her mother to help her stop. She placed her hand gently on Lally's hand and said:

> "I see you remember, no throwing spoons on the floor. I will help you stop yourself."

Lally smiled and continued to eat her yogurt. It is of interest that when a mother prevents her daughter from following through on a disapproved of intention that she has signaled, the child usually does not protest. There is mutual agreement – a meeting of minds. The baby signaling and then not protesting indicates that her mother's prohibition is becoming the baby's own self-prohibition. The details of such complex intersubjective interactions can contribute to teaching the do's and don'ts of everyday life and will be discussed in greater detail in chapters by age.

Creating Shared Memory Narratives – Pointing to the Past

Memory narratives are the stories about experiences that include words to identify the feelings that were elicited. Mothers co-create memory narratives with their babies and toddlers. The memory narratives they co-construct together help the children to adapt to disturbing experiences. While remembering together – a pointing to the past – babies and toddlers can feel safe, understood, and in control. Shared memory narratives of experiences that were difficult to understand can help babies and toddlers make sense of them. Experiences that were frightening can be remembered rather than relived. The contents of memory narratives become increasingly detailed with age, and the children's contributions change as they develop.

Marigold was one year old, had gone to the zoo, and was frightened when the lion roared. When Marigold's mother was telling the story about what happened, she said to Marigold, "Remember when the lion roared so loud. You were very scared and cried? Show everybody how loud the lion roared." Marigold imitated the lion's loud, ferocious roar. Feeling safe while remembering together and pretending to be the scary lion helped Marigold process her experience. The next time they went to the zoo and the lion roared, Marigold did not cry; she held her mother's hand and roared. Without words Marigold was communicating, *I remember when the lion roared and I got scared. Mommy remembers also. I can hold Mommy's hand. I can roar too. I am safe.*

Sometimes mothers wish that their children will not remember an event. Well-meaning others may try to convince a mother that her baby or toddler will not remember. In some ways, wishing or believing that a baby will not remember substitutes for wishing the event had never happened. There is overwhelming evidence that babies and toddlers do remember (Coates, S. 2016). Remembering together with words and pretend play about having been scared or hurt is less disturbing than re-experiencing the painful feelings and can help a child realize that she is now safe.

Language Acquisition

Babies are surrounded by language and repeat the sounds that they hear. When a mother is uncertain about the meaning of her baby's sounds, she may rely on the context to attribute meaning to them. A baby's approximation of a word, in combination with the mother's enunciation of the word and attribution of meaning to it, creates a new word for the baby. When the mother imagines that her baby said,

"Mama," and responds, "Yes, Mama is coming!" as if her baby said, "Mama," they have created a new word together. Often, mothers are the only ones who understand their toddlers' emerging language. We can imagine what it might feel like to a toddler when her mother is the only one in the whole world who understands. In these ways, the language acquisition process is about attachment, meaning making, and feeling understood – all elements of intersubjectivity.

First smiles, pointing, communicating intentions, creating shared memory narratives, and language acquisition are mother-daughter joint focus of attention interactions about meanings, feelings, and the shared emotional connection of intersubjectivity.

5   Birth to One Year

Among the first decisions a woman makes about her baby is whether to learn the sex before or at birth. Although there is little research about the reasons for the choices women make, studies suggest that decisions to know before or at birth are about equally frequent with first pregnancies. While pragmatic reasons are often cited, the more complex psychological reasons for either choice, including those that are related to childhood memories or to traumatic experiences, are usually not discussed.

During a mothers' group, the women talked about knowing the sex of their babies. Renata was almost three months pregnant and was frightened in different ways about having either a boy or a girl. Renata explained:

> "I waited as long as I could to get pregnant. I had so many fears. Growing up my brother always hurt me. When I was 5, he broke my arm. When I was 10, he gave me a black eye. For me, girls were vulnerable and boys were dangerous. As a child, I never felt safe. I want to know the sex of my baby as soon as possible. It is easier since I'm pregnant to imagine a girl as safe, and a boy as gentle. I feel stronger than I have ever felt. I don't feel as afraid as I did before I got pregnant. If I have a girl, I will be able to help her to feel safe and to be safe; if I have a boy, I will help him to not hurt girls. The sooner I know the sex of my baby, the better; I know my feelings of safety will keep getting stronger. The more practice I have feeling safe, the safer I will feel when my baby is born whether a boy or a girl."

As a child, Renata was not protected when she needed to be. With the help of therapy, Renata's lifelong fear of her brother, which she had extended to other boys and men, and her fears about being a girl, which meant being weak and vulnerable, had abated. However, her fears were reactivated in anticipation of having a baby. She feared that she would be afraid of her son and afraid for her daughter. Nevertheless, being pregnant, she felt powerful. She believed that knowing the sex of her baby while she was still pregnant would provide more time to resolve her reawakened childhood fears:

> "I must be strong. I'm creating a new life and childbirth requires strength. My fears are memories of when I was a frightened little girl."

DOI: 10.4324/9781003687603-6

While there are definite risks to pregnancy and childbirth, for Renata, her childhood fears felt more threatening.

Another mother in the group, Corina, described her decision not to know the sex of her baby before birth:

> "I really want a girl. If I find out before the birth and it's a boy, I will be so disappointed. But, if I find out after he's born when I can see him and hold him, it will be easier for me to tolerate the disappointment and bond with him."

Corina was aware of both her preference for a girl and her coexisting ability to love her baby when born, whether a boy or a girl. Tatiana, in contrast, thought that knowing the sex of her baby while she was pregnant would give her the needed time to adjust:

> "I definitely want to know before. I really want a boy, but if she's a girl, I want more time to adjust before she's born. I just realized: my father really wanted me to be a boy. Maybe that's why I want a boy: to please him. I'm not sure what I want. I like the idea of having a girl that's wanted."

Tatiana's poignant insight about her reason for wanting a boy resolved her strong preference for a boy and reinforced her decision to know the sex of her baby before birth. Tatiana had a baby girl and adored her daughter in a way that she had wanted to be adored herself, but never had been.

Justine described her choice:

> "I have decided not to know the sex of my baby before birth. That way, throughout my pregnancy I can play with the possibility of both. In a sense, I will be able to have a little bit of each before the reality of one."

For each mother, whatever decision she makes about whether to learn the sex of her baby either before or after birth, she claims her actual baby as "my baby" (Baradon, 2005). After birth, a mother's claiming of her baby girl includes all the ways in which her baby is the same and different from how she had imagined and wished, and all the ways in which her daughter is actually the same and different from herself.

It's A Girl

After her daughter is born, a mother's thoughts about her baby being a girl in some moments may be vivid and at other times fade into the background. Some reactions may be surprising and rarely, if ever, talked about. When her daughter is naked and her mother views her vulva, inner labia, clitoris, and vagina, her baby's femaleness can be striking and inescapable. As is true of all body parts, there is huge individual variation in the details of female genitals. The ways in which her daughter's genitals are the same and different from her own may evoke strong reactions. No pubic hair is expected, other differences may not be. The variety of mothers' reactions to seeing their baby girls' naked bodies is enormous; sometimes childhood memories are awakened: "I like the way she looks naked. She reminds me of myself when I was a little girl." Or: "She looks so different from the way I look. Her clitoris looks bigger than mine. I think she will be very sexy." Sometimes concerns are triggered: "Her vulva looks wrinkled; something looks wrong." Or: "When I change her diaper she always touches herself; I'm afraid she will hurt herself." A mother's reactions to her daughter's naked body may be related to feelings she had about herself when she was a little girl or that she currently has. Sometimes reactions include feelings about male-female genital differences.

In many moments, a mother may barely notice or think about her baby's sex. However, when a mother views a physical or behavioral trait that her daughter has as particularly feminine, or a trait that violates her own sense of femininity, her baby's femaleness may rush to the front of her mind. Mothers may be surprised by their own male and female stereotypes that get triggered, as well as those of others. Tamara commented, "I like that Laura's cry is soft and gentle, it's more feminine." Surprised and disapproving, Chiara said, "When my daughter is distressed, or has anything to say, I want her to have a strong voice."

Mothers may be alarmed by attitudes they never knew they had. Liz, who had attended a family Thanksgiving dinner with six-week-old Maxine, described what happened:

"My whole family was meeting Maxine for the first time; I was so excited. When we walked in, everyone rushed over to see her and my cousin said, 'Why do you have her dressed in a brown and beige striped onesie? We can't tell she's a girl; especially when you call her Max.' I was horrified. I don't like pink; I have no pink for her. I would never put a bow in a baby's hair. She's too little to wear a dress. I prefer more gender neutral clothes. I thought her nickname was cute. I never knew I had such negative feelings about many girl things; I wonder why I do. I definitely want people to know she's a girl."

Liz began to identify childhood memories about her brother that motivated many of her decisions about how to dress Maxine, for example:

"My brother had the best black leather jacket, but my mother wouldn't buy one for me. She said it was only for boys. She bought me a pink one; I hated it."

Liz began to realize that feelings she had toward her brother were influencing her attitudes toward her daughter's "femininity" and the decisions she was making.

Gradually, as a girl develops, she becomes more recognizable as a girl to others and she increasingly self-identifies as a girl. With huge variations, characteristics that identify her as female emerge. This process is a combination of the choices that her mother makes for her, her own preferences, and innate traits. Furthermore, the process includes a little girl's responses to the expectations of others and culturally determined symbols that surround her including hairstyle, clothes, body gestures, and play preferences. Her evolving sense of self that includes *I am a girl* and her own developing ideas about what it means to be a girl become increasingly apparent during the first three years.

Once a mother knows that her baby is a girl, she makes decisions collaboratively and independently, consciously and unconsciously, about her baby's name, how she is dressed, and the toys that she is given. These decisions are influenced by a mother's own feelings about being female, her personal history, her gender politics, and the surrounding culture. For example, a mother chooses whether to name her baby a typical girl's name or a more androgenous name. She makes decisions about whether the color and style of clothes chosen for her daughter make her more or less identifiable to others as a girl. We may wonder about the impact that these decisions and a mother's thoughts and feelings that motivate the decisions have on a little girl's developing sense of self. There are no right or wrong choices, but they all have meaning.

For each mother, the moments in which her baby being a girl are prominent in her mind and the moments in which her daughter's femaleness retreats to the back of her mind are of interest. Malinda had an insight that was emotionally meaningful to her:

> "I just realized that whenever I am dressing Arabella to go to a party, I think more about her being a girl and start to worry about whether I am dressing her pretty enough. Sometimes I even change her outfit two or three times. My twin sister was the pretty one and I was the smart one. I don't want Arabella to worry about being pretty or smart. I guess I worry."

Malinda became aware that her activated childhood memories about being smart and being pretty were influencing her interactions with her daughter. She realized that in moments when Arabella being a girl came to the front of her mind, she worried about whether Arabella was pretty enough – a remnant of her own childhood feelings. She took Arabella's intelligence for granted, but worried about how she looked and what she wore.

In a mothers' group discussion about pet names, Gina realized that "All my nicknames for Anita are sweet foods: cupcake, muffin, sweety pie, and honeybun." With a gasp, she suddenly remembered her own mother always saying, "You are such a sweet little girl; I'm going to eat you up!" Gina believed that being a "sweet girl" meant that she was being a "good girl" and that her mother was being affectionate; but she also remembered worrying about being eaten. Her worries intensified when her mother read Hansel and Gretel to her. Gina explained:

> "Hansel and Gretel were clever enough to escape the witch who was planning to eat them, but I was worried. Being a sweet girl was not all good; it might make it more likely that I would be eaten. But being a bad girl was dangerous also, I could be eaten for being bad."

For Gina, being a "bad girl" and being a "sweet girl" were dangerous. Being a sweet girl meant concealing her "not so sweet" angry feelings in order to appear "good," and intensified her fears about being eaten for being a "bad girl." As Anita reflected on her childhood memory, she thought about her reactions when her 11-month-old daughter got angry. Gina realized that she thought her daughter was being "bad" when she got angry and that by calling her sweet foods she was repeating her own childhood conflicts about being "good," "sweet," and "bad." Gina's childhood feelings about the importance of a girl being good and the idea that having angry feelings meant that she was bad were reawakened during interactions with her daughter. Gina recognized that Anita was not a "bad" girl when she appeared angry, but emotionally she reacted as if Anita was being "bad." Gina's insight was useful:

"Intellectually I know that having angry feelings is normal, but emotionally I think I still feel like it's being bad."

Gina began to use words to identify Anita's angry feelings; they no longer felt as dangerous as they had. Her little girl's angry feelings could be acknowledged.

Breastfeeding, Bottle Feeding, and Pumping

The decisions a woman makes about breastfeeding, bottle feeding, and pumping are influenced by pediatric recommendations, work schedules, surrounding cultural attitudes, a mother's personal history, and her relationship with her own mother. Decisions are influenced further by both her baby's response to nursing and the ways in which her own body responds. Nadine, for example, described having been told throughout her childhood that she was breastfed:

"It aways made me feel special that my mother nursed me when I was a baby: especially since as I got older she yelled at me so much. When I was 15 years old, I told my mother that I had the strangest dream; I was a baby breastfeeding, but the breast felt hard and cold. My mother said, 'That's because you were bottle-fed.' Shocked, I said, 'Then why have you told me my whole life that I was breastfed?' My mother defended herself by saying, 'I breastfed your baby brother and did not want you to feel bad.' I felt so betrayed; in a way gaslighted. I decided then that I would definitely breastfeed all my babies."

While Nadine's decision to breastfeed was rooted in her own childhood experiences, Billie, another mother in the group, was influenced by cultural norms:

"I never thought I would nurse, but that's what everyone is doing."

For the first five months of her life, Billie and her baby Jinni settled into nursing easily. Jinni focused on sucking vigorously; nothing distracted her. When Jinni was about five and a half months, Billie felt that everything had changed. Jinni periodically stopped sucking and turned her attention to gaze and smile at her mother. At times, Jinni twisted her entire body around to scan the room; in the process, she yanked Billie's nipple, and then resumed nursing. Jinni's developing social interests and curiosity changed the way she liked to nurse. Feedings took much longer. Billie enjoyed the playful interactions that were part of their attachment relationship and her baby's growing interest in the world, but she sometimes felt more in a rush. In addition, she did not like the nipple pain from Jinni's yanking. Some of Billie's friends suggested that she stop nursing, but Billie wanted to continue; she liked nursing and she knew that Jinni liked it too.

However, in addition to the time it took and the nipple pain, there was something else about nursing and socializing that Billie did not like, especially when her husband was watching. Billie wondered:

> "Maybe I have some uncomfortable feelings breastfeeding because Jinni is a girl. In some ways, it feels sexy in a way that I don't like."

Over time, Billie and Jinni established a rhythm that included some long playful feedings, some quick snacks, and some long drowsy wake-sleep feasts. Billie learned to break the suction created by nursing before Jinni twisted completely around, and Jinni learned not to yank Billie's nipples when she wanted to look around. Both Mother and baby contributed to this mutually regulated, pleasurable pattern. Billie's increased awareness of her uncomfortable feelings about breastfeeding a girl contributed to the establishment of nursing interactions that satisfied them both. Billie described:

> "Sometimes I end a feeding and sometimes Jinni does. Sometimes they are long and sometimes short. When other people are around they are definitely shorter. Maybe I would feel differently breastfeeding a boy. I'm not sure exactly what that's about."

Jinni was beginning to learn about her own intentions and the reciprocity in relationships, and Billie was managing her feelings, which included emotional intimacy and bodily pleasure with a girl. Each phase of nursing has different pleasures and different stresses. Some may be specific to breastfeeding a girl. It has been found that in general, girl babies are weaned younger than boy babies.

Mirror Gazing

A mother's evolving identity that expands to include *I am the mother of my daughter* expresses itself in many ways. During a mothers' group, Jessica described her experience of self-identifying as a mother:

> "I was registering for a mother-baby class and the form that I needed to fill out asked for Mother's Name. I wrote my mother's name instead of my

name. My unconscious really surprised me. I know I'm Merrie's mother, but I guess my own mother is still the first mother that comes to mind."

Suzannah commented:

"Maybe that's why I keep standing in front of the mirror holding Jane. It's wonderful to see us together in the mirror; Jane looks like a little girl and I look like her mother. Seeing what we look like from the outside, makes it feel real on the inside in a different way."

Katrina added:

"I have wanted a baby for so long, seeing Talia and myself in the mirror together is like a wish come true. I'm seeing myself as others see me, and as I want to be seen. In all the videos of me with my mother when I was a baby, we are never looking at each other."

Katrina and Suzannah did not have the experience as babies that most babies have of feeling themselves as loved reflected in their mother's gaze; their mothers were depressed. When Katrina and her mother looked at each other, all Katrina saw was a "frozen stare." Suzannah's mother always looked "angry." Suzannah recounted that as an adolescent (another transition in identity), she often looked deeply into her own eyes in the mirror. Suzannah realized:

"I think I was searching without my mother's angry sneer to see who I was and who I was becoming."

The experience of a mother seeing herself in the mirror holding her baby, seeing herself from the outside the way she feels on the inside, or seeing an external image of her new identity that is coming into being – I am the mother of my daughter – is satisfying to many mothers. This new facet of a woman's identity is part of her expanding sense of self.

Mothers' Fears

In addition to the pleasurable experiences of new motherhood, during the first year, mothers may also have nightmares or daytime fears about bad things happening to their babies. Olive, the mother of a three month old, announced during a mothers' group that every time she walked past a door while holding her baby, she thought about the possibility of her baby's head banging against the door frame. Similarly, Nickie added that every time she closed the car door, she imagined that she had slammed it on her baby's hand. Frightening thoughts about hurting her baby may be triggered by a mother's own childhood memory of a painful accident. Her own accident may not be remembered in the moment, but the feelings may be awakened. While these typical frightening thoughts for mothers with babies are disturbing, they can increase mothers' vigilance to protect their babies.

In addition to powerful feelings of love and attachment, and fierce motivation to protect their babies, mothers' feelings during the first year also include boredom, loneliness, guilt, anger, and anxiety. While mothers' frightening thoughts about their babies getting hurt or lost are typical, the angry feelings and resentments that mothers have can increase their fears and feelings of horror about their fears. As their babies develop and as mothers discover how common their frightening thoughts and angry feelings are, the frightening thoughts typically diminish. For many mothers, while the disturbing thoughts and feelings are stirring, the pleasurable mirror image of themselves with their baby is a comfort.

Emotion Regulation

Emotion regulation is the process by which a state of equilibrium is maintained and, when disrupted, can be reestablished. Throughout the day, feelings vary, and their intensity fluctuates. Feelings of love, joy, sadness, curiosity, anger, and fear well up and subside. The emotional bonds of mother-baby attachment are at the center of a baby's developing inner world of thoughts and feelings, and create the foundation for emotion regulation. A mother's attachment to her baby promotes the mother's interest in and attention to her baby's thoughts, feelings, and intentions that motivate behavior. Another way of saying this is that mother-baby attachment promotes the mother's ability to reflect on her baby's inner world and to respond sensitively to the thoughts and feelings underlying her baby's behavior. As a mother communicates her reflections about her own and her baby's thoughts and feelings, she awakens her baby's self-reflection and activates her baby's curiosity about her own inner world. For example, during a feeding, when her baby tried to grab the spoon, and the spinach splashed all over, Fallon said:

"I see you are very hungry and you want to feed yourself."

When Allegra's baby pushed the spoon away, Allegra said:

"I see, you don't want to eat the spinach; you pushed my hand away. You can eat your pasta."

Clementine, while eating the spinach herself after Carin pushed the spoon away, said:

"Spinach is a new taste. Maybe tomorrow you will try it. I like spinach."

Despite the similarities in these babies' responses to being fed spinach, each baby's behavior was motivated by different thoughts, feelings, and intentions, and meant something different to her mother. For Stacey, Carola, and her grandmother, a similar mother-baby interaction resulted in an angry fight. Stacey was feeding

Carola pureed carrots, which she loved, and spinach for the first time. As soon as the spinach touched Carola's mouth, with a shiver and a look of disgust, she spit it out. Stacey said, "You didn't like the spinach." Grandma, wiping Carola's face, said, "Not very lady-like Carola! Stacey, you better teach her not to spit." Stacey exploded:

> "Mom, she really didn't like it, she's 10 months old: being a lady is not the point. Even ladies spit and fart. The pressure you always put on me to be proper, and the endless criticisms, made me feel so insecure. I will not let you do that to Carola."

The personal meaning to a mother of her daughter's rejection of food and how a mother responds to her little girl's messiness are often rooted in the mother's own childhood memories.

Mother-baby attachment, which includes a mother's physical and psychological holding of her baby, is at the center of her child's inner world. A mother holding her baby in mind – that is, her ongoing thoughts and feelings about her baby's experience and her empathy for her baby, promotes her baby's attachment and self-regulation. The mother-baby relationship is unique. A mother's ability to see the world through her baby's eyes can be extraordinary. Her impulses to protect her baby can be fierce. A baby's reactivity to her mother's emotions is also highly sensitive.

Even in moments when her baby's thoughts, feelings, and intentions are unclear, or her baby's behavior is disturbing, oppositional, or messy, the mother can seek to know her baby's inner experience. In other words, when her baby's behavior triggers the mother's anger or anxiety, the mother can remain curious about her baby's thoughts, feelings, and intentions that are underlying the behavior, and she can communicate her empathy. A baby's developing emotion regulation is intricately linked to this aspect of mother-baby attachment.

When a mother holds her baby girl and feels her small, contented body cradled gently in her arms, she may feel a surge of tender love, a sense of pride, and satisfaction. The same mother in other moments may have a different experience. Impressed by the helplessness and vulnerability of her little baby and the enormous responsibility of being a mother, the changes in roles and identities, the sleepless nights, and inconsolable crying, she may feel helpless herself and want to escape. Her job, other relationships, competing responsibilities, personal care necessities and luxuries, and other pleasures that are interfered with may add to the stress of caring for her baby. The origins of these different feelings may not be obvious as they are occurring, but upon reflection, can be traced to memories. June wondered:

> "When I was growing up, I always needed to take care of my baby sister: I wanted to play with my friends. I think my mother didn't like taking care of us, or maybe she was depressed. She was always in her room with the door closed. I want to be the kind of mother that I wanted my mother to be, but sometimes I think I feel the same way my mother felt."

June's childhood memories about needing to take care of her sister were reactivated when her baby was born. She recognized that other mothers had some of the same feelings that she had, but realized that the degree of her current anger and resentment was influenced by her childhood memories. She also knew that her feelings of anger and resentment that she had about taking care of her sister when she was a child were not the same feelings she had as a mother taking care of her baby. Self-reflection helped her to disentangle her past from the present and to be the kind of mother that she wanted to be.

Obstacles to Attachment Resolved

Mother-baby attachment is a powerful and resilient dynamic: it can be fortified by self-reflection, established when there are obstacles, and repaired when ruptured. For Cora and Lizzie, there were obstacles. Cora entered the mother-baby room for her pre-group individual visit carrying five-month-old Lizzie on her hip. Lizzie's lower body was wedged in the crook of her mother's arm; her upper body was at a distance from her mother's. Cora, dressed for her executive job, adjusted her light beige gabardine suit, hiked up her skirt, kicked off her heels, and joined me on the carpeted floor. Lizzie was dressed in coordinated colors and wore a delicate baby-barrette to keep wisps of blond hair off her face. As Cora and I chatted breezily, she propped Lizzie on the edge of her lap facing toward me.

Lizzie remained completely still, her rosy face unexpressive, and her gaze riveted on me. There was a distinct disconnect between Cora and Lizzie; an absence of any sense of being emotionally connected with each other. There were no tender caresses and no moments of shared smiles or mutual gaze between them. Cora was lively and engaging with me; Lizzie was quiet and still, with an intense seeking of sustained eye contact with me. Both the disconnect between mother and baby and Lizzie's intense seeking of mutual gaze with me were unusual for mothers and babies of this age.

Our light conversation ended when Cora told me that she had returned to full-time work when Lizzie was ten days old. Cora explained:

"I'm different from most mothers. I'm like my Mom, I work all the time. Sometimes I don't see Lizzie for four or five days."

Underlying Cora's surface indifference to what she was describing seemed to be a suffering that was too painful to be acknowledged, but was revealed in her next sentence:

"When I do see her, she won't look at me, there's no eye-contact. No matter what I do, Lizzie won't look at me."

As we spoke, Lizzie's gaze remained focused on me. I asked:

"How does it happen that you don't see Lizzie for four or five days?"

Cora replied:

"If I leave for work before she wakes-up and return after she's asleep, I don't see her for days. When I get home and she's already asleep, I wonder why I made my last appointment so late."

I probed further: "Why do you think she won't look at you?" Cora confided, "She's angry at me. I'm like my Mom, I work all the time." Cora's efforts to maintain her attachment to her own mother by being like her mother, "working all the time," were interfering with having the kind of relationship that she wanted to have with Lizzie. Cora's self-questioning about why she comes home too late to see Lizzie, though spoken almost in passing, indicated her growing wish to have a different kind of relationship with Lizzie than she had with her own mother. The self-blame in questioning why she comes home too late to see Lizzie may have been a remnant of blaming herself as a child for her own mother's absences. Her self-blame also reflected her new perspective as a mother, which included that it is the mother's wish to be with her baby and the mother who can arrange it. In addition was Cora's dawning self-awareness that she was not only like her own mother, whom she had described as working all the time, but also that she was like she imagined Lizzie and had angry feelings toward her own mother. Cora's conviction that Lizzie was angry reflected her emerging feelings of closeness to Lizzie; They both had angry feelings.

Seeking an answer to Cora's rhetorical self-questioning, "Why do I come home too late to see Lizzie?" I asked about Cora's childhood memories, "Who took care of you when you were a little girl?" Cora began:

"Not my mother, other people. I remember when I woke-up in the morning, my Mom was still asleep, and when I came home from school she wasn't there."

Cora confirmed a connection between her childhood memories and her interactions with Lizzie. Although they occurred at different ages, the way in which Cora remembered the lack of contact with her own mother was almost identical to the way in which she described her lack of contact with Lizzie: "If I leave for work before Lizzie wakes-up and return after she's asleep, I don't see her for days…" And when describing her childhood memories: "When I woke-up in the morning my Mom was still asleep and when I came home from school, she wasn't there. I didn't see my mother for days." The narrative structure and words of both statements, the lyrics and the music, were similar.

As Cora and I spoke, the absence of any emotional bond between mother and baby continued. Lizzie remained on the edge of Cora's lap facing away from her mother and seeking eye contact with me. Cora went on to describe the physical distance combined with emotional closeness between her own mother and herself, who had lived in different cities at opposite ends of the country since Cora was 16 years old. Cora explained: "I moved to New York with my dad, my Mom stayed in Oregon to work." While Cora was describing the extensive physical distance between herself and her mother since she was a teenager, she emphasized:

"We are very close. We have a very intimate relationship. We talk on the phone every day."

Cora's description of current interactions with her mother mirrored aspects of her description of interactions with Lizzie. Her belief that Lizzie was angry because they did not see each other encapsulated her childhood memories and her current feelings of anger and disconnectedness from her own mother – feelings she struggled with and disavowed. At the same time, Cora's desire for emotional connectedness with Lizzie was apparent. I said:

"You describe a very close, intimate relationship with your mother that takes place mostly on the phone. There is no eye-contact possible on the phone." (Their phone conversations occurred without FaceTime.) "When you and your mother are talking, you don't see each other. You also tell me about wondering why you come home too late to see Lizzie, and moments when you want Lizzie to look at you and she won't."

Although Cora had just described the interactions with her mother and with her baby, she looked surprised at, but curious about the similarities that I was identifying between her relationships with her own mother and with her daughter, and invited me to continue. Lizzie was intensely focused on me. I added:

"It sounds like you want Lizzie to look at you and you want to look at Lizzie, but something interferes."

I said to Lizzie, another way of speaking to Cora:

"Mommy wants to look at you, and Mommy wants you to look at her."

At this moment, Lizzie leaned back against her mother and twisted her entire body around to face her mother. It is unclear whether Lizzie rotated toward her mother and then Cora's arms embraced her, or Cora's arms embraced Lizzie first, and then Lizzie rotated toward her mother; they seemed simultaneous. Either way, now Lizzie was cradled close in her mother's arms, and Cora and Lizzie were facing each other and smiling in mutual gaze for the first time. They lingered for many moments in this shared pleasurable interaction of emotional connectedness. I talked to Lizzie again with words that earlier had expressed both mother and baby wishes, but now were an affirmation of their experience:

"Mommy wants to look at you, and you want to look at Mommy."

Cora's conflict between maintaining an attachment to her own mother by being like her and working all the time, or having a satisfying attachment relationship with Lizzie, had crystallized. The mutual gaze between Cora and Lizzie was a moment of intersubjectivity that Cora experienced as, "… beginning to bond."

It is not clear what exactly had prompted the surprising close body contact, intense mutual gaze, and shared smiles between Cora and Lizzie, or the feeling of bonding that Cora described. Perhaps Cora felt seen by me in a way that she was only dimly aware of herself. I saw her as a mother who wanted to and could connect with her baby, but was having trouble because her way of feeling connected to her own mother, "working all the time," was interfering. Gradually, Cora began to feel increasingly gratified by her relationship with Lizzie, but sad and angry about the distance from her own mother. Cora's impulses to escape from Lizzie faded; in four months, she found a new job with shorter hours. After Cora recognized how she was reliving her childhood memories with Lizzie, and as she became aware of aspects of her current relationship with her own mother which were painful and she had been disavowing, loving moments of mutual gaze with Lizzie became possible and feeling bonded emerged and gradually intensified. Lizzie was enlivened; she began to sparkle and explore the world around her.

Although the impact of a mother's own attachment history can interfere with mother-baby attachment, a mother's awareness of the links between her past and the present can lead to change.

Restoring Disrupted Attachment

Whereas Cora was able to develop an attachment bond with her daughter once she understood more about aspects of her relationship with her own mother that were creating obstacles, sometimes a developing mother-baby bond is disrupted by current events in a mother's life. Such disruptions can also be repaired. When Mackenzie was six months old, her mother, Doris, discovered the affair that her husband had been having for two years. When he asked for a divorce, she became depressed. Doris stopped playing with Mackenzie and delegated her care to others. Mother-baby attachment was disrupted.

When Mackenzie was nine months old, Doris joined a mother-baby group. During the group, Doris ignored Mackenzie's distress and rejected her efforts to get close; Mackenzie withdrew and looked deflated. Her flat expression mirrored her mother's depressed expression – they both appeared joyless. Because her mother did not respond when Mackenzie needed her, she was learning not to signal or approach her mother when she felt distressed. Mother-baby attachment interactions and emotion regulation were disrupted. In order to change this pattern, I described what was happening and identified any indication of Mackenzie's attachment to her mother. For example, when Mackenzie glanced fleetingly at her mother, or slightly moved toward her, I said:

"I think Mackenzie feels scared surrounded by strangers and wants to be close to you to feel safe. You are her secure base."

The other mothers commiserated with Doris' anger at her husband and her sadness. However, Doris was not able to be friendly with the other mothers, or to feel loved and needed by Mackenzie, or loving toward her. Doris continued to ignore Mackenzie and sat at a distance from the other mothers; she was quite depressed. The anti-depression medication she had been taking for three months was not working.

After six weeks in the mother-baby group, something changed. For the first time, sitting close to the other mothers, smiling, and holding Mackenzie tenderly on her lap, the way some of the other mothers were holding their babies, Doris had a new idea:

> "Mackenzie has discovered her bellybutton. Maybe she remembers being attached to me."

Doris's image of prenatal umbilical attachment with Mackenzie reflected the activation of their earlier bond and the evolving psychological repair of their ruptured emotional attachment. While it had taken several weeks for mother-baby interactions to change, the activation and repair of their earlier mother-baby attachment relationship had been developing gradually throughout the time Doris and Mackenzie had attended the group. They never missed a group. Mother-baby interactions began to include mutual gaze, shared smiles, and affectionate physical contact. Mackenzie's joyful smile and curious play emerged. Doris resumed making entries in Mackenzie's baby book.

Imitation

A baby feeling emotionally close to her mother promotes emotion regulation. When a baby girl imitates her mother, we can imagine that she feels emotionally close to her mother. Being imitated by her baby can promote the mother's feelings of being seen, known, and emotionally connected. When Stella was two months old, her mother, Grace, began to sing a song to her with repeated words and hand motions including: tap your nose, tap your head, tap your tummy, and clap your hands. When Stella was 11 months old and her mother sang the song, Stella began to imitate her mother's hand motions. Grace was surprised:

> "I was amazed that I felt so close to Stella when she imitated me. It was the first time I felt that she wanted to be like me and she was really seeing me."

A baby playing with things that she mentally connects to her mother also promotes feelings of mother-baby emotional closeness. A baby's experience may be: *When I do the same thing Mommy does, I feel close to Mommy even if she is busy cooking. Feeling emotionally close to Mommy helps me feel safe and loved – a sense of comfort and the security of ongoingness.* Remington was cooking and needed to put 11-month-old Mika on the floor while she stirred a pot of boiling pasta. Mika cried until Remington gave the same kind of pot and spoon that she was using to Mika. Because they were both doing the same thing, "cooking," Mika felt emotionally close to her mother while physically separated.

When a mother puts her own bracelet or scarf on her baby girl, something she views as particularly feminine, her daughter's femaleness may come to the front of the mother's mind. In addition, being a girl like Mommy may be part of her daughter's play. Her daughter may have an emergent sense of, *When I play with Mommy's bracelet or scarf, and she puts it on me, in addition to feeling close to Mommy, I know I am a girl like Mommy.* It may be of interest which particular items that a little girl plays with evoke her mother's sense of her daughter's femaleness. Are the items cultural symbols of femininity, are they related to family gender role activities, or are they more personal, idiosyncratic objects with gender meaning?

Being Soothed and Self-Soothing

Babies have an inborn system to maintain a state of equilibrium. When a baby's equilibrium is disturbed, this system is activated. Although a baby's system is immature, it is active. When her equilibrium is disrupted, she cries. Mothers have an innate response to comfort their babies when they cry. When a baby's cries are responded to, her expression of distress increasingly becomes a communication about distress. This process within the baby combined with mother-baby interactions creates the foundation for developing emotion regulation.

Both being soothed and self-soothing are part of the system to maintain, and when disrupted to return to, a state of equilibrium. Experiences of being soothed promote the capacity for self-soothing and experiences of self-soothing promote the capacity for being soothed. Some aspects of a baby being soothed are internal. In other words, there is a self-regulating part when being soothed by someone else. When a mother is comforting her baby and her baby is comforted, the internal self-regulating processes within the baby cannot be seen.

A baby may also have developed some observable self-soothing behaviors, for example, sucking a finger or pacifier, rubbing a piece of soft fabric, or an attachment to a cuddly treasured toy. While these toys have appealing features, it is the meaning that a baby is able to attribute to the toy and the baby's capacity for attachment to the toy that make it treasured and promote emotion regulation.

Treasured Toys

Babies' attachments to their treasured toys, first described by Donald Winnicott as transitional objects (1953), reveal important aspects of their developing minds including their growing abilities to tolerate frustration, anxiety, sadness, intense anger, and terrifying fear. Because of these developing mental capacities and the baby's soothing attributions to the toy, the baby is better able to manage these emotions when close to the toy. The toy may have accompanied feedings since infancy or may have remained among many toys huddled on a shelf and then claimed by the baby. Either way, attachment to the toy is created by the baby and the emotion regulation capacities that are attributed by the baby to the toy increase during the first three years.

Lyla had conflicted feelings about 12-month-old Marcie's growing attachment to a soft, cuddly bunny and was preventing her access to the bunny. Lyla required that the toy stay in Marcie's crib and was warning Marcie about it getting lost:

"I know an attachment to a toy is considered an important part of development, but Marcie wants it with her all the time. I'm afraid she is becoming too attached; it would be unbearable if it got lost."

As Lyla spoke these words, she remembered her own lonely grief when her teddy bear was repeatedly lost:

"My older sister teased me all the time. She also tricked me. When I couldn't find my teddy-bear, she would tell me she found it; I would get very excited and then she would say, 'just kidding'. I know now that she hid it all the time. It's great to have a special toy but I've been trying to protect Marcie from the pain of losing it. Actually I think I've been frightening Marcie by repeatedly warning her that her bunny will get lost. I want to stop threatening her and do what I can to prevent her bunny from getting lost but if it does get lost, I will help her cope. Maybe there's no such thing as too attached."

Lyla's reflections about her sister's role in the loss of her own treasured toy enabled her to recognize that she was frightening her daughter about losing her treasured toy, as her sister had frightened her by actually hiding her treasured toy. Lyla decided to let Marcie keep her treasured toy close. Marcie developed a strong attachment to her bunny. Her attachment to the bunny contributed to her sturdy, easygoing ability to regulate emotions. She recovered quickly from frustration, separations from her mother were relatively easy, and her sleep was uninterrupted.

Social Referencing

During the first year of life, babies initiate emotion-regulating mother-baby interactions called social referencing (Klinnert, M.D. et al. 1986). While a baby explores her surroundings, practices crawling, interacts with other people, and learns about the world, in moments of uncertainty or anxiety, she gets reassurance and security from her mother. She engages her mother in a mutual gaze interaction and with emotional facial expressions, her mother communicates safety. In response, the baby continues her explorations, interactions with others, or play. The dramatic "visual cliff experiment" illustrates the power of a mother's reassurance of safety to her baby. When a baby approaches the visual cliff, if her mother smiles and encourages her, the baby will crawl across it. If her mother looks frightened and signals danger, the baby will stop. Frequent, everyday mother-baby interactions are similar to the "visual cliff experiment" in that a baby uses her mother's facial expressions of safety and assurance, or fear and danger, to guide her behavior (Gibson, E. and Walk, R. 1960). This is part of the mother-baby attachment relationship.

Because a mother is tracking her baby's well-being, either up close or from a distance, her baby initiates interactions with her mother as needed to feel secure, and her mother signals assurance of safety and approval: this is social referencing. In other words, a baby checks in with her mother to confirm her safety, the suitability of her behavior, and an assessment or acknowledgment of her pleasures and pains. These mother-baby interactions are subtle but full of meaning. A baby's mother is her self-regulating other and safety check on the world. When her mother is not available, a baby will social reference with another caregiver with whom she has formed a secure relationship.

All human beings, including babies, children, and adults, at times benefit from emotion-regulating interactions with others. When uncertain or distressed, empathy from a friend, a hug from a spouse, or kind words from a stranger can be soothing for adults. Soothing mother-baby interactions create the foundation for both a baby's developing ability to self-soothe and a baby's growing capacity to elicit comfort from others when needed. Both are vital.

When a Baby Cries

A baby crying is stressful for the mother; it triggers empathy for her baby and elicits strong motivation to soothe her baby. This is a valuable system – the baby crying and the mother's response – because it can promote sensitive caretaking; however, it is a fragile system. When her baby continues to cry, a mother's feelings of helplessness and anxiety can become overwhelming. Since mothers' well-being is essential, also built into the system is a mother's increasing ability to understand her baby's distress and to find ways to comfort her. Sometimes mothers' childhood memories can promote this process.

During a first mother-baby group three-month-old Candi began to cry. Candi's mother, Regina, explained: "See, this is what happens. She just cries. She's very difficult." After a few minutes of loud crying, Regina stood up and began walking back and forth gently rocking Candi in her arms. After a few more moments of loud crying, Regina said, "Maybe I should leave." The other mothers urged Regina to stay and commiserated with her distress. I added:

> "You are welcome to stay. During our group, the babies are going to do all the things they do – cry, poop, eat, spit-up, sleep, smile, coo, and more. Babies 3 months old are learning how to transition from being awake to sleeping and from sleeping to being awake. They are learning about what it feels like to poop and to burp. They may have strong reactions to these internal experiences. They are also learning about what it feels like to be in a mother-baby group for the first time."

This allusion to the mothers' feelings and implicitly to mother-baby mutual arousal triggered the mothers' recognition of some discomfort and a shared laugh. Everyone relaxed. I continued:

> "These may be some of the meanings of Candi's crying. We are going to talk a great deal about the meanings beneath the surface of the babies' behavior: what we imagine and what research has found."

Mothers' imaginings are important; they can have elements of empathy, fragments from childhood memories, and can indicate ways for a mother to respond.

In a few minutes, but what seemed to Regina like forever, Candi calmed and then fell asleep in her mother's arms. Regina was in a sweat as she criticized herself:

"I guess I'm just not a natural mother. I need to teach her to behave better."

After Regina criticized herself, her negative attributions to Candi intensified and she blurted out:

"She looks like a crazy baby. Her stringy blond hair is so wild."

Regina tried to minimize her own painful feelings about herself as "not a natural mother" and bolster her positive self-feelings by attributing negative traits to Candi.

When the mothers' discussion shifted to childhood memories, Regina recalled:

"My mother only cared about how I behaved. She never cared about how I felt. When I was in a school play, as I was walking on stage, I told my mother I was very nervous. She told me that there is nothing to be nervous about; I had a nothing part. I was so hurt and angry."

Regina began to realize that her anger and feelings of inadequacy as a mother that were triggered when Candi cried were rooted in childhood memories of anxiety and ridicule. With this new way to think about her childhood memories that were being activated when her baby cried, gradually Regina shifted her focus from an evaluation of Candi's behavior to empathy for how Candi felt. Over time, Regina became more empathic when Candi signaled distress. Her own mother's impatience and criticisms, and Regina's reactivated anger toward her mother could be identified. Her long-held feelings of inadequacy that were linked to feelings of anger and anxiety were no longer activated by Candi's cries. Her reactions to Candi became increasingly disentangled from her childhood memories; she became more empathic to Candi and better able to soothe her. Emotion regulation for both mother and baby improved.

Developing Expectations

Mother-baby interactions lead to the development of a baby's expectations. That is: babies make mental predictions based on their experience. Even a very young baby begins to expect a repetition of what has already been experienced. A baby who is fed when hungry will begin to expect the breast or bottle when feeling hungry. This expectation of pleasure helps the baby's expression of hunger – crying, to become a communication and gradually helps the baby to wait to be fed.

After a good sleep, a ten-month-old baby may awaken, play alone for a short while and then signal Mommy with a cry. After hearing her mother's voice,

"I'm coming," the baby stops crying. Her mother's voice reinforces the expectation that the baby will see her mother and helps her to shift attention from feelings of hunger to the expectation of seeing her mother, feeling the nipple, and the flow of milk. The expectation calms the baby. The satisfied expectation of her mother's arrival intensifies the pleasure of their reunion and is reflected in their joyful greeting. Expecting safety, shared pleasure, and the gratification of needs promotes mother-baby attachment and emotion regulation.

A mother may wonder about her baby acquiring certain expectations. In the following example, the mother's worries about "spoiling" her six month old and her conflicts about responding to her baby's cries were activated. Zina wondered:

> "When I'm in a different room and Callie cries, I always feel she is calling me a bad mother. I am not sure if I should go to her. I don't want to spoil her, but when I don't go to her, she gets hysterical."

Zina's childhood memories were activated; she continued through tears:

> "My mother always called me a bad, spoiled little girl. The only thing I ever expected was to be yelled at. I tried to be good, but I was never good enough. I think Callie needs me; she's not being bad; she should be able to expect me to comfort her when she's distressed."

By reflecting on her own childhood memories, including frequent accusations that she was a bad girl, Zina recognized that neither she nor Callie was a bad girl and that she wanted Callie to be able to expect comfort and care.

Words to Identify Feelings

A baby's early emotions include happiness, joy, curiosity, sadness, anger, surprise, fear, uncertainty, frustration, and affection. A baby learning words to identify emotions can contribute to her developing emotion regulation. With words, in addition to being experienced, her feelings can be thought about and talked about; that is, reflective functioning becomes possible and promotes emotion regulation. When mothers identify their own emotions with words, their babies can begin to think about Mommy's emotions in addition to having a reaction to their mothers' behavior. Emergent thoughts, such as *When Mommy feels angry, sometimes she yells at me, and I feel frightened,* become possible and help to protect the development of a positive sense of self. When mothers talk about emotions, they help their babies begin to learn that everyone has feelings and reflective functioning – thinking about feelings is promoted.

While a group of mothers were talking about identifying their babies' emotions with words, Darlene had an insight:

> "I just realized that I often tell Kitty she's sad when really I know that she's angry. Maybe I want her to feel sad rather than be angry. I'm embarrassed

to say this, but in some ways a girl being sad seems better than a girl being angry. She's entitled to be angry."

Denni had a different experience:

"When Freya cries, it feels like she's yelling at me. I always tell her she's angry. It was my mother who was always angry! Maybe Freya is feeling something else when she cries. I don't feel comfortable telling her that I'm sad or angry, but I'm sure she can tell when I am not my usual self; she always wants me to hold her. Maybe saying something would feel better to us both."

The mothers' reflections about their own and their babies' feelings deepened their understanding and led to new ways of thinking about their interactions.

During the first year of life, babies become increasingly motivated to communicate or share their subjective experiences with their mothers – their pleasures, interests, fears, pains, and uncertainties. They want to know that Mommy understands them, and they want to understand Mommy. Babies sometimes participate when mothers talk to each other, they join the conversation even before they can speak words. For example, Patricia was describing to a group of mothers how angry and embarrassed she was when 12-month-old Lulu had her first temper tantrum in the supermarket.

"Lulu was having fun loading the shopping cart with me. As she sat on the shopping cart seat pointing to items on the shelf, I handed each item to her, and she threw it into the cart. But it was enough, and it was time to leave. I had already collected many items we didn't need because Lulu was having so much fun. When I told her no more and refused to give another item to her, she began to kick and scream."

As Patricia was describing this scene, Lulu crawled past the other mothers and babies to get next to her mother. She looked at her mother intensely, lay on the floor, kicked her feet, and let out a long, loud shriek. I said:

"Lulu, it looks like you want to join our conversation and show us what happened in the supermarket. You remember; you and Mommy were having so much fun filling the shopping cart. It was time to stop and both you and Mommy were angry."

Even before they can speak, babies are beginning to learn that angry feelings can be talked about together and memory narratives can be co-constructed. A baby's emotions gradually become part of her developing sense of self (Emde, R.N. 1983). A baby also becomes aware of her mother's empathy. We can imagine a baby's emerging experience of this process: *Sometimes I feel happy, affectionate, curious, surprised, sad, angry, frustrated, or afraid. These feelings are all part of me. Mommy knows all my feeling parts.*

Empathy Without Words

A baby can sense her mother's feelings even when her mother does not explicitly communicate them or tries to conceal them. For example, Erika realized that when she is going out for the evening and wants to leave after 11-month-old Julianna falls asleep, it always takes Julianna longer to fall asleep. Erika wondered:

> "Julianna seems to know that I am going out after she falls asleep so it takes longer. I'm tense and I'm rushing her to sleep so I can leave without saying goodbye. It's so hard for me to say goodbye; in a way I'm sneaking out. I just remembered, my mother never said goodbye; all of a sudden I would realize that she had left. I was always surprised, maybe stunned. Saying goodbye while Julianna is awake might be better for us both."

While saying goodbye is difficult because of the feelings that are aroused in anticipation of a separation, the sudden realization that Mommy has left, being unable to anticipate a separation, or to rely on being told, adds to the stress of separations.

Talking about angry feelings can also be difficult. Adrianne, another mother in the group, realized:

> "Whenever I am angry at my husband, Jesse wants to be held. I think she feels scared. Maybe she thinks I am angry at her. I always felt frightened when my parents fought. I do hold Jesse, but maybe I should also say something to her. I could say, Daddy and I were very angry at each other. We were shouting loud. Now we are talking gently."

These mothers were realizing that their babies understood a great deal about feelings and that there was potential value in speaking about feelings.

Loving and Angry Interactions

Like all relationships, mother-baby love relationships include angry interactions (Gold, C. 2020). Ongoing loving interactions are ruptured and repaired. Often, the ruptures are triggered by the baby's "No" or the mother's "No." For example, when it was time to leave the playground, nine-month-old Kenzie screamed and flailed when her mother, Roxanna, tried to take her out of the swing. Neither her mother's empathy, physical strength, nor coaxing helped; Kenzie continued to scream and hold on to the swing – her little fingers gripping tight. Both Kenzie's and Roxanna's anger escalated. Kenzie hit her mother's arm as she tried to pick her up, and Roxanna yelled at Kenzie. It may be surprising how angry mothers and babies can feel toward each other. Roxanna, startled by her own reaction, calmed and said:

> "I know you are angry. You really want to keep swinging. I'm going to swing you for one more minute, then it's time to leave."

Kenzie calmed while her mother pushed her in the swing. After one minute, Roxanna eased Kenzie into the stroller with her special doll, and while Kenzie continued to scream, her mother said:

> "I know you want to keep swinging, but it's time to leave. Now, you can have a ride in your stroller with Baby Doll. Tomorrow we will come back for more swinging."

Kenzie screamed the whole way home. Roxanna described what happened the following day:

> "Before it was time to leave the playground I told her what to expect, 'Kenzie in three minutes it will be time to stop swinging and go home for lunch.' In three minutes, I stopped the swing and Kenzie began to cry. I lifted her gently and said, 'Now it's time to leave, here is your Baby-Doll' and put her in the stroller while she continued to cry. I couldn't believe it: she cried for a few minutes, then calmed. She must have felt assured by my staying calm, and telling her what was going to happen. Also, she may have not wanted a repetition of what happened the day before."

The distress for both mothers and babies caused by angry feelings and the rupture of affectionate interactions may be eased by the knowledge that anger is normal and universal. The expectation that ruptures of loving interactions get repaired and loving interactions will return is a comfort to both mothers and daughters. However, the history and details of this process have been different for men and women, and anger is experienced by men and women differently. Angry men and angry women are responded to differently. An angry man may be viewed as strong and assertive, and an angry woman as hormonally cranky or a bitch. A mother's personal history and cultural history influence angry interactions with her daughter.

Shifting a Baby's Attention

A baby's angry feelings are often triggered and emotion regulation disrupted when her mother takes something away from her. When this happens, there is a potentially useful distinction between the idea of distracting a baby from what she wants and helping a baby to shift her attention. A baby who is being distracted is passive, without agency or control: distraction is being done to the baby. The goal of distraction is to obliterate what is on the baby's mind. In contrast, helping a baby to shift attention includes the acknowledgment and validation of what the baby wants and the recognition of the baby's agency; the baby does the shifting of attention. The baby is not tricked, the limit is explicit, and the baby's agency is supported. For example:

> "I know you want to play with my eyeglasses. My glasses are not for playing; I am stopping you. You can play with these toy glasses."

As a baby develops, feeling that what is on her mind is understood by her mother can help a little girl to discover her own mind, support her autonomy, and self-assertiveness. Feeling understood will not always help a baby to shift her attention, accept a substitute, or wait for what she wants. Furthermore, communicating understanding may not always be practical. However, a baby feeling understood can provide valuable experiences that can come to mean: *Mommy understands me, I understand myself. Mommy knows what I want, but Mommy's 'No' is clear. I have choices; I can have fun with something else that I like.*

Mothers and babies learn to adapt to angry outbursts, their own as well as each other's. They develop ways to repair the ruptures in their loving feelings and return to loving interactions. They learn to expect the repairs. Angry interactions intensify as children develop. During a mothers' group, one woman confessed, "I now understand why some mothers spank. I would never do it, but I never could understand it before, but now I understand it. I never imagined how angry, helpless, and frightened mothers could feel." The other mothers agreed.

Sibling Interactions

Babies who have siblings may have a range of everyday loving and angry interactions with each other. Sometimes siblings feel like rivals for Mommy's affection and attention, at other times they band together. Babies gaze adoringly at their older siblings and older siblings who enjoy being adored and admired, protect and teach the younger ones.

Babies bring their experiences with siblings to their interactions with other babies. Jazmine was ten months old and had a three-year-old brother who frequently grabbed toys from her. Her mother Zoe thought it was "No big deal" because Jazmine did not seem to care. She enjoyed her brother's attention and picked up another toy. When Zoe and Jazmine joined a mother-baby group, Zoe changed her mind:

> "Jazmine keeps grabbing toys from the other babies and they cry. It's as though she has learned that grabbing is what you do. It looks as if she doesn't care when her brother grabs from her, but maybe she does. All the other babies care when she grabs from them. Maybe she thinks it's okay when her brother grabs from her because I act as if it's okay, but it's not. I definitely don't want other boys to grab from her. I want her to know it's not okay with me when her brother grabs from her and when she grabs from others."

Zoe's insight about the way she was communicating approval when Jazmine's brother grabbed from her changed the way she responded to both children. Zoe described what happened:

> "The next time Jake grabbed a toy from Jazmine, I told her 'It's not okay for Jake to grab from you. You are busy playing with that toy. Jake, there is no grabbing. It's Jazmine's turn. You need to wait.' Both children know grabbing is not okay with me."

As Jake stopped grabbing from Jazmine, her play with toys became more focused. She explored them more fully and played for a longer time with each toy. Jazmine's mother believed that this change in her play was significant and would extend to other activities and even to school and work. Jazmine no longer expected toys to be grabbed away from her and she knew that it was not okay with her mother. She could invest more attention and interest in her activities. In addition, Jazmine stopped grabbing toys from other babies. Furthermore, Jake was assured that his mother would not let Jazmine grab from him.

Separations and Reunions

Families have different patterns of separating from and reuniting with each other. In some families, three generations live together. In others, parents, children, and siblings live in different cities or countries. In some families, people announce when they intend to leave a room, even if briefly, and where they are going. Some parents travel without their babies and little children; others do not. Reunions in some families always include a kiss. In others, reunions are more casual or are not acknowledged. Annise had a vivid childhood memory:

> "When my mother came home from work, she was so quiet that I never heard her come into the apartment. All of a sudden she would come into my bedroom in her exercise clothes. I never knew when she got home. I didn't like it. My husband and I always shout 'Hi, I'm home' when we walk into the apartment, and whoever is home runs to the door. We never planned it; it's what we both want, so we just do it."

Annise and her husband established satisfying reunions unlike those in her childhood. Understanding the ways in which patterns of separation and reunion have evolved and what they mean may be useful in making decisions about separations and reunions.

During the first year of a baby's life, mothers may want to return to work, may need to work but not want to, may have decided not to work, or may be ambivalent about working. Childcare arrangements and feelings about this mother-baby separation can be complicated. Integrating parenthood and work has been different for men and women, and continues to be.

As mother-baby attachment develops, babies begin to react to separations from their mothers. Distress reactions can begin as young as six weeks old, reach a peak of anxiety at around eight months, and escalate to include intense fearful protests. Babies gradually learn that their unseen mothers still exist and to expect that separations will be followed by reunions. This knowledge eases their stress reactions to separation. Fears that *Mommy is gone forever* diminish.

Saying Goodbye

As discussed earlier, saying goodbye helps a baby to prepare for an imminent separation. While it may be upsetting to a baby and mother to say goodbye, having some of the anticipated distress before separating may lessen the stress during the separation. Furthermore, knowing when to expect a separation protects babies from unnecessary anticipatory anxiety and hypervigilance. Routinely saying goodbye before separations gradually enables a baby to know that she can expect to be told before separations. Being cared for during separations by someone the baby knows and likes makes it easier for a baby to adapt to the stress of separation. A baby may protest a separation vigorously, but a protest is different from being overwhelmed with anxiety or grief. Gradually, as she develops, a baby can evoke the memory of her mother when separated from her. The baby can think about her mother and remember what it feels like to be with her. This way of being with her emotionally and mentally makes separation easier.

Reunion Reactions

A baby's reaction after a separation from her mother may be surprising. Rita described 12-month-old Adeline:

"I went away for the weekend; when I came home, Adeline looked totally confused. She didn't recognize me."

Other mothers in the group had similar experiences. Kristen added:

"Kiara was angry at me, not confused. She wouldn't even look at me."

Another explanation for the kinds of reunion reactions that Kristin and Rita describe is that, during separations, babies are beginning to envision Mommy in order to feel close when separated. The mental image or sense of Mommy that a baby imagines is a composite that is based on the many different ways that her mother has looked: happy, angry, busy, and playful; Mommy with wet hair, dry hair, etc. When a baby is reunited with her mother after a separation, she may be trying to reconcile her composite mental image with the actual, specific way that her mother looks when they are reunited. A baby's and young toddler's facial expression and reaction after a separation may reflect this adaptive mental process.

Adults can have a similar experience. For example, if the only time together that two new friends have had is at the beach with windswept hair and wearing bathing suits, and they unexpectedly see each other at a formal restaurant in the city, it might take them by surprise. They may need a few minutes to reconcile their inner images of each other with how they look in the present moment. Intellectually, they know that their friend is the same person they knew at the beach, but emotionally, there may be a disconnect. With development, a baby can more easily reconcile her imagined composite image of her mother with the actual specific way that her mother looks at reunion; the baby's mental image of her mother becomes both more constant and flexible.

Separations from One Generation to the Next

Mothers' decisions about when and for how long they separate from their babies and to whom they entrust their care are determined by many factors, some are intergenerational. Kate, who was uncertain about returning to work, explained:

"My grandmother wanted to be a doctor and got into medical school. Her parents warned her that since her husband did not get into medical school, she shouldn't go; they said it would ruin her marriage. She didn't go and instead got a Ph.D. in biochemistry. My grandmother had a good job doing research and teaching medical students, but her entire life she regretted not being a doctor. My mother wanted to be a different kind of woman than her mother, (my grandmother). My mother always said that her mother was too ambitious, and it ruined her life. My mother decided when she was young not even to go to college, what good did a Ph.D. do her mother; she wanted to be a tradwife. Her mother had a good career but her husband cheated for years, then divorced her, and married a young doctor. My mother took care of me and my sister, eventually divorced my father because she did not want to be controlled by him anymore, and when I was in college, she established a thriving business. I met my husband in law school, and when we graduated I got a great job. I'm not like my mother or my grandmother. My daughter is almost 6 months old and my maternity leave is about to end. I'm not sure what I want to do about my career. I'm not sure what it will mean to my husband if I return to work or if I don't. It seems like such a big separation from my daughter; I know it will be hard for her and for me. I'm sure we will adjust, but that's my biggest concern. I don't know what I want to do."

Kate's story illustrates that intergenerational family histories reverberate and may continue to influence a mother's decisions about separations from her baby and career choices. Decisions made and the ways in which each family member responds can be influenced from one generation to the next and by changing cultural views.

Riley also told an intergenerational story about separation:

"When my grandmother was 8 years old she travelled with her father, mother, and brother from Scotland to the United States. When they arrived at Ellis Island, my grandmother was diagnosed with chickenpox and could not enter. She was quarantined alone for 10 days in the infirmary. I was horrified to hear this story about an 8-year-old with chickenpox having just left her home, and separated from her family. I imagined how frightening this could be, but my grandmother told me that she was never scared. I thought that my grandmother needed to remember it this way in order to cope. My mother told me that she was often left alone when she was too young and that my grandmother, her mother, could not understand why my mother always cried. My mother was sent to sleep-away camp every year beginning when she was 6 years old. She cried all the time and my grandmother would not take my mother home. My mother did the opposite with me. She never did anything without me. She refused to let me have sleepovers with friends and would not let me go to sleep-away camp. I thought that my grandmother was traumatized by separation, but had no memory of being afraid. My grandmother left my mother alone prematurely, and my mother remembered her fear and anger, and never let me separate from her. I'm not sure what I want to do with Layla. Right now, she's in daycare and I work four days a week. When my husband and I go out for the evening, she always has the same babysitter. Separations go easy for us. I am very different from my mother and my grandmother."

Riley uses her family's intergenerational stories and her own childhood memories to help her make decisions about separations from her daughter. She integrates her reflections about her grandmother's and her mother's reactions to separation with her own experiences and combines them with her understanding of child development. Processing or reflecting on her memories and her thoughts and feelings about her grandmother's and mother's separation experiences guides her to make decisions about separations from her daughter that have been successful. In Riley's words, "Separations go easy for us."

Sleep

Sleep is a kind of separation, and a baby's reactions to separation may influence her sleep-wake patterns. Bedtime routines can help babies develop expectations about sleep including the separation from their mothers. Sleep routines that might include dimmed lights, a feeding, and a song or story with a cuddle can promote a readiness to sleep by lowering excitation and providing a sense of coziness and security. The sense of security comes from a baby's expectation of her mother's availability when needed and her mother's continuing care and protection while she sleeps. Although mothers can create sleep routines that promote a readiness for sleep, falling asleep is something the baby does. Babies gradually establish sleep patterns that fit with adult sleep schedules and family lifestyles. There are maturational, behavioral, physiological, and psychological components to sleep. In addition, the meaning of sleep to a mother can play a role in her baby's sleep patterns. Therefore, the process of developing sleep patterns is different for each mother and baby.

When Ester was nine months old, she was waking every three hours. Her mother, Adrianna, was unaware that her "checking" on Ester by tiptoeing into her room throughout the night was waking her. She was also unaware that her "checking" was related to childhood memories. While describing Ester's "sleep problem," Adrianna recalled that when she was five years old, her mother had a stillbirth. Adrianna realized that her memories of what she was told about the stillbirth throughout her life and her mother's ongoing depression and anxiety were disrupting her own sleep to "check" on Ester. With this new way of thinking about her own worries, Adrianna resolved the "sleep problem."

Mothers who have experienced the death of a parent or sibling, or some other significant loss or separation, may have interactions with their babies that affect both of their sleep patterns. Mothers' memories of nightmares can also influence sleep patterns. A baby's innate traits, mothers' and babies' everyday experiences, and more significant life events can influence sleep patterns. A mother's awareness of these influences can help to establish, and when disrupted to restore satisfying sleep patterns.

Mothers' Childhood Memories and Babies' Emotion Regulation

A mother's thoughts and feelings in response to her baby contribute to her baby's developing emotion regulation. Every mother, however positive most of her thoughts and feelings, has moments of negative and dysregulated reactions to her baby. When a mother understands the impact of her own childhood memories on reactions to her baby, she can lessen their influence when useful. Morgen was born with a red birthmark on her face. Her mother, Emersyn, was worried and explained:

> "When I look at Morgen, sometimes all I see is her birthmark. I wish I could get over it; my husband doesn't even notice it. I would like to have it removed, but my husband won't agree. Morgen is 10 months old and I'm afraid that as she gets older my reaction to her birthmark will influence how she feels about herself. When we look in the mirror together, I don't know what to say. When people ask about it or are too shocked to say anything, I just freeze."

As Emersyn talked about her concerns, she was reminded about her own acne when she was a teenager. She described the "disgusting and painful" treatments her mother required that she get, and her mother's accusations that the acne was her fault because she ate sweets and touched her face all the time. Emersyn remembered:

> "I never thought I had such bad acne, but my mother did! She was ashamed of me. I felt ashamed and wanted to hide. I couldn't stand to be seen. My mother kept telling me how awful I looked. Eventually, I believed her. She never cared about my brother's pimples."

Emersyn realized that her reaction to her daughter's birthmark was a reliving of her memories about her own teenage acne and her inability to manage her feelings. Furthermore, she realized that her mother's reaction was specific to her being a girl. With this insight, the birthmark on Morgen's face seemed to fade for Emersyn. She felt increasingly confident that she could help Morgen to integrate the blemish on her skin with a positive sense of self and prevent her daughter from suffering the way she had with her mother's reactions to her acne. Emersyn agreed with her husband to wait until Morgen was a teenager to decide together about cosmetic surgery.

Emersyn's story illustrates the ways in which a mother's childhood memories can explain the intensity of her reactions to her daughter and, when useful, can help to moderate her own unregulated emotions. Every woman has things that she likes and things that she does not like about her own and about her daughter's body. And while a mother's likes and dislikes will influence her daughter's developing sense of self, a mother's related childhood memories can be helpful to understand the impact of her past on the present and to lessen its unwanted influence. In this way, a mother can help her daughter manage her feelings and develop a positive sense of self. A positive sense of self can help to create a foundation for emotion regulation.

Summary: Emotion Regulation

Mother-baby interactions create the foundation for a baby's developing emotion regulation. A mother's interest in her baby's thoughts, feelings, and intentions, and using words to identify them, leads to a baby's awareness of her own inner life and a sense of self that includes, *These thoughts and feelings are all part of me. Mommy can know my thinking and feeling parts.* A mother's understanding of her own childhood memories and the feelings that are re-activated with her baby helps to regulate her own emotions and facilitate her daughter's sense of well-being and emotion regulation.

Meeting of Minds and Separateness of Minds

The shared pleasures of a mother and baby meeting of minds are experienced during the first year of life. As described in Chapter 4, mutual gaze and smiles that create moments of intersubjectivity can be described as a meeting of minds. While smiling with each other, a mother and her baby are both aware of their own and each other's shared pleasurable emotional state. When a baby points, and the mother follows her baby's point, they share a perception and an awareness that the same object is in each of their minds – their minds are in sync. The mother-baby joint focus of attention on an object that is initiated by a baby pointing to the object is a frequently repeated interaction because of its pleasurable significance. A baby discovers that she can let her mother know what is in her mind, and what is in her mind can be known by her mother.

A baby also discovers the separateness of minds. That is to say, a baby discovers that she and her mother can have something different in mind. In addition, a baby discovers that her mother cannot know what is in her mind until she lets her mother know. Babies are learning about both the meeting of minds and the separateness of minds. Importantly, understanding someone and feeling understood by someone, while creating feelings of emotional closeness or connectedness also maintain the boundaries of their separateness of minds.

Pointing

Babies begin to point at around seven months of age. In Chapter 4 Moments of Intersubjectivity, ideas about pointing, communicating intentions, and asserting and substantiating the separateness of minds were introduced; the discussion continues. A baby pointing creates a mother-baby joint focus of attention on the object that the baby has chosen for their attention. Often, the objects that a baby first points to are at a distance, for example, a ceiling light or wall clock, and may start to include airplanes and birds. Pointing to objects at a distance highlights that the primary aim and pleasure of early pointing is not to get the object, but to achieve a joint focus of attention: a meeting of minds. Both mother and baby have a strong conviction that they are both looking at the same object. The pleasure of their meeting of minds motivates frequent pointing.

A baby's pointing is insistent and calls for a response. When a baby points at a ceiling light, her mother may say some version of, "Yes, I see the light." Her implicit communication – *I know what you are looking at, and you know that I am looking at the same thing* – is satisfying to both mother and baby. Whereas discussions of pointing often highlight a baby's discovery that each object has a word, I am highlighting the emotional significance of pointing that includes the mother-baby shared experience. A baby's repeated aim of pointing is to have what is in her mind understood – an aim later pursued through verbal conversation. The shared focus of attention that is achieved by a baby pointing is a precursor to the development of language. This connection between the finger pointing gesture and language acquisition is supported by the observation that among the first words that many babies say is the word "this" or "that," words that symbolically designate or point to an object.

Communicating Intentions – Pointing to the Future

A baby signaling an intention is a kind of pointing to the future. Once a baby discovers that her thoughts can be communicated, she may practice communicating her intentions frequently. For example, Geraldine gets her mother's attention with a smile from across the room, mutual gaze, and a glance at the dog's food to signal that it is her intention to play with the dog's food. Geraldine is letting her mother know what is in her mind. Her mother has been teaching Geraldine not to touch the dog's food. As discussed earlier, a baby's signal of an intention to do something that she knows her mother will disapprove of is simultaneously a confirmation that she remembers the prohibition, an assertion of her autonomy, and an indication that her mother's disapproval is becoming her own self-disapproval. A baby communicating her intention to do something that her mother disapproves of also has the potential to create a mother-baby meeting of minds where the mother communicates, "I see you remember there is no touching the dog's food. I will help you to stop yourself."

Furthermore, a baby signaling her intention to do something that she knows her mother disapproves of reveals the tensions between her attachment to her

mother and her autonomy strivings. Signaling also indicates a compromise between pleasing herself and pleasing her mother. She pleases herself by having the
idea and initiating the behavior, and pleases her mother by providing the opportunity for her mother to stop her. Importantly, a baby's communicating an intention to do something that her mother disapproves of indicates that the mother's
disapproval of the behavior is becoming the baby's own self-disapproval. The
do's and don'ts that her mother is teaching are becoming her daughter's own
codes of behavior.

Asserting and Substantiating the Separateness of Minds

As discussed earlier, a baby's ongoing explorations and discoveries about the
separateness of minds are an important developmental process which contributes to individuating. Mother-daughter interactions that assert and substantiate
the separateness of minds become more nuanced and complex with age. Ten-
month-old Carina and her mother Shira provide an example. It was dinnertime,
and the family was gathered around the table. Carina pointed to a basket full of
bagels. Her mother, Shira, offered her a bagel, but Carina rejected it and pointed
to another bagel. Shira offered the bagel to Carina that she believed Carina was
pointing to now and Carina rejected that bagel and pointed to another. This interaction was repeated several times until Carina accepted a bagel. Mothers often
experience this kind of mother-baby interaction as their baby's deliberate attempt
to annoy her or as her own inability to understand her baby. However, another
explanation of this interaction is that the baby is practicing having something in
mind that Mommy cannot know until the baby decides to let her mother know
what is in her mind. In other words, the baby may not have a specific bagel in
mind, but wants the experience of her mother trying to figure out what is in her
mind and, at some point, deciding that the bagel that her mother offers to her
is the exact bagel that is in her mind. The baby has created an interaction that
asserts and substantiates the separateness of their minds and also creates a moment where she enables her mother to know exactly what is in her mind. In other
words, she decides that the bagel she wants is the exact one that her mother gives
to her – that her mother understands her. Shira liked this explanation, but was
not convinced:

> "Your explanation makes sense and may help me not get so frustrated, but
> I'm not sure it's really true that a baby is doing that. That reminds me that
> it makes me so angry that my mother often thinks she knows what's in my
> mind, when she doesn't. She acts as if she can read my mind, but sometimes
> she just doesn't understand me."

Shira's comment highlights how difficult it is to know what is in a baby's mind,
as well as the ongoing importance of mother-daughter recognition of their separateness of minds, and the essential need to feel understood.

Saying "No"

A baby gesturing "No" and then saying the word "No" are significant developmental achievements. "No" indicates a baby's awareness of her own mind, and her self-assertiveness; in addition saying "No" highlights the separateness of minds. Daisy was nine months old and needed to take antibiotics for her sore throat. When her mother tried to give the liquid medicine to her on a spoon, Daisy sealed her lips and turned her head. When Daisy's mother put the medicine into an eye dropper and handed the eye dropper to Daisy, she eagerly took it and sucked in the medicine all by herself. Daisy felt in control: actively doing, rather than passively being done to. Feeling in control can promote awareness of one's own mind and autonomy. The gesture and word "No" express and communicate autonomy, separateness of minds, individual wishes, and assertiveness. I am highlighting the exciting developmental meanings of "No," not the mother-daughter conflicts that come with it.

When a mother says "No" to her baby, communicating that she understands what her baby wants – what is in her baby's mind – and offering a substitute can help the baby accept her mother's "No" and shift attention. For example, 11-month-old Charlotte pulled the lid off her sippy cup and delighted in spilling and splashing puddles of milk on the table. Her mother Christina explained:

"At breakfast when Charlotte spilled her milk and was making a mess, I grabbed the cup out of her hand and yelled at her. She got very frightened and cried hysterically. It reminded me of the times my mother yelled and terrified me. I was older, but still it frightened me. When Charlotte did it again at lunch, I decided to respond differently; I did not want to frighten her. I gently took the cup away from her and said, I see you want to spill and splash. Messy splashing can be fun. I think that means you are all finished with lunch. There is no spilling milk. I'm going to clean this mess and get a basin of water and some cups for spilling. It was amazing. She watched while I cleared away her plate and cleaned the milk. That was three days ago, she's not spilled the milk again, but she has played with water every day."

While an 11 month old may not understand all of the words, the complex meaning of her mother's words that included disapproval and prohibition of spilling milk, validation that spilling and splashing are fun, and the choice of playing with water were clearly communicated by the mother and understood by the baby. In addition, her mother's soothing voice helped Charlotte shift her attention and have fun playing with the water.

Awareness of the separateness of minds also enables a mother to see the world through her baby's eyes. She can rediscover the wonder of splashing in puddles or watching a bubble float through the air and the thrill of popping it. In this way, the discovery of her little girl's mind can become part of a mother's expanding sense of self. Her own playfulness can be enlivened.

Summary: Meeting of Minds and Separateness of Minds

Mothers and babies begin to share the pleasures of a meeting of minds during the first year of life. Mutual gaze and smiles, and a joint focus of attention initiated by a baby pointing, are frequent pleasurable moments of emotional bonding. Each becomes aware of what is in the other's mind and their shared pleasure. Babies also discover the separateness of minds and initiate interactions that demonstrate: *Mommy cannot know what is in my mind until I let her know. We can have the same thing in mind and we can have different things in mind.*

Play

Emerging mother-baby face-to-face affectionate playful interactions are a complex, intuitively improvised dance. The specifics of mother-baby play are original for each mother and baby. Both the mother and the baby contribute to the details. These mutually pleasurable interactions are part of their developing attachment relationship. The primary elements are mutual gaze, a mother's lilting words, a baby's expressive sounds, facial expressions, and synchronized smiles (Beebe, B. 2016). These ways of being together are not explicitly taught, they are implicitly known by mothers and passed from one generation to the next. The mother's feelings of connectedness with her baby might be, "I am your mommy; you are my baby; we go together."

Robyn described the most pleasurable play she had with three-month-old Sloane:

"I lie on the sofa with a pillow behind my head and my knees bent. Sloane is seated on my lap, leaning back against my thighs. It is a perfect position for a conversation and a song. We hold hands. Our eye contact is intense and intimate. Actually, I think it's the first time in my life that I have had such an experience of connectedness. At this age, other kinds of play can be boring for me."

Robyn's mother had died when Robyn was two years old and she had no explicit memories of her mother other than photographs she had seen and stories she had been told. Her intersubjective play with Sloane, that included, mutual gaze, smiling, and tender touching, may have been a pleasurable reliving of early play with her own mother that had been implicitly known but not consciously remembered, or even imagined as possible in her romantic relationships. The deeply satisfying, intimate bond that she created during play with her baby enabled her to ignite more satisfying intimate interactions with her husband.

Laughing

At around four months of age, babies begin to laugh. Mother-baby interactions that evoke repeated laughter can be thought of as emotion regulation play. The mother initiates and repeats a comical action, and her baby's laughter repeatedly erupts in response to the simultaneously expected and surprising elements. For example, while maintaining mutual gaze, Londyn puts five-month-old Skye's pacifier in her own mouth, and as Skye reaches for it, her mother spits it out with a loud, playful popping sound. Skye laughs uproariously. This playful interaction is repeated several times. The essential elements of this pleasurable game include the intuitively well-synchronized rhythm of their turn-taking, the loving playfulness of the unusual, but repeated and therefore expected popping noise, and the pacifier in the right place (a mouth) but also the wrong place (Mommy's mouth). When unpleasure that includes fear, frustration, or hyperarousal is too intense or predominates an interaction that evokes laughter, the baby's laugh can sound more like crying. A baby's laughter can have different meanings.

Peek-a-Boo

Mother-baby play is an opportunity for babies to have fun, learn, and master everyday stress. As described earlier, when mother-baby attachment develops, babies begin to have stressful reactions to separation. Peek-a-boo, the classic game about separation and reunion, first reported in the early 1500s and played throughout the world, is one of the earliest games introduced by mothers. While each mother and baby play their own version of peek-a-boo, and while the specific differences may have meaning, they all share the main elements of the game: the separations are brief and the reunions are joyful – separations are followed by reunions. The universal appeal of peek-a-boo is its meaning about separation. As a baby learns that Mommy and what is important about her continue to exist when they are separated from each other, hiding and finding games increase and help babies to cope with the stress of separation.

The following description of a first game of peek-a-boo illustrates some of the details. While face-to-face with her baby, the mother momentarily covers her face with her hands. She and her baby no longer have emotional contact with each other; their facial expressions, which ordinarily communicate enormous emotional meaning and vitality, cannot be seen. While the rest of the mother's body remains visible, the momentary loss of their emotional connection activates the baby's experience of distress that she has during separations. Seeing the rest of her mother's body while unable to see her face supports the baby's emerging understanding that her mother still exists when they are separated from each other. This very brief loss of emotional relatedness is immediately repaired when the mother removes her hands from covering her face, her eyes brighten, and she smiles. Her baby's gleeful reciprocal smile reveals the significance of the game. The singsong words, "peek-a-boo" and "I see you," that accompany the hand motions accentuate the rhythm of the game. Games of peek-a-boo are often elaborated into hiding and finding games.

For example, Harper watched her mother hide her favorite baby doll under a blanket, and with great delight, Harper pulled the blanket off. After mastering peek-a-boo with her mother and with her doll, ten-month-old Harper created a new game. She repeatedly threw a small, hard ball far and fast across the room and crawled to retrieve it. Harper was a delicate little girl and the ball made a loud crash when it hit the floor and rolled under the sofa, out of sight. We can imagine what it felt like to Harper, *I am strong. I can throw the ball hard. I can make the ball go away, and I can get it back.* Harper's mother liked seeing that her gentle little girl could also be strong and assertive. In addition to the pleasure of mastering the physical feat, Harper's play had meaning. Her game reinforced her learning that the ball existed even when it rolled under the sofa where she could not see it, but could reach and retrieve it. Furthermore, Harper turned her passive experience of being left into an active experience. Harper controlled separating from and reuniting with the ball, unlike when separated from her mother, which she could not control; Harper was playing peek-a-boo with the ball. A baby's pretend play has particular learning power. Harper continued to play peek-a-boo with the ball for about two months. Separations from her mother became easier, and Harper stopped playing the game.

Another variation of peek-a-boo is the turn-taking game often initiated when a baby hands an object to her mother: "I give it to you; you give it to me." Although the object is not hidden, as it is handed back and forth between mother and baby; the object is possessed by one and then the other. When it is received by the mother, she may say "thank you," and in time, the baby imitates "thank you." The melodic words become part of the play. The turn-taking in this pass-the-object game is similar to that in a conversation in which thoughts are passed back and forth between two people (Bergman, A. and Lefcourt, I. 1999).

Play with Toys

Beginning play with toys provides the opportunity for babies to learn about how things work and promotes a sense of self that can make things happen such as shake a rattle and make it jingle. Sometimes, trying to manipulate a toy is frustrating. Marilyn realized that her uncertainty about whether to help nine-month-old Aimee turn the crank on the activity box or to let her struggle to do it herself was related to her memories of her own struggles about what it meant to her and to her mother to do homework by herself or with her mother's help. Marilyn recalled:

> "My mother thought that I needed her help with homework. If I got her help, I felt completely inadequate. If I did my homework by myself, I was afraid it would be unacceptable. I never felt this way with my son, but I do with Aimee all the time. I guess I identify more with her because she is a girl."

Understanding the link between her childhood memory about homework and her conflict about helping Aimee with a toy enabled Marilyn to make decisions about when to help Aimee that were based on her interactions with Aimee, rather than in response to her reactivated childhood feelings of inadequacy. She realized that Aimee was challenged by various tasks and motivated to work hard to master them as she had assumed with her son. Marilyn's childhood experience had influenced her interactions with her daughter, but not with her son.

There are two complementary patterns of mothers' play with their babies and toys: following their baby's lead and expanding their baby's play. A combination of both kinds of play promotes a baby's play, learning, and pleasure, and simultaneously contributes to mothers' interest in the play.

Play with Mommy's Things

A baby may want to touch and fondle an object that her mother wears, for example, a shiny necklace. The intrinsic properties of the object may be appealing, but in addition, a baby's interest comes from growing mother-baby attachment and the baby's beginning ability to mentally connect the object with her mother (Bergman, A. and Lefcourt, I. 1999). The baby mentally links the object with her mother, but the object is also separate and therefore can be possessed by the baby. A daughter's developing ability to mentally connect an object with her mother, and to use that mental connection to feel emotionally close to her mother while touching the object, is an emergent developmental step that may be practiced frequently. When the object is linked to something typically only women do, for example, wear lipstick or carry a purse, a little girl's play with the object may acquire this additional meaning. When Wynona mastered walking at 11 months, an activity of separation, she insisted on carrying her mother's purse as she walked from room to room around the apartment. When she was 18 months, she put lip gloss in the purse to take to the playground with her. Wynona's choice to carry two items linked to femininity as she separates from her mother indicates a facet of her emerging self-identity: *I am a girl like Mommy.*

Pretend Play and Gender

A baby's imitations of her mother clapping or waving and imitations of a dog barking or a cow mooing are linked to the progressive development of pretend play. Babbling on her mother's cell phone is a precursor to role-play. A baby may imitate her mother by pretending to feed a baby doll or toy animal. If a mother pushes a toy car along the floor and makes an engine noise, her baby may imitate the sound. Mother and baby are building a repertoire of everyday pretend play scenarios.

Beginning pretend play with toy animals and dolls includes the possibility of gender related themes. The labels male or female, and related traits and roles, may be assigned to the dolls and animals deliberately or inadvertently by the mother. Current cultural influences and mothers' childhood memories are enmeshed in the play scenarios that are created. A mothers' group discussion shed light on this idea and triggered the mothers' insights. Wren described her pretend play with one-year-old Reese:

"We play with the little doll family every day. Reese loves the stories I make up about going to the playground, eating dinner, and going to the zoo. Because lately separations have been difficult for Reese, yesterday I made up a story about saying goodbye. However, I kept having the Daddy doll go to work. I was totally surprised because I go to work every day and she cries when I leave. Reese's father often works at home. I'm not sure why I did that."

After a moment's thought Wren remembered:

"My mother didn't work, but my father went to work every day. He loved his work. I think that my mother resented it. She wanted to work, but believed that mothers should be home with the children. My Mom is always support-ive of me working and proud of my successes at work, but I think she is also critical of me working, and maybe envious that I am doing something that she always wanted to do. I love my work like my Dad, but I feel guilty about working and leaving Reese. I don't think my Dad ever felt guilty. Maybe that's why I pretended that the Daddy doll was going to work."

Wren's description of her play with Reese, her related childhood memories, her guilt about working, and her insight about the meaning of having the Daddy doll leave to go to work opened group discussion about the ways in which mothers' ideas and memories about gender can be reflected in mother-baby pretend play. Harriet commented:

"Whenever I play with Eden with the toy dog-family, I always have the mommy-dog playing with her puppies. They jump together, run together, and rollover together. I never have the daddy-dog take care of the puppies, or play with them. I'm not sure why I do that. Maybe I like having more control and involvement with Eden, even though I complain that my husband doesn't do enough."

Theresa added:

"I just realized that I always refer to the animals that we play with as 'he.' I don't know why I do that. Maybe I should make some of them girls."

Marissa said:

"It's almost Halloween. It's Josephine's first Halloween and we are going to a party; I bought a beautiful princess costume for her. Josephine is only 1-year-old and I usually dress her so gender neutral, but I made a totally girly-girl costume choice, and I am so excited about it. I didn't realize I would have these feelings. My Mom never allowed me to buy the very feminine, pretty clothes. Maybe that's why I dress Josephine so gender neutral and why I chose the princess costume for Halloween. A princess costume is pretend, but I realize that I would like to see Josephine in real dresses."

The group discussion about beginning mother-baby pretend play and gender awakened the mothers' related childhood memories and their current conflicts of which the mothers had not been aware but had included in play with their daughters. Wren had introduced separation into the pretend play scenarios to help Reese cope with the stress of separation every morning when she went to work, but in the play, Wren had the Daddy go to work. The daddy-doll going to work was a re-enactment in play of her own childhood experiences that included her mother's resentment of her husband, who worked without guilt, and her mother's belief that mothers should not work. Harriet realized that while she wanted Eden to know that daddies want to take care of and play with their children, she did not include it in their play. Harriet became aware of her own wishes for exclusivity with Eden that conflicted with her wishes for her husband to do more with Eden. Marissa, who dressed Josephine in gender neutral clothes as her mother had dressed her, became aware of her pleasure in her stereotypic girl costume choice for Josephine and began to dress her in some pretty dresses.

These few examples illustrate some of the ways in which ideas related to gender are handed down from mother to daughter during early pretend play. The personal and cultural elements are entangled from one generation to the next.

Play Alone in the Presence of Mommy

Babies play with their mothers and they play alone. Both kinds of play are pleasurable and promote development. A third category of a baby's play is: alone in the presence of Mommy; mother and baby are together, but each one is focused on something different. They are physically together, intermittingly interactive, and emotionally connected. For example: while the mother is reading the newspaper, her baby is emptying and filling a basket full of blocks as they have done together. Occasionally, the mother and baby look at each other, or the mother says something, or her baby gives a block to her mother. There are simultaneous feelings of emotional connectedness with each other and solitary pleasure – alone, but not alone. Alone in the presence of Mommy has been described as contributing to the developing capacity to be alone (Winnicott, D.W. 1990). We can imagine that alone in the presence of Mommy promotes a baby's internal image of her mother that includes what it feels like to be close to her. The baby's internal sense of her mother is becoming part of the baby's sense of self. Ongoing feelings, *Mommy keeps me safe; I am safe and Mommy loves me; I am lovable* are becoming part of her daughter's sense of self.

Summary: Play

The most distinctive characteristics of play are that it is pleasurable and self-motivated. When babies play, they learn about the world and themselves; they learn about their bodies and their minds. When babies play with others, they learn about turn-taking and other aspects of pleasurable social interaction. Beginning pretend play includes events of a baby's daily life and the possibility of gender related themes, including gender roles. Peek-a-boo is the earliest play to master stress – the stress of separation.

Codes of Behavior

During their first year, babies gradually begin to learn codes of behavior – the do's and don'ts of everyday life. Codes of behavior, or social rules, are the needed guidelines to live in the world with other people in the family, the sandbox, school, and eventually the wider world. There are cultural norms and personal codes of behavior. The codes of behavior a mother teaches her daughter often clash with her baby's own wishes, impulses, and intense curiosity.

Babies learn about ways to behave by observation and by instruction, and they gradually learn to expect approval and disapproval for specific behaviors. As they develop, babies are highly motivated to behave in ways to get approval and enrich their feelings of self-worth. This may be difficult to believe because babies so often behave in ways that get disapproval. This paradox can be explained by child development theories about a little girl's developing sense of self: a girl who has likes and dislikes, and ideas and intentions of her own that conflict with pleasing her mother. When mothers are teaching and babies are learning the do's and don'ts of everyday life, emotions can run high. Gradually, the codes of behavior that her mother teaches mostly become a little girl's own codes of behavior.

Behavioral Do's and Don'ts, and Emotional Development

The overarching goal when teaching behavioral do's and don'ts to a baby is to promote emotional development. Emotional development includes the mental capacities needed to regulate emotions, and wishes to please Mommy – an aspect of attachment. It also includes the ability to inhibit behavior when impulses are strong, to achieve adequate resolution of ambivalence, to tolerate frustration, to wait, to get satisfaction from substitute gratifications when needed, and to develop a personal sense of right and wrong – a conscience. These mental abilities are the pillars of socialized behavior. A baby's behavioral obedience without underlying emotional development is flawed and therefore fragile. Sensitive and attuned mother-baby interactions while teaching codes of behavior promote the baby's development of these mental capacities that are essential for socialized behavior. However, it is important to note that the converse is also true: learning the behaviors promotes emotional development. Therefore, the convergence of codes of behavior and emotional development is the model for teaching and learning codes of behavior.

When a baby feels understood – when a baby's thoughts and feelings are recognized and accepted as understandable, even when disagreed with – it is easier for a baby to learn her mother's codes of behavior. For example, while 11-month-old Aurora was in the highchair drinking from her sippy cup, she repeatedly threw the cup on the floor and leaned over the side of the highchair to watch it crash. Her mother, Brook, kept telling her to stop, but Aurora kept throwing the cup. Since Aurora was drinking her water and was interested in the spectacle she was creating, rather than take the cup away from her, Brook decided to give a small rubber toy to Aurora to investigate gravity. She told Aurora:

"It is so interesting to watch the cup crash on the floor. Cups are not for throwing; here is a toy you can throw."

In this way, Brook supported Aurora's self-initiative and cognitive learning, and at the same time taught her about not throwing cups. Aurora may not have understood all the words, but she understood their important meaning: no throwing cups, and some version of, *Mommy thinks I had an interesting idea and knows why I wanted to throw the cup.* After lunch, Brook elaborated Aurora's play with the block by giving a soft toy to her that landed on the floor quietly. For a few days, Aurora alternated throwing the hard rubber toy and the soft toy. A mother's attention to both the external behavior she wants her baby to learn and simultaneously to her baby's inner world of thoughts, feelings, and intentions can result in complementary behavioral learning and emotional and cognitive development.

Because babies want and need their mothers' approval, they become increasingly self-observant. A little girl develops internal conflicts between pleasing her mother by doing what her mother wants, and pleasing herself by satisfying her own curiosities, wishes, and impulses that are unacceptable to her mother – for example, throwing sippy cups on the floor. Through repeated supportive teaching-learning interactions, interpersonal mother-baby conflicts about behavior increasingly become a child's own internal conflicts – *I can please myself and throw the cup on the floor or I can please Mommy and get her approval. Mommy knows that throwing things is fun and I had a good idea. I can throw something else.* The repetition of supportive teaching-learning interactions promotes this process and results in the mother's codes of behavior becoming the child's own sense of right and wrong. In addition, a little girl learns it is important to please herself.

Signaling Intentions to Misbehave

As discussed earlier, one indication that a baby is learning her mother's codes of behavior is when she signals an intention to misbehave before she misbehaves. In this way, she asserts her wish to misbehave – an act of autonomy – and at the same time enables her mother to stop her before she misbehaves so that she can do what is expected and thereby get her mother's approval. Londyn had been repeatedly shown how to pet the family dog gently and was always stopped when she tried to pull the dog's tail. After many repetitions, Londyn began to signal her intention to pull the dog's tail instead of doing it. Londyn was aware of her thinking, differentiating her thoughts from actions, communicating her thoughts about pulling the dog's tail, preventing herself from doing it, asserting her autonomy, and simultaneously engaging her mother's help to stop herself and thereby earn her mother's approval. When she signaled an intention to pull the dog's tail, her mother gently embraced her and said:

"I see, you remember no pulling Flossy's tail. I will help you to stop yourself."

A mother's expectations of her baby's behavior gradually become her little girl's own standards of behavior. A baby communicating an intention to defy her mother indicates her internal conflict about the behavior, her beginning ability to stop herself, and a step in the process of developing her own codes of behavior.

Consistency and Inconsistency

Consistency is often described as the best approach to establishing routines and teaching codes of behavior. However, at times, there are useful inconsistencies. There are inevitable disruptions of routines, and many rules are context dependent. For example, as described above, rules such as no pulling dogs' tails are non-negotiable and are consistently upheld. However, patting a dog's back gently is okay; but it may not be okay when a dog is eating. In addition, rules about petting dogs are different if the dog is a family pet or an unfamiliar dog in the park. Mother-baby teaching-learning interactions about petting dogs may be inconsistent in a variety of contexts.

In order to be responsive to a baby's developmental changes, shifting emotional states, and life experience, a mother's routines need to be flexible – another way of saying inconsistent. For example, Quincy had established a bedtime routine with ten-month-old Helena that included: while Helena held her soft teddy bear, Quincy held Helena on her lap. As she read two books to Helena, they gently swayed in the glider, and then Quincy dimmed the lights, nursed Helena, and, while placing Helena in her crib with her teddy bear sang their special goodnight song. Quincy left the room while Helena was still awake, and in a few minutes, she fell asleep. This well-established routine was disrupted when Quincy went away with her husband for a romantic weekend without Helena. After she returned, separations became difficult and bedtime became a disaster. As soon as Quincy finished reading the second book, Helena began to cry, grabbed the book, and refused to nurse. Changing the routine helped. The new routine included: reading three books – the third of which Helena chooses. While being held in her mother's arms, Helena puts the books back on the shelf and her teddy bear into the crib. Quincy then sits back on the glider and Helena nurses. After nursing, Quincy sings their goodnight song and as Quincy lowers her into the crib, Helena reaches for her teddy bear and snuggles up as her mother leaves the room. Quincy's ability to flexibly change the routine and Helena being more active in the new routine helped to establish the new routine that preceded bedtime separation. However, a change in the routine that had been associated with the stressful separation may have been more important than the details that changed.

Reliable routines help babies to develop expectations and adapt to everyday events. Being able to adapt to the inevitable changes in routine is also essential and promotes emotion regulation. Some inconsistencies in rules help children to be responsive to everyday variation and nuance, such as some things are okay in private, but not okay in public; it is okay to eat French fries with fingers, but not soup; some things are okay with Mommy but not with Daddy. To learn the non-negotiable, the negotiable, and the context-dependent rules requires multiple teaching-learning interactions. There are a few non-negotiable, non-flexible routines, rules, or ways of being. Changes in routines and rules, whether in response to child development, a mother's stress, or changing personal preferences, can promote a baby's ability to adapt to changing life experiences.

Internal Conflict

In addition to internal conflicts between pleasing oneself and pleasing others, and between attachment and autonomy, babies begin to have other ambivalent feelings. Recognizing a baby's ambivalent feelings can be useful. For example, a baby may be frightened by the noise of the blender, but may also be curious about it. Cynthia was ten months and cried every time her mother, Austin, turned the blender on, but when the blender was off, she was curious about it. Cynthia was delighted by the power she had to turn the ceiling lights on and off with the quiet flick of a switch. By further stimulating Cynthia's curiosity about the blender, Austin helped Cynthia put the cover on and off, and drop strawberries into it. Austin pretended to make the blender's noise, and Cynthia imitated her. After having fun with the blender, Austin taught Cynthia how to turn the blender on and off. While being held in her mother's arms, Cynthia was helped to master her fear of the blender's noise by imitating and controlling it.

Internal conflict and ambivalent feelings are universal. Mothers also have internal conflicts. A mother's internal conflicts can affect setting limits, establishing routines, and teaching codes of behavior. A mother may find it more challenging to recognize the impact of her own internal conflicts on interactions with her daughter than to recognize her child's internal conflicts. For example, Jillian believed that it was best for babies to sleep in their own beds, a routine that she wanted to teach her daughter, Samantha. She did not think that co-sleeping was good for children or parents. By four months of age, Samantha was sleeping through the night in her own crib. After her last nursing for the day, Jillian changed Samantha's diaper and lay her down in her crib awake. As Jillian left the room, Samantha quickly drifted off to sleep. However, this well-established routine changed when Samantha was around eight months old, an age when, typically, there is an increase in a baby's stress reactions to separation that can affect sleep routines. As soon as her head touched the mattress, Samantha sat herself up and began to scream. Jillian returned to Samantha, comforted her, lay her back down, and began to leave the room again. After many repetitions, Samantha fell asleep. When this pattern was repeated during the middle of the night, Jillian was frustrated and exhausted. Her own conflict, of which she had been unaware, emerged. Determined not to take Samantha into her and her husband's bed, she moved a recliner into Samantha's room and fell asleep on it with Samantha. Jillian described her conflict and its connection to a childhood memory:

"I'm not sleeping with Samantha in my bed, but I am sleeping with her on the recliner and not sleeping with my husband. I don't know what I want to do. I was never allowed in my parents' bed. I didn't think I would ever want to sleep with Samantha. Maybe I did and didn't know it. Actually, I remember when I was about 6 years old and my baby teeth started to get loose and fall out, I was very scared and wanted to sleep in my parents' bed. I was afraid my teeth would all fall out in the middle of the night. My parents would not let me. They said it was no big deal, all children lose their baby teeth. It was a big deal for me."

Recalling her childhood memory helped Jillian to give the additional support to Samantha that she needed and to reestablish Samantha's ability to sleep in her own bed. Jillian created a separation routine that included a goodbye song. She always used the same babysitter who played with Samantha for half an hour before going out. In addition, Jillian and Samantha began to play peek-a-boo and other games of separation several times a day. Separations became easier.

As described above, a baby girl wants to please her mother, but not always. Sometimes her explorations, curiosity, attachment needs, and autonomy strivings are so compelling that they conflict with her wishes to please her mother and compete with following her mother's rules and routines.

Summary: Codes of Behavior

A baby begins to learn codes of behavior during the first year of life. Valued routines and rules that are being learned get disrupted by development, life events, and a baby's own passions. Mother-daughter relationship themes: being the same and being different, attachment needs and autonomy strivings, identifying with and individuating from, and pleasing oneself and pleasing others are activated. Mother-baby interactions about the do's and don'ts of everyday life gradually become an internal process for the baby. As a little girl is increasingly able to: benefit from her mother's approval, tolerate frustration, resolve ambivalent feelings, and get satisfaction from substitute gratifications, her learning codes of behavior progresses and she develops a conscience. During the first three years of development, a mother's codes of behavior gradually become her little girl's, and she develops her own internal sense of right and wrong.

Sense of Self

A baby's emerging sense of self includes her body sense of self and all that her body can do and feel; a mind sense of self that has thoughts and emotions, likes and dislikes, intentions and agency, and an evolving sense of self in interaction with others. Before language, a baby may imitate sounds and participate in turn-taking sound interactions with her mother – a conversation without words. She may discover with delight her exuberant squeal. When she begins to crawl, she practices accelerated approaches to and separations from her mother. Her sense of self is invigorated. In addition, gradually, she is developing a gendered sense of self. A mother's thoughts and feelings about her baby contribute to her baby's developing sense of self. Though not spoken, words to describe a baby's emerging sense of self include: *Mommy loves me, I am lovable. Mommy protects me, I am safe. Mommy is proud of me; I can do many things. Mommy is my mommy; I feel good.* These ideas are experienced bodily, mentally, and emotionally.

Sense of Self, Sex, and Gender

Designating the biological sex of a baby occurs either before or at birth, but at what age a baby girl self-identifies as a girl is difficult to say. In recent years, there has been increased attention to and controversy about the meanings of gender in medicine, law, politics, and child development. Picture books for young children and the marketing of toys have been influenced by shifting cultural attitudes. While in 1967 the box cover of the game Battleship showed a father and son playing the game, and a mother and daughter washing dishes in the background, today this would not occur. Some of the societal changes and controversies among experts have raised questions for parents.

Over 25 years ago, I conducted a written survey among the 60 mothers and fathers attending my groups with their children between 1 and 3½ years of age. To the questions, "Does your daughter know that she is a girl?" and "Does your son know that he is a boy" all of the parents answered, "Yes." In response to the questions, "How does your daughter know that she is a girl?" and "How does your son know that he is a boy?" they filled in the blank, "Because I tell her" or "Because I tell him." However, what is left unanswered is the multiple ways in which parents "tell" their children explicitly and implicitly, deliberately and inadvertently: you are a girl or you are a boy.

When mothers tell their daughters directly that they are girls, it is clear. For example, Joyce noticed that whenever nine-month-old Janice did something clever, she told her, "You are such a smart girl." Joyce always put a bow in Janice's hair like many of the other girls they knew. When Janice protested, her mother said, "All the girls wear a bow." Undoubtedly, Janice did not understand these words at nine months of age, but for her mother, the idea that being a girl means you wear a bow in your hair was clear. When Valerie tried to feed herself with a spoon for the first time, her mother said, "You are a bigger girl." While the mothers had many examples of the ways in which they tell their daughters directly that they are girls, the ways in which they tell them indirectly and the ways in which they tell them what it means to be a girl, were less noticeable.

Identifying Mommy as a woman, Daddy as a man, and the baby as a girl may be everyday occurrences. Gender is in our consciousness. Allusions to what it means to be male or female begin to surface. Many things influence the ways in which gender is expressed and communicated in mother-baby interactions. For example, Willow's mother Piper was distressed that people frequently thought ten-month-old Willow was a boy. Piper dressed Willow in what she considered "gender neutral" clothes, but clothes that the world around her seemed to view as boys' clothes. Piper resented "gender stereotyping" and did not want to conform to it until she realized that her nickname for Willow since she was two months old was Will:

"I just realized I am calling Willow a boy's name! My husband really wanted a boy; maybe that's why I call her Will. I want her to be recognized as a girl. I want her to know she's a girl."

Piper's insight about what motivated her to choose a boy's name as a nickname for her daughter enabled her to realize that it was important to her that Willow be recognized as a girl.

Whereas some mothers may avoid gender-linked references, others may highlight gender (Coates, S.1997). Another mother in the group, Lesley, noted:

"I just realized that I usually refer to Jackson as a baby, not as a girl. I love her name; it was my mother's maiden name. It sounds strong to me. I never thought of it, but we are starting to call her Jack for short – clearly a boy's name. I thought I chose the name Jackson because it was my mother's maiden name which she gave up when she married my father, but I guess the name Jackson has many meanings to me."

Lesley realized that her choice of Jackson's name had gender meaning in addition to being her mother's maiden name. Jackson sounded like a "strong" name to Leslie because it sounded like a boy's name. A mother's understanding of the influences that her life experiences have on her views about gender can be informative. As a baby girl's awareness of and reactions to gender develop, important information about what gender means to her will be revealed.

Mirror Image and Developing Sense of Self

A new perspective of self was emerging for 11-month-old Dakota as she explored her mirror image. When Dakota had been younger and her mother held her in front of the mirror, she seemed to focus on her mother's reflection. This time was different. With determination, Dakota crawled very close to the mirror. Anticipating a moment of discovery, her mother videotaped what happened next.

Dakota, with her forehead almost touching the mirror, looked carefully at her own reflection. She stuck her tongue slowly in and out several times. Her concentration intensified. She moved her head gently toward the mirror until her forehead and nose touched it softly. Her mother said, "Yes, you see your nose."

Dakota wiggled her nose. She repeated, ever so slowly, sticking her tongue in and out and gently kissed her reflection. Her mother joyfully commented, "You are giving yourself a kiss." Dakota turned away from the mirror and looked at her mother with a big smile. The video recording captured Dakota's new mirror play and revealed a facet of her emerging sense of self that may not have included being a girl, but did reflect seeing herself from the outside while experiencing herself on the inside. Her mother watched with delight.

Summary: Sense of Self

Mother-baby interactions and their attachment relationship are at the core of a baby's developing sense of self. Although being seen as a girl starts at the beginning of life; self-identifying as a girl gradually develops. She has been told directly and indirectly that she is a girl and what it means to be a girl. A baby's first birthday is a milestone in this process and includes both beginning to identify with and to individuate from her mother. She has discovered the beginnings of her own sense of agency: she can make things happen. She has begun to discover her own mind, she has experienced pleasurable mother-baby meeting of minds, and she is exploring their separateness of minds. She has a beginning body, mental, and interpersonal sense of self.

6 One to Two Years

The transition from baby to toddler includes walking and beginning to talk, and makes possible new experiences of autonomy and new kinds of mother-daughter interaction. Attachment intensifies. The exhilaration of upright mobility, impassioned curiosity, and exciting new discoveries are characteristic of this phase. In order to organize all that she is learning, a little girl begins to create mental categories based on similarities and differences. "Baby" is one of the first categories created; mommy and daddy categories quickly follow. Boy and girl categories begin to emerge. Other categories include big and little, animals, colors, and body parts. During this year, a little girl's sense of self is beginning to include, *I am a girl.*

Mother-toddler interactions provide the secure base from which a little girl learns about the world and practices her rapidly developing abilities. As she explores her surroundings, first crawling then walking, a little girl keeps her mother emotionally with her and remains in her mother's emotional orbit. She is held in her mother's mind, and she holds her mother in her mind. If in the same room, when she needs to, she signals her mother and together mother and daughter share a moment of mutual gaze that is full of meaning, often without words – social referencing. If physical contact or proximity is needed, she approaches her mother. Mother-toddler attachment is an organizing element of her emotional inner world and is reflected in her behavior. Her attachments to others also deepen.

Discovery of Girl-Boy Differences

Based on their own observations and what they are being told, toddler girls begin to self-identify as girls. They also begin to identify other children as either girls or boys. They create female and male categories based on culturally prevalent styles of clothes and hair, and on designations they hear. Toddlers are interested in girl-boy differences. For example, in New York City, *Girls wear dresses and pants. Boys wear pants, they don't wear dresses. Girls have long hair; boys have short hair.* Little girls are also interested in differences between men and women, *Mommies wear lipstick. Daddies shave their faces.* Whether this interest in male and female categories is environmentally determined, innate, or a combination of both is hotly debated. Some toddler categories may seem rigid in that they do not include all possible variations, but they serve toddlers' needs and their beginning ability to make

DOI: 10.4324/9781003687603-7

sense of the world they perceive. Categories become more complex with development. For example, *Most boys have short hair, but some boys have long hair.*

Awareness of Female-Male Genital Differences

Discovery of female-male genital differences is thought to occur at around 16 months of age (Roiphe, H. and Galenson, E. 1981). A little girl assumes that all the parts of her body are exactly the way they should be. And just as she has learned to expect that people have a head, two eyes, a nose, and a mouth as she does, she expects others to have the same genital body parts that she has. Girl-boy genital differences are not what she expects. When she discovers that a little boy does not have what she has, this violation of an expectation contributes to her interest; awareness of *not like me* evokes curiosity. In addition, awareness of her pleasurable genital sensations stimulates a little girl's increasing awareness of and interest in girl-boy genital differences and contributes to self-identifying as a girl. Consider the pleasure during the first three years that a little girl experiences being naked, and the pride she takes in her naked body.

Reactions to Nudity

The new awareness of female-male genital differences during this phase of development can influence a little girl's reactions to seeing other children naked. Teri had bathed with her five-year-old brother since she could sit in the bathtub. When she turned 16 months, she began to try to touch her brother's penis. The bath toys no longer interested her. At times, this annoyed her brother and he yelled at her to stop. At other times, he giggled and began to splash the water out of control. There were definite changes in both children's reactions to being naked together. Teri's mother decided to bathe them separately because she thought it was "preoccupying" for her daughter and "overstimulating" for her son.

Awareness of female-male genital differences also influences how a little girl reacts to seeing her mother and her father naked. During a mothers' group, the women described their experiences of how their little girls' reactions to seeing them naked had changed. Larissa had bathed with Julia since she was a baby. It was a pleasurable time for them both. While Julia contentedly played with the bath toys, her mother washed her and relaxed. Julia seemed to have had no reaction to seeing her mother naked until she was a little over 17 months and she began to try to touch her mother's pubic hair. Julia's reaction to her mother's naked body had changed; she had become curious about that part of her mother's body. Larissa understood Julia's interest in her pubic hair; it was something she had never noticed before; it was different from her body. Larisa did not want her daughter to explore her pubic hair; she stopped her and said, "That's my pubic hair. All women have pubic hair on their vaginas." Larissa told the mothers' group her thinking:

> "I understand that because Julia is older now, she is curious about things that she was not curious about before. She notices things now that she didn't

notice before or didn't care about. Now she's curious. I want Julia to know it's okay to be curious, we can talk about all parts of her body and mine. She can touch all parts of her own body, but she cannot touch all parts of my body."

Kara added:

"I agree, children need to learn that many curiosities are not best satisfied by action; for example playing with matches would be too dangerous. But touching your body is not dangerous; why not let her do it?"

Larissa answered:

"I don't think Julia's curiosity about my body will be satisfied by touching it once; she would want to do it more. Curiosity about sex is endless. Exploring my body won't satisfy all her curiosities about bodies. And anyway, it does not feel right to me. It's too sexy."

Claudine added:

"Maggie has become very curious about my body also. She watches me undress, go to the toilet, and we bathe together. She tries to touch my nipples, my pubic hair, and my butt. I've been ignoring it because I don't want to make a big deal about it, but she's doing it more and more. My husband and I like to be naked. We both grew up in very up-tight homes and don't want that for Maggie, but maybe she's being overstimulated. She used to watch my husband pee. Once she tried to touch his penis, so he doesn't pee in front of her anymore."

Claudine decided to limit being naked in front of Maggie and stopped bathing with her even though it had been very pleasurable. She remembered that the increase in Maggie touching her breasts and pubic hair had occurred after having changed a tampon in front of her. Claudine realized:

"I really liked the feeling of intimacy bathing with Maggie. I never felt close to my mother. She's always very formal and distant. I realize now that I have many other ways of feeling close and being intimate with Maggie that don't include being naked or changing tampons."

Sometimes the amount of nudity that feels comfortable for adults is too much for children. For Maggie, watching her mother remove a bloody tampon and insert a new one may have triggered disturbing thoughts and feelings that she was trying to cope with by touching her mother's genitals. After Claudine limited family nudity, the many moments of emotionally intimate interaction that she and

Maggie shared and their many tender physical interactions became more obvious and fulfilling to Claudine. Maggie stopped trying to touch her mother's breasts and genital area.

Mothers often wonder whether parent-child same-sex nudity and opposite-sex nudity should be thought about differently. In fact, children have reactions to both; a naked body is not a neutral object. Mothers have childhood memories of seeing both their mothers and fathers naked, and remember a range of feelings that were evoked in response to each parent's naked body. Toddlers are curious about the bodies of their same-sex parents and their opposite-sex parents. Both arouse interest and stimulate a toddler's thoughts, feelings, and sometimes worries. Frequently, mothers question whether a little girl's responses to nudity are sexual, sensual, or sensorial. This question may arise because it may be disconcerting to think about such a young girl in terms of sex. One way to answer the question – do little girls have sexual thoughts or feelings – is to consider the idea that because awareness of genital differences relates to the sex organs, and sex organs have specific pleasurable sensations, these experiences are sensorial, sensual, and sexual.

When Jayne was 17 months old, she stood in front of the toilet with her hands on her genitals and said, "Making pee-pee." Jayne's mother Harmony thought that Jayne was asking a question that she could not ask in words, but a question that she could answer in words. Harmony said:

> "Daddy makes peepee standing up. Girls make pee-pee sitting on the toilet, you are a girl like Mommy. You can sit on your potty and make peepee."

While the world may be more complicated, Harmony believed that her response that highlighted a female-male sex difference, acknowledged a gender difference, and designated her child a girl, was the best response in the moment.

Awareness of female-male genital differences and child-adult genital differences can influence children's interest in their own genitals, can stimulate increased awareness of or focus on their own genital sensations, and can promote their interest in the genitals of others. Alecia and Tim were twins, and their mother, Cara, always bathed them together. It was convenient, and they had fun. After they turned 18 months, Tim began to hold his penis whenever he and his sister were naked together, and Alecia began to masturbate frequently. Bathing with her brother may have stimulated genital sensations, and the arousal of those sensations, combined with her reactions to the girl-boy genital differences, led to increased masturbation. The change in Tim's behavior may have been a reaction to a new awareness of the male-female genital differences and their meaning to him – concerns about losing his penis. Their mother, Cara, decided to bathe them separately. She described what was happening and her decision during a mother-toddler group. Patsy, another group-mother, confronted her:

> "Isn't it better for Tim to learn about boy-girl differences and for Cara to enjoy her genital sensations?"

Cara clarified her thinking further:

"Yes, but it's important to learn about boy-girl differences in a way that's comfortable, not in a way that makes him so nervous. It's great for Cara to discover genital pleasure, but not to be over-stimulated in a way that preoccupies her and interferes with other activities."

Brice, another mother, added:

"Ellie acts as if she doesn't notice when we bathe together, but I'm sure she notices that I'm naked. Maybe that's her reaction to noticing – tuning it out. I wonder what it means. I had three older brothers, and they were always naked."

As Brice talked about the details of her childhood memories of her brothers "always naked," including her fear of her brothers and her mother's rage at her brothers, she recalled memories she had forgotten about her brothers "sexually taunting" her. Like her daughter, Brice had not been noticing or remembering her reactions to nudity. As Brice began to remember more, Ellie began to point to her father's penis when she saw him naked, which gave Brice the opportunity to tell her, "That's Daddy's penis. Boys have penises; girls have vaginas."

Mothers have their own preferences about being naked in front of their children and their children being naked with each other. Their own childhood experiences – the pleasures, excitement, curiosities, as well as worries – motivate their decisions about family nudity. Recognizing the changing behavior of their children that may be reactive to seeing parents and siblings naked can be useful when making decisions about family nudity at each stage of development.

Gender Role Identity

Observations of female-male role differences begin to capture a toddler's attention. This is true whether children have same sex or opposite sex parents. Family composition and the tasks fulfilled by each member of the family can influence a toddler's awareness of and interest in gender roles. The first gender roles a little girl identifies are those of Mommy and Daddy. The specifics of those roles are different in each family. The discovery that mothers had been little girls who grew up and became mothers is made early. What this means to a little girl about herself evolves. A little girl's earliest ideas about the role of a mother are determined by the details of her individual life experiences that are generalized; for example, *Mommies feed their babies milk from their breasts. Daddies carry their babies on their shoulders.*

As a little girl observes other mothers and fathers, the differences from and similarities to her own mother and father are processed. Gradually, early stereotypes expand and include more variation. *My Mommy feeds me milk from her breast, Suzette's Daddy gives her a bottle. Bernadine's mommy gives her a bottle. Babies drink milk from breasts and bottles.* In some families, a frequent observation is, *Mommy drives the car and Daddy drives, but when Mommy and Daddy are together, Daddy always drives. Some families have two mommies. Some families have two daddies.* What this means to each member of the family may be different. Mothers' preferences to avoid gender themes, or to highlight or blur gender differences and similarities, and what gets talked about and what does not, may influence the meanings toddlers attribute to their observations of gender roles.

There are many contradictory ideas about the development of gender identity and gender role identity in both professional publications and public discourse. There is much that is unknown. Importantly, each little girl indicates her own developing thoughts and feelings about gender.

Temperament

Innate temperament and life experience both contribute to development. Mother-toddler interactions are an enormous part of life experience for a toddler. These interactions are influenced by the toddler's temperament, the mother's temperament, and the fit of each one's temperament with the other. Temperament includes the innate traits that are relatively predictable ways of behaving, such as activity level, novelty seeking or novelty avoidant (sometimes called shy or slow to warm up), persistence or distractibility, reactivity to sensory stimulation, and predominant mood. A mother's temperament and her child's temperament can align, complement each other, or clash.

Lynda was a quiet, gentle musician. Her daughter Kiki was an active, loud 22 month old. Lynda described their clashing temperaments:

> "She's all over the place, all the time. She climbs on everything and messes everything up. She never sits to listen to a story or to music. Her cry is so harsh it hurts my ears. Other little girls, I hate to say it, are more lady-like. She's very outgoing. I'm so different."

The innate temperament differences between Lynda and her daughter had created ongoing conflict between them until Lynda thought about her comment, "Other little girls, and I hate to say it, are more lady-like," and she remembered:

> "When I was a little girl, we had a jungle gym in the backyard and I learned how to hang-upside down on the trapeze. It was my 7-year-old birthday party, and I was wearing a dress. I hung upside-down on the trapeze and my dress fell all the way up and my panties showed. My mother was furious and yelled, 'You are not very lady-like!' Being accused of not being lady-like is the worst part of my memory. Maybe I was naturally more active and became less active to be more lady-like, or maybe I was always less active, but certainly my mother's comment influences my reactions to the differences between me and Kiki."

Lynda realized that her reactions to the temperament differences between herself and her daughter were intensified by the gender related meaning of her childhood memories and her mother's words, "You are not very lady-like." Being accused of not being the right kind of girl was the most painful part of her memory and the part that was reactivated with her daughter.

A Dress – Symbol of Femininity

Wearing a dress is a symbol of being a girl. While wearing a dress provides easy access to her genitals and visibility of her panties, dresses come with repeated in-structions: "Keep your legs closed and keep your panties covered." This apparent contradiction does not prevent little girls, and may pave the way for them, to pick up their skirts, sit with their legs spread, and spin around to fan out their skirts in gleeful peek-a-boo and hide-and-seek games with their dresses. For example, as Kellie lifted her dress, twirled around the room, and announced with pride, "I have a vagina, boys have a penis!"

A Mother's Sibling Rivalry, Temperament, and Pride Being a Girl

Sometimes a mother's rivalry with her own sister is infused with conflicts about showing off femininity, and is reactivated and repeated with her daughter. Joyce characterized herself as shy and reserved. She described her two-year-old daughter Jill:

> "She's such a showoff. Jill's always trying to be the center of attention. She wants to wear party dresses and twirl around all the time. I don't like it. I'm not like that."

Joyce's reserved demeanor was different from her exuberant outgoing daughter's and triggered memories of her older sister, whom she believed:

> "… did everything better and was always in the spotlight, especially when she twirled around and picked up her skirt."

Joyce's feelings about her sister had activated a ferocious rivalry with her daughter that Joyce felt she was losing. As Joyce began to recognize that she had displaced feelings that she had toward her sister onto her little girl, she became able to differentiate her painful childhood memories and continuing competition with her sister from the normal needs of a two year old that include an emerging sense of self as a girl to be admired.

Emotion Regulation

A toddler's temperament that includes high activity and hypersensitivity to sensory stimulation and emotional arousal may make emotion regulation more difficult.

For toddlers with more low-key temperaments, emotion regulation can be easier. As has been emphasized, a primary way in which emotions are regulated is through language: words to identify feelings and memory narratives to process feelings. Identifying feelings with words can create experiences of being understood, *I feel better when Mommy knows how I feel.* However, not always; when Justine's cookie crumbled, her mother, Marianna, said:

> "Your cookie broke into little pieces; I know you are disappointed. You want the big cookie. You can eat all the little pieces; and I think they taste yummy."

While these words may be complicated, the soothing quality of a mother's voice and her empathy can comfort her daughter and promote emotion regulation. But this is not what happened. Justine screamed and threw the cookie pieces on the floor. Marianna realized that while she had said understanding words, she felt angry at her daughter. Marianna had baked the cookies specially for Justine, and she was angry. Justine was not reacting to her mother's words: she was reacting to and mirroring her mother's underlying, authentic feelings of anger.

The mother-daughter relationship is at the center of a little girl's emotional life – both identifying with her mother and individuating from her. A mother's emotions and the ways in which she reacts to her own feelings have an impact on her daughter. Little girls are sensitive to their mothers' feelings even when their mothers are unaware of their own feelings or are trying to conceal them.

Attachment and Autonomy, Proximity, and Exploration

Toddlers are motivated by their attachment needs, autonomy strivings, and the tensions between them; their mothers are motivated to support their toddlers' autonomous explorations, as well as to keep them close. Sometimes these aims are in conflict and a little girl's exuberance, activity level, and autonomy strivings clash with her mother's needs for quiet closeness. Wendy described:

> "I keep saying I want Mia to play with the other children, but whenever she is on my lap touching base with me for security, I keep caressing her. I am trying to reassure her, but maybe I'm keeping her too close by caressing her."

Wendy's insight – the new meaning of caressing Mia to keep her close when Mia was ready to resume play after a cuddle – triggered Wendy's childhood memory:

> "I remember that I always wanted more physical contact with my mother. I must have been about 5 years old; we were at a party and there were so many people. I wanted to sit on my mother's lap, but she didn't want me to mess up her clothes. Now she doesn't want me to mess-up her apartment. She's

always telling me to use a coaster. Maybe that's why I don't get a coaster when I'm in her apartment; it's really about wanting to sit on my mother's lap when I was 5 and she cared more about staying neat. I always use a coaster in my own apartment."

Wendy's childhood memory helped her to understand interactions with her daughter and current interactions with her own mother in a new way. She began to help Mia return to play after a cuddle, and she started to use coasters in her mother's apartment.

Collecting Treasures

When babies begin to walk, they collect many treasures as they explore their surroundings. A toddler may deposit many items on her mother's lap; to a toddler, they are all precious – dirty sticks and stones, scraps of paper, toys, etc. While a mother holds her little girl's collection, and a little girl feels held by her mother as if in her arms and in her mind, the toddler's explorations continue and expand, and emotion regulation is sustained. In this way, toddlers maintain and refuel their internal mental sense of Mommy and create a bridge connecting the wider world with Mommy. This invisible bridge enables a little girl to feel emotionally close to her mother when she is at a slight distance playing and learning about the world (Bergman A., and Lefcourt I. 1999).

April and her mother, Taylor, were in a mother-toddler group for the first time. April was 15 months old and whimpered as she wandered aimlessly around the room. She was unable to play with the toys and unable to be close to her mother. April and her mother had no secure base or social referencing interactions. After a while, April approached her mother and dropped a doll next to her. Her mother did not respond; April walked away, quietly crying. A few minutes later, April dropped the doll on her mother's lap. Her mother removed it and placed it on the floor. April walked away and continued to wander and softly cry.

Mothers' group discussion focused on the possible meanings of April dropping the doll next to her mother and on her lap. The idea that April wanted to watch her mother hold the doll in order to feel close and safe triggered Taylor's frightening memories of her father's alcoholic rages and her mother's fear and helplessness – memories of how unsafe and frightened she herself felt:

"One night my father threw a lamp at the window. Shattered glass flew across the floor. My mother screamed. I'm not sure if the light bulb or the window broke, but I was terrified and felt so alone."

Both April's frightened, wandering aloneness and Taylor's ignoring the doll that April gave to her were enacted remnants of Taylor's childhood memories of fear and aloneness. Taylor's response to the links between her childhood memory and her interactions with April, combined with mothers' group support, enabled her to respond to April intuitively and empathically. Taylor said:

> "I think April feels the same way here as I remember feeling when my father threw the lamp: scared and alone. I'm ignoring her as I was ignored."

The next time April dropped the doll on her mother's lap, Taylor held it. Her initial awkwardness holding the doll revealed the remains of her childhood terror and aloneness. Gradually, as Taylor felt safer in the group, she embraced the doll tenderly. April began to hand the doll to her mother frequently and then to sit on her mother's lap. Her mother cuddled and caressed her. April began to explore the toys and when at a distance from her mother, they began to connect emotionally with mutual glances and smiles. The mother-daughter "doll-play" had provided a symbolic bridge to secure base attachment interactions.

April was no longer distressed; she felt held by her mother and safe. April's independent play became more organized and focused. She was able to both initiate physical contact with her mother when she needed it and to connect with her emotionally from a distance; social referencing became part of their ongoing interactions. Mother and daughter were able to share moments of intersubjectivity through mutual gaze and smiles, which meant: *I see you, you see me, you are thinking about me, I am thinking about you, we are safe, we are emotionally connected.* In time, the doll remained mostly on the shelf. April's mother had become a secure base for April, both in their interactions and in April's mind. Emotion regulation was restored.

Protection from and Coping with Emotional Pain

A mother's ability to tolerate her daughter's distress influences the moment-to-moment decisions that she makes to either protect her little girl from feeling distressed or help her cope with feelings of distress. Children need both protection from and learning to manage many kinds of distress. A few drops of water splashing on a toddler's face during a bath may communicate it is okay when your face gets wet; more water may be overwhelming; preventing a toddler's face from getting wet at all or quickly drying it may intensify discomfort or anxiety about getting wet when it is not warranted. Rochelle described the following situation with her daughter:

> "Amanda was playing with a helium balloon tied to her stroller. She repeatedly pulled it close and then let it fly up. All of a sudden the balloon came untied. Amanda cried as she watched it float away. I needed to decide whether to buy her another balloon or help her to cope with the loss. I decided to help her cope with her feelings. I said: The balloon came untied and floated so far away. Only balloons can float away like that. You are so sad."

Decisions about trying to protect a toddler from painful feelings or helping her cope with them may be related to a mother's own childhood memories and reactivated feelings of loss, fear, and anger. Unlike Rochelle, Marjorie realized that her impulse to buy another balloon when Sharon's flew away was triggered by her own childhood experiences when the family dog died and fears of becoming untethered from her own mother were reactivated:

"When Sharon's red balloon flew away, she was so sad that I quickly bought her another one; I didn't think she could tolerate it. There were no more red balloons, so I bought a blue one. When I gave the blue balloon to Sharon she screamed and refused to take it. She became hysterical. It seemed to me that her reaction was more than to losing a balloon; it was like in that moment she realized that she could lose me forever. All of a sudden I remembered that when I was about 10 years old and our dog died, my parents bought a new dog but never told me that our dog had died. I knew it was a different dog, it looked the same but it was different. It was never talked about. We needed to pretend it didn't happen. I did the same thing with the balloon and Sharon. I wonder how else not talking about painful things when I was a child has affected me."

Marjorie's insight about the link between her reaction to Sharon's lost balloon and her childhood memory about her dog's death, and her parents' decision to re-place her dog without talking about its death, increased Marjorie's curiosity about her childhood memories and their impact on interactions with her daughter. She also recognized that the loss of a balloon can trigger fears of other losses, and that helping young children cope with emotional pain of loss was important.

Shared Memory Narratives

Children, even very young children, are helped to cope with emotional pain by mother-daughter co-construction of memory narratives. Words that describe events and identify feelings help toddlers to cope. Frightening experiences, sad events, ongoing stressful situations, and anxious anticipation can cause distress. Detached freezing and overwhelming feelings in response to stress that cause "meltdowns" can be soothed. Emotion regulation can be restored. Wishing or believing that a baby or toddler will not remember a frightening, sad, or incomprehensible experi-ence may substitute for wishing the event had never happened. Babies and tod-dlers do remember either as a verbal narrative or as a feeling (Coates, S. 2016). Remembering together with words and pretend play about how something felt is less disturbing than re-experiencing the painful feelings.

When Lucy was 19 months old, she tripped in the playground, fell, and cracked her tooth. After the accident and dental procedure to file her tooth down to the gum-line, which were both painful and frightening, Lucy's behavior changed dramati-cally. Her activity level became generally low, she became clingy to her mother in new situations, and hypersensitive to noises that had never bothered her before. Lucy began to startle easily, wake during the middle of the night crying, and was difficult to comfort.

Lucy's mother, Geri, believed that Lucy was reacting to the kind of accident that often raises a toddler's body anxieties: falling, cracking a tooth, and having it filed down almost to the gumline with a loud, painful drill. Geri used pretend play and a shared memory narrative to help Lucy cope with her intensified body anxieties. Geri described:

> "I told Lucy, 'you had a scary accident. You tripped and fell and broke your tooth. It hurt!' It surprised me but Lucy added, 'My tooth is gone.' I guess that's the part that was most upsetting to her. I explained, 'the dentist needed to file your tooth. The filing made a loud noise and made your tooth very little. You can barely see it. The dentist said a big new tooth will grow. It will take a long time, but in a few years, you will see your new big tooth."

This may seem like a long memory narrative for a 19-month-old, but Lucy used the parts of it that she needed and added the part that was particularly distressing to her, "Can't see my tooth. It's gone." Her mother addressed her concern about losing a part of her body and reassured her that a new tooth would grow. Lucy and her mother's pretend play included taking her special doll to the dentist, filing the doll's tooth, and a big-girl tooth growing. Lucy particularly enjoyed making the loud drilling noise, which seemed to represent her fear and feelings about losing a part of her body. Lucy's disturbed sleep, startle reaction to noises, and difficulty being comforted in the middle of the night subsided and then disappeared. Lucy had an experience of resilience that was documented in their co-constructed evolving narrative – "It hurt, but I'm okay. It is getting better." Lucy was hurt, she felt scared, her mother knew how she felt, and she got better. An experience of resilience documented with an explicit memory narrative can promote emotion regulation.

Children Lucy's age – whatever their innate temperament, external behavior, or life experiences – have thoughts and feelings that may trigger anxiety about parts of their body breaking. When an accident occurs or surgery is required, body anxieties may intensify, and a sense of body damage may persist. A toddler might feel, *There is something wrong with my body, there is something wrong with me.* Creating shared memory narratives and pretend play scenarios can promote emotion regulation and healing. When Lucy was 3 years old, she told this memory:

> "When I was very little I fell in the playground and my tooth broke. I was very scared. There was a lot of blood. It hurt so much; it was hard to eat. Mommy gave me ice cream; I love ice cream. The dentist fixed my tooth with a loud, scary, machine. Mommy said it would get better. My new big tooth didn't grow yet, but I'm okay. It takes a long time to grow."

Lucy's memory narrative includes her accident, her feelings, her mother's supportive words, and ice cream. A stage of development and a life experience can intensify a toddler's worries about body damage. Awareness of boy-girl genital differences can add to the worries. If a mother feels guilty about her daughter's experience, co-constructing a memory narrative may be difficult, but might be even more useful to both mother and daughter.

Mothers' Guilt

Many things trigger mothers' feelings of guilt. If not excessive, maternal guilt can signal awareness of a toddler's need. On the other hand, maternal guilt can be punishing self-criticism linked to childhood memories. Ricky had worked hard since getting her MBA and had built a successful business. She loved her work and was eager to keep growing her business. Ricky was worried about 20-month-old Brianna's development:

> "She just doesn't talk or play like other children her age. Work is so important to me; it pulls me away from her. I feel so guilty. Even when I'm with Brianna, I'm not really with her. When I'm at work I'm anxious and guilty about not being with her. Either way, I'm not with her. Brianna's suffering and I'm guilty."

I asked Ricky what it would be like in moments when Brianna was content playing for her to think about something she needed to do at work; a memory was triggered and Ricky responded:

> "I was so angry at my mother who was always working at home, right there behind a closed door. I cried for her, but she would not open the door. When I'm with Brianna, I'm trying so hard not to think about work that I'm not really with her; I'm talking at her and telling her what to do, but not really with her. Maybe I'm trying to not think about how angry I was at my Mom when she was right there, but not with me. Maybe I'm still angry."

Ricky's efforts to manage her guilt about work were keeping her emotionally distant from Brianna. The entanglement of her childhood memory, "... my Mom was right there, but not with me ..." and her reactivated anger at her own mother fueled and perpetuated her guilt about work. With these insights, combined with her pleasure in talking to me about her work while she interacted with Brianna, Ricky's focus shifted from guilty attending to Brianna, to emotional connecting with Brianna. Brianna began to thrive.

Reactivated Childhood Sexual Guilt

Many things influence mothers' reactions to their toddlers' sexually related behavior. As an adult, Kathleen knew that childhood genital exploration and touching for pleasure were considered normal, but her own childhood memories of shame and guilt were activated when 16-month-old Amber started to masturbate:

> "Amber has started to rub herself. She likes it, but I'm afraid she is going to hurt herself. I think it's normal but I'm worried. I was not allowed to do that."

When Amber developed some genital irritation and the pediatrician wanted to catheterize her to make a diagnosis, Kathleen was unable to tell him that she thought the irritation was from her "rubbing," not from an infection:

"I felt too embarrassed and guilty to tell the doctor."

The terror and pain that Amber experienced being catheterized and the fact that she did not have a urinary tract infection, amplified Kathleen's guilt:

"It's all my fault. If I had told the doctor, she would not have needed to be catheterized."

Genay had similar childhood memories of shame and guilt, but a different response to her daughter Charlene's genital explorations. Genay remembered:

"I had my first orgasm when I was 10 years old. I discovered while lying in bed before sleep, if I rubbed my legs together in a special way I had this amazing feeling. I was so excited; I told my mother. She told me never to do it again. It was a bad thing to do, and I could hurt myself. I tried not to do it, but it felt too good to stop. I never told my mother again. When Charlene touches herself I tell her that I know it feels good. I don't want her to feel the guilt, shame, and fear that I felt."

Reactivated childhood sexual guilt is a common experience and can take many forms. During a mothers' group discussion about their little girls beginning genital exploration and touching for pleasure, Autumn had a shameful memory that she related to childhood sexual guilt:

"Jayden has started to pick her nose. She's only 23 months but she really likes to do it. I'm so embarrassed when she does it in public. I think it's disgusting. Every time she does it I have a flashback. When I was a child, I picked my nose in bed and reached my finger with the mucus on it below the side of my bed, and rubbed it on the wall. No one could see it and I never did it in public. But when I was 11 years old and we were moving, the moving men came into my bedroom to pack my bed. As they moved my bed away from the wall, all the mucus that I had rubbed on the wall showed. I was so embarrassed. I think my memory is really about childhood masturbation. I don't actually remember picking my nose or masturbating as a child. I only remember the shame I felt when the wall was exposed and was all dirty."

The new meaning Autumn attributed to her "flashback" memory was triggered in response to her daughter's nose picking, and her impulse to shame her daughter about the pleasure of nose-picking. Autumn's memory about her bed being moved, the "dirty wall" that revealed that she had rubbed body fluids all over it, and her intense shame is consistent with experiences of childhood sexual guilt. Autumn's memory has narrative truth – it reflects real feelings. That is to say that her memory captures her feelings about body pleasure of which she was unaware, guilty, and ashamed. Whether every detail of her memory has historical truth is not known. The new meaning of Autumn's memory – childhood masturbation guilt – lessened her own feelings of shame about nose-picking and helped her not to shame her daughter.

Life's Big Questions

Toddlers are beginning to grapple with life's big questions. They are aware of natural phenomena that cannot be controlled, are sometimes frightening, and whose explanations are complicated. Day changes into night, thunder booms, big waves noisily crash on the beach, mommies get pregnant, and babies are born. Flowers bloom and die. Toddlers begin to wonder about death. There are everyday opportunities to have conversations that lay a foundation for open, truthful information about death. Hearing about disturbing facts of life from their mothers, with all the comfort and security provided, paves the way for resilience when harsh realities of life are experienced. It is easier to talk to a little girl about death and for her to process the information in the context of everyday happenings before experiencing a death that creates a personal loss.

During a mothers' group discussion about toddlers' emerging ideas about death, Esme described her experience with 24-month-old Sabrina:

"Last week we visited a neighborhood pet store that had a goldfish aquarium. Sabrina likes to watch the fish swim around. Last week Sabrina noticed that one of the fish was not moving and said, 'Mommy, something is wrong.' I took a closer look. One fish was floating on top of the water. I told Sabrina that the fish was dead and we can tell the shop owner. I explained that dead means: the fish's body stopped working. Sabrina knows that when flowers die we throw them out, but that's different; flowers don't move. I think this was a good experience with death for Sabrina. The fish dying was not a personal loss. I want Sabrina to learn about death from me. When we got home, Sabrina told her father that a fish died. Sabrina said that the fish's body stopped working and was floating on top of the water. She repeated exactly what I had told her. I was glad Sabrina talked about it with her father. When I was growing up, death could never be talked about and it made me very scared. I felt okay talking to Sabrina about it."

Talking is a major way in which feelings are processed and worries are soothed. When a mother is talking to her daughter about things that could be disturbing, being aware of her own anxieties and how they are linked to reactivated childhood memories can be useful. An adult perspective can be gained. The challenge in talking to young children about death is to be truthful and at the same time reassuring (Lister, E. 2022).

Things Mothers Dread Talking about with Their Daughters

Mothers are often aware of specific topics or events that they dread talking about with their daughters. A prior marriage, alcohol and drugs, or traumatic accidents that were associated with guilt may seem difficult to talk about. There may be things mothers wish their daughters will not notice or will never know. There is much evidence that children do notice important things around them, especially things that their mothers have reactions to, even when they try to conceal their reactions. Grandma may drink too much, and the change in her behavior may be obvious not only to the adults around the dinner table, but also to a toddler. Having a way to understand what is happening can be a comfort to a young child:

> "I see you noticed Grandma is acting different. You look scared, but you are okay. Grandma has a problem when she drinks wine; sometimes she drinks too much and gets loud and scary. Her doctor is helping her."

Mothers may dread talking about menstruation, sex, pregnancy, or childbirth with their daughters because of their own difficult experiences. Memories of conversations with their own mothers may arouse concerns. A mother creates a foundation for talking about these topics when her daughter is a baby. Her intimate contact with her baby's body combined with emotional attachment, and both mother and daughter being female, pave the way. Tender touching and words to identify feelings are the beginnings of future conversations. A mother's self-awareness about her own concerns eases them.

Family Secrets

Every mother may have things in her past or current life that she would prefer never to talk about with her daughter or want to delay talking about for as long as possible. Beginning conversations about prior marriage, surrogacy, adoption, donor egg and sperm, physical and emotional illness, death, and other life events that affect young children and their families can create relationships that promote adaptation and resilience when faced with life's inevitable difficulties. Some information may be embarrassing and some events might be private. Maintaining privacy is different from keeping a shameful secret. Choosing what, when, and how potentially disturbing information is given to toddlers can be a challenge. Although living with and keeping family secrets can be stressful and intensify disturbing feelings about the facts, providing information prematurely or inappropriately can also create problems. Often, children are aware when something important that surrounds them is not being talked about. They may experience the feelings but have no way to make sense of them. They may be unable to formulate a question, believe it is not okay to talk about, or have their own explanation. A little girl's explanation to herself may be more disturbing than knowing the actuality. In addition, thinking something or knowing something she believes she is not supposed to think or know can be stressful. Yet, with all of these potential complications, talking about disturbing events that continue to reverberate in the family or currently surround a little girl can provide comfort and build a foundation for open communication.

Learning about potentially stressful information from her mother – a daughter's secure base – can provide the most comfort. A mother understanding her own feelings before talking to her daughter can enable her to destigmatize and de-catastrophize the information, formulate it in a way that can be meaningful to a little girl, and answer questions simply and honestly.

Memories and Concerns about "Spoiling"

Mothers' worries about "spoiling" their daughters may be related to their own childhood memories. Concerns may be focused on children's demands to have their own way or to acquire things. Mothers' childhood memories of unmet emotional needs can lead to worries about little girls being spoiled by having things. Adults may describe a child as "spoiled" when she behaves entitled, selfish, or demanding – especially when the child is a girl. These traits may be viewed as innate or the result of overindulgence, but may also be acquired by deprivation. In some ways, all toddlers, and all people, have these traits to varying degrees at various times.

During a mother's group discussion about spoiling, Miranda described her concerns about her 18-month-old daughter Charlize:

"Charlize is very demanding and greedy. She screams for ice cream as soon as we get to the playground. In a toy store she wants me to buy so many things. I'm worried that she is spoiled."

As Miranda described her relationship with her own mother she had an insight:

"I don't think my mother ever really liked me. We are basically very different. I never felt valued or approved of. My mother showered me with things, but not with feelings. Maybe that's why I have such a negative reaction to Charlize wanting things. I never wanted the things; I wanted to feel valued."

Until this moment, Miranda was not aware of the connection between her own feelings of emotional deprivation and her responses to her daughter. When Miranda realized that her painful yearnings related to her own unmet emotional needs that were triggered when her daughter cried for things like ice cream and toys, her concerns about "spoiling" slowly dissolved. Miranda was able to make decisions about buying things for her daughter based on other criteria. In addition, Miranda realized that she often deprived herself of things that she wanted. In Miranda's words, "I have become more generous to myself."

Angry Feelings

Toddlers are learning more about the pleasures of loving interactions with their mothers and the feelings of safety that their mothers provide. They are also learning more about the angry interactions that may begin to increase in frequency and intensity during this phase of development. Loving feelings predominate, angry feelings erupt, and loving feelings are restored; the anger dissipates.

The magnitude of mother-toddler anger may be surprising. A frustrating element may be that an intelligent little girl can seem completely irrational, while at the same time, from a developmental perspective she makes sense. Toby and 17-month-old Emily were ready to go on a picnic. Their picnic basket was packed with Emily's favorite snacks. However, as they approached the door to leave the building, it was pouring rain. Toby, being totally rational, said:

> "Look, it's raining. We cannot go to the park for our picnic. We can eat our picnic upstairs."

Emily screamed for what seemed like a long time: "No, stop the rain. Stop it, stop it." A toddler views her mother as omnipotent. From a toddler's point of view, Mommy is all-powerful – she can kiss a booboo and it feels better, so certainly she should be able to stop the rain. Toby, on the other hand, felt unjustly accused of not stopping the rain. Toby reminded herself that toddlers are not always rational from an adult perspective and reassured herself that Emily's anger would subside. She did not mount a defense, instead, she said, "I know how disappointed you are." Emily calmed. She may not have known the meaning of the word disappointed, but she did know how she felt. In addition, she felt that her feelings were understood by her mother. Emily also learned that the feeling she was experiencing was called "disappointed." Through repeated experiences of angry interactions, the rupture of loving feelings, and the repair of loving feelings, children learn to expect that angry feelings do not last – they are remembered but do not persist. Mothers' and toddlers' expectations that loving feelings will return help to lessen both of their emotional reactions to angry flare-ups and promote the return to loving interactions.

Overwhelming Feelings

When feelings are overwhelming, a toddler may do things that hurt herself. Tammy was 17 months and frequently pinched and hit herself creating red blotches on her arms and legs. When this happened during a mother-toddler group, her mother, Linda, froze in an angry frightening glare. Tammy had no way to process her feelings or to regulate her emotional state without her mother's help. During further mothers' group discussion, Linda became aware that she felt anxious when Tammy pinched and hit herself because it seemed "inexplicable and crazy." In addition, Tammy hitting and pinching triggered Linda's memories of being hit and pinched by her sister when they were little girls. It had been easier for Linda to feel angry at Tammy rather than scared and helpless, as she had felt as a child when her sister pinched and hit her. This insight helped Linda to temper her own reactivated fear and anger that frightened Tammy.

After identifying both Linda and Tammy's fears of each other, it became clear that the immediate trigger for Tammy hitting and pinching herself was the approach of another child. Tammy seemed afraid that she would be hit, that a toy would be taken from her, or that she would grab a toy from or hit the approaching child. In response to her fears of other children, and to control her own impulse to hit them, which also frightened her, Tammy hit and pinched herself. With these new meanings of Tammy's behavior, Linda was more empathic, less frightened and angry, and therefore less frightening to Tammy. Linda began to protect Tammy from her fears of other children and fears of her own aggressive impulses toward other children. For example, Linda said:

"I am not going to let Sammy take the truck away from you; I'm going to help you to keep it."

Linda also helped Tammy to wait her turn for a toy that she wanted:

"I know you want the puzzle Josie is playing with; I will help you to wait. We can play with the shape-box while you wait."

Feeling protected by her mother helped Tammy feel safer. She felt protected from the aggression of the other children and from her own aggressive impulses toward the other children. Emotion regulation was now possible. Pinching and hitting herself abated and then stopped. With her mother's help, emotion regulation and self-assertiveness replaced self-injury.

Intergenerational Fear

As Roberta entered the mother-toddler room, she was reprimanding two-year-old Jade, but her disapproval and warnings were unsuccessful. One by one, each child came to her mother crying because she had been hit by Jade. The hitting happened so unexpectedly that it was difficult to anticipate or to see what had triggered it. The mothers were sympathetic to Roberta, but they were also angry. Roberta was perplexed by Jade's seemingly unprovoked "aggressive behavior" and frustrated by her own inability to "discipline" her:

"I've tried everything: time-outs, no iPad, I even threatened to take her special teddy-bear away. I would never really do that."

Roberta was focused on threats, discipline, and punishments. To understand more about what might be motivating Jade to hit, I asked Roberta about Jade's play at home. Roberta described the details:

"Hide-and-seek is great. I often hide behind a door, and when Jade enters the room I jump out at her and shout boo. She always startles. I played it with my dad. Jade plays tickle torture with her dad. He runs after her, catches her, and tickles her while she squeals."

In addition to these "games," the videos that Jade watched included a selection of cartoons and fairytales often frightening to two year olds. Roberta's description of Jade's play included the following significant elements, "She always startles, I played it with my dad, and tickle-torture." A startle is a noticeable indication of hyperarousal, "tickle-torture" alludes to pain and horror, and "I played it with my Dad" suggests that childhood memories are being relived. I offered the following child development information: "These sound like exciting games that sometimes scare little children." Roberta quickly disagreed and contradicted me, "Jade never gets scared." With mock surprise and disbelief, I challenged Roberta, "Really? Never?"

My gentle confrontation of Roberta's disavowal of Jade's fear awakened childhood memories that flooded out:

> "My father wanted a son. He taught me to be tough like he was, not weak and scared like my mother. He taught me to do scary things like climb trees and ride my bike down a steep hill with no hands. We always watched horror movies together. At the amusement park near our house we went on the big roller coaster and sneaked around the haunted house avoiding the moving skeletons and booby traps. My dad always got me past the ticket collectors because he lied about my age. It helped me to feel strong."

Recounting memories may have triggered remnants of Roberta's feelings and ideas about what it means to be a girl – "weak and scared." I said:

> "It seems like appearing not scared and sharing frightening experiences with your father helped you to feel strong and loved and accepted by him, and maybe protected by him. I wonder whether Jade might be feeling some of the same things."

This was a new way for Roberta to think about her memories, and it seemed to strike a chord. I provided additional child development information that emphasized an aspect of Jade's experience of which Roberta had been unaware:

> "Sometimes children hit when they are frightened. Punishments won't help them to stop hitting if they're scared. Acknowledging scared feelings, feeling protected, and safe might."

As we began to consider the activities and situations that might be frightening to Jade, and other group mothers described their toddlers' typical fears, a distant memory of Roberta's began to emerge:

> "I just remembered, when I was a little girl I had a music box with a twirling ballerina. It was kept on a high shelf in my bedroom: it was rarely taken down. I never played with it. It was fragile and delicate. I remember the beautiful music."

At the same time, the music box memory was coming into focus, Roberta began to recognize moments when Jade was scared. Feelings could be identified;

emotion regulation was now possible. Recognizing vulnerabilities can be a strength. Roberta began to limit the frightening videos and modified the scary games. She also began to help Jade talk about her scared feelings. By next week, the hitting had stopped. The joy returned to the group and the warm support among the mothers was restored. The music box memory that had remained in the shadows too fragile to appear, emerged with all its delicate details. It represented the little girl, who on the surface appeared brave and tough but who also had frightening feelings that had needed to be kept far away, on a high shelf, out of reach, and out of memory. Frightening feelings were no longer dangerous; they could be acknowledged.

Hitting and Early Trauma

The ongoing impact of a newborn's medical trauma on her mother can be triggered throughout the first three years and after. Ginny weighed two pounds at birth and had many related medical complications. Her mother, Miriam, was convinced that Ginny would be small and vulnerable her entire life. Miriam wanted to do everything she could to help Ginny to be able to defend herself. However, when Ginny was 20 months old, Miriam said:

"She's too aggressive with other children and nobody wants playdates with her anymore."

As Miriam described Ginny's hitting and grabbing behavior in the sandbox, she noted:

"I just realized, since Ginny was born I have always done everything I can to help her feel strong. She is so tiny. I see her as so vulnerable. I don't want her to be bullied. Maybe I am promoting her hitting and grabbing. I was tough; nobody ever saw me as vulnerable or bullied me. If anything, I did the bullying. Maybe I was a bully because I felt vulnerable and maybe Ginny is not as vulnerable as I see her."

Miriam's childhood memories of her own bullying and vulnerabilities, and her new way of thinking about her worries that Ginny would be bullied, helped her to modify the ways in which she was promoting Ginny's aggressive behavior. Miriam was able to disentangle her childhood memories, her memories of Ginny's fragile and vulnerable beginnings, and her own feelings of vulnerability from her view of Ginny as currently, only, and forever being vulnerable. Her vivid image of Ginny in the NICU, tiny and helpless, hooked up to wires and tubes, began to fade. The idea that Ginny was strong to have survived her vulnerable beginnings emerged. Miriam moved the framed NICU photo of Ginny that she had kept next to her bed since she was born into a photo album kept in the living room. The album also included pictures of Ginny's thriving development. Ginny's hitting and grabbing stopped.

"Hitting Is Not Allowed But Self-Protection Is Important"

Kaylee was 17 months old and busy playing in the sandbox. Alyssa tried to take Kaylee's shovel as she had successfully done several times before. This time, Kaylee said "No," held on to the shovel tight, hit Alyssa gently on the wrist, and ran to her mother. Kaylee's mother, Marietta, believed that hitting was not the way to resolve disputes and that toddlers need to be taught not to hit. But Marietta also strongly believed that children need to feel entitled to protect themselves and to stand up for themselves:

> "I always teach Kaylee there is no hitting, but I also try to teach her to feel entitled to protect herself. Hitting is not allowed, but self-protection is important. I think that's why she said 'No' very loud and hit Alyssa so gently. Kaylee wanted to know what I thought, and I was confused about how I wanted to respond. I tried to describe what happened. I said: 'Alyssa is not allowed to grab your shovel. You told her No very loud! You also hit her. You know hitting is not okay so you hit her very softly. I think she heard you."

Marietta believed in this situation, apologies and reprimands for hitting were secondary to the importance of Kaylee feeling entitled to protect herself. Mother-daughter meeting of minds about this significant issue is an important and gradual process.

Being Excluded

Mothers have activities that do not include their children. Toddlers learn about their mothers' interests and relationships from which they are excluded. For example, a special hug with Daddy, a passion for work, and exhilaration going for a run or playing tennis. Little girls approaching two years old may also begin to develop passionate interests that do not include their mothers. India could play with her baby-dolls for 20 minutes. Her mother, Anika, thought something was wrong:

> "It seems like India is obsessed with her dolls. She plays with them all the time. I'm worried that she has an obsession. If she was obsessed with puzzles, I don't think I would care."

Unlike an obsession, a passionate interest is balanced with other interests. It does not intrude or take over, it enriches. During the mothers' group discussion, with many examples of the other mothers feeling excluded, Anika realized that her anxiety reaction to India's doll-play that did not include her, was a revived feeling of being rejected by her sister:

> "My sister always played for hours with her friends with their baby-dolls and would never let me play with them. It's like I'm reliving my past! India really likes to feed, undress, and bathe her doll. She even changes the diaper. She's very good at it. Maybe she's pretending to be me."

Anika's realization that her feelings about being excluded were a revival of painful childhood feelings, and the idea that her daughter might be pretending to be a mother when she played with her baby doll, helped her to recognize India's doll-play as an indication of India's identification with her. Anika's worries about India having an "obsession" faded. In addition, Anika's ability to satisfy her own needs and wishes that did not include India increased. Relationship themes of attachment needs and autonomy strivings, identifying, and individuating were activated.

Needs and Wishes

Whereas it is optimal that a child's physical, cognitive, and emotional needs are met, it is not necessary, possible, or practical for all wishes to be gratified. Many things that a baby or toddler wants are not good for her. Toddlers have frequent experiences of not getting what they want – there are many potential opportunities to learn this important life lesson. However, differentiating between wishes and needs is sometimes difficult. Children learn to differentiate between what they experience as a wish and what they experience as a need, in part, by what their mothers recognize as wishes and needs. Sometimes a mother's own feelings of emotional deprivation contribute to worries about her daughter learning that she cannot have everything she wants. Joy voiced a concern about Wellesley that many mothers have:

"I'm worried. She needs to learn she can't have everything she wants."

As Joy and 19-month-old Wellesley were entering the mother-toddler room, Wellesley looked up at her mother and reached to hold her hand in order to feel safe while walking into the loud, crowded room. Joy gently moved her hand away, and her painful memories followed:

"When I was a little girl my older sister tripped me all the time. When I told my mother that I needed her help, she always told me, 'You can't have everything you want. Don't be a tattletale, handle it yourself.' I knew I couldn't have everything I wanted. There were a zillion opportunities to learn it, but I needed my mother's help to feel safe. I could not do it myself. I felt so abandoned and ignored by my mother. What I really want is to help Wellesley feel safe and understood. I don't think she needs to hold my hand."

After a moment's thought Joy added:

"I could say to her, I know you want to hold my hand because it's so loud here and there are so many people. I am going to stay very close to you and help you walk in all by yourself."

Differentiating between needs and wishes was useful for Joy. Wellesley needed a secure base; she wanted to hold hands. Joy thought of another way to meet Wellesley's needs to feel safe and to be emotionally supported. Joy's childhood memory of feeling emotionally ignored by her own mother enabled her to recognize the variety of ways in which she was meeting Wellesley's emotional needs and, at the same time, was teaching her that she could not have everything she wanted:

"I remember just yesterday Wellesley wanted more French fries and there were no more. She was so angry at me. I offered her potato chips which she didn't want. I told her that I understood how hard it is when you want French fries and there are only potato chips. After a few minutes she re-regulated and ate some of the chips. I guess she is learning that she can't have everything she wants. I also realized that I always say, I need a cup of coffee. I don't need a cup of coffee, I want it."

Joy's new awareness about the ways in which Wellesley was learning that she cannot have everything that she wants helped to lessen Joy's worries and enabled her to find more ways to meet Wellesley's emotional needs. Her recognition that she desired a cup of coffee and that desires can be passionate but are not needs, led to more pleasure and satisfaction with her morning coffee.

"I Didn't Need Her To Be Wrong For Me To Be Right"

A mother's expanding sense of self can emerge from a childhood memory. Randi described an interaction with 20-month-old Davina:

"Davina wanted to walk up the slide rather than climb the steps and slide down. She saw her older sister do it and she was determined. As Davina lifted her foot onto the slide, I reached for her hand. She went into total meltdown. She threw herself on the ground and screamed. All I did was try to keep her safe. I understood she wanted to walk up the slide herself, but it was too dangerous to let her do it. This time, instead of trying to convince her that I did the right thing to protect her, I told her I knew she did not want me to help and I understood why she was angry. I couldn't believe it, she stopped crying. I know it won't always help, but this time simply saying I understood helped. I didn't need her to be wrong for me to be right."

Randi went on to describe many childhood memories of being accused by her mother of being wrong and her unsuccessful angry efforts to convince her mother that she was right. Randi realized that her mother could not recognize that she was right because it made her mother feel wrong. With this insight, Randi no longer needed to convince Davina that she was right to hold her hand or to convince Davina that she was wrong to want to walk up the slide by herself. They could both be right. Emotion regulation was restored.

Shared Wishful Fantasies

Mother-daughter shared wishful fantasies can provide a substitute for the actual fulfillment of a wish, "It would be great to have all the cookies in the world!" Sometimes adding a touch of irony is fun, "Of course, we want Grandma to have some of the cookies so she can give them to us!"

Mother-daughter window-shopping can include shared wish-fulfilling interactions. A mother's simple words, such as "It might be fun to have that big jungle gym," can provide momentary shared wish fulfillment. Elena was 23 months old and wanted a puppy just like her cousin had. Elena's mother, Lydia, was definitely not going to get a dog. There was a pet shop in their neighborhood with a large window filled with six playful, adorable puppies. Every day for a week, Elena and Lydia stood at the window gazing at and talking about the puppies. Elena called them, "My puppies." They gave names to each one. Elena told her father about them. At home, Elena set up a corner of her room with three stuffed toy dogs and a bowl with pretend dog food. With her mother's help, she made a cozy bed for the toy puppies. In a short while, Elena stopped asking for a dog.

Sometimes the wish-fulfilling element of a toddler's play is to be like her mother. For example, to pretend to drive a car, go to work, or be a mommy. The wish to grow up is deep-rooted and strong. To a little girl, being like her mother is part of the meaning of growing up.

Treasured Toys

Soft brown teddy bears with shiny noses, pink bunnies with silk lined ears, plush satin blankets, and tattered old receiving blankets are among the treasured toys of young children. As described earlier, attachment to a treasured toy reveals aspects of a baby and young child's developing mind. A toddler's attachment to a treasured toy indicates – and further promotes – her developing capacity for emotion regulation. The toy may have objective qualities that make it appealing, but the toddler creates its meaning. Whereas many of the words a toddler speaks have been learned, the name and exact pronunciation of a treasured toy name often are created by or co-created with the toddler. This co-created name may be part of a treasured toy's special meaning to the toddler and the entire family.

A treasured toy may be a valued sleep partner and frequent play companion, but may seem to be ignored in moments even as it is carefully guarded. For example, Clarissa was 16 months old. She slept with her Blanky every night, dragged it around the apartment, and took it with her outside. When distressed, she snuggled with it. Sitting on her bedroom floor, Clarissa played with her baby-dolls while her treasured Blanky remained cast aside among a bunch of scattered toys. However, the moment her mother picked it up to return it to Clarissa's crib, Clarissa shouted "No!"

A toddler keeps track of her treasured toy to the best of her ability. She may protest it being thrown into the washing machine or left at home when she leaves. Even when she is prevented from physical access to her treasured toy, a little girl can always reclaim it. A treasured toy is never preoccupied with other things. The ability to self-regulate while holding a treasured toy is embodied in the toddler's mind.

Not all children have treasured toys. Those who do not form an attachment to one special toy create other ways to achieve the same emotion regulation capacities. Thumb sucking, pacifiers, and bottles are similar to treasured toys in some ways, but different because of the ongoing direct body pleasure since infancy that they provide.

A young toddler's attachment to a treasured toy, including her ability to endow the toy with emotion regulation capacities, increases during the first three years. Later, the little girl becomes able to mentally perform the emotion regulation functions without the treasured toy. In other words, while a little girl is attributing soothing to her blanket or soft cuddly toy, she is developing the needed mental capacities for emotion regulation without the toy. Words to describe this process are, *I am loveable, even when Mommy is angry at me. I am lovable, even when I am angry at Mommy. I am safe, even when I feel scared. I love Mommy and she loves me, even when we are angry. Holding my blanket helps me have these feelings.*

A toddler's emerging capacity for empathy may be seen with a treasured toy. When Andrea's mother was chopping onions and tears were rolling down her cheeks, Andrea handed her treasured stuffed animal to her mother and said, "Kiss Bunny." Andrea could identify with what she believed were her mother's distressing feelings that were making her cry and wanted to comfort her. Andrea demonstrated her awareness of her own emotion regulation capacities by offering her treasured toy to her mother to kiss.

Separations and Reunions

From one to two years old, a little girl's distress reactions to separations from her mother can reach new intensities as struggles between her autonomy strivings and her attachment needs increase. She has learned from experience that she can get hurt. She has discovered how much she needs her mother. Little girls this age have more angry interactions with their mothers, which also make separations fraught with fear: fears about losing their mother's love. The developing expectation that loving feelings return when anger subsides can buffer the impact of angry interactions, but desperate reactions to separation may erupt. Goodbye routines and familiar caregivers ease the stress of separation.

Mother-toddler separations often get more attention than reunions, but both are important. Peggy and 20-month-old Bonnie walk Daddy to the elevator every morning when he leaves for work. He lifts Bonnie to press the button and kisses her. Bonnie giggles. Saying goodbye to Daddy is easy; it is a frequent routine and Bonnie is staying with her mother. Reunions with Daddy at the end of the day when he returns home are difficult. Peggy explained:

> "Bonnie and I are happy playing in her room. Her father has not seen her all day and arranges his schedule so they can play before dinner. But, as soon as he walks into her room she crawls into my lap and clings. Bonnie won't play with her father. I think the transition is hard for her."

When I asked Peggy about establishing a reunion routine that might make the transition easier and more joyful for them all, she said:

"My mother was always so angry that my father was working all the time. I thought she missed him, but I think she also resented him and envied him. We never had happy reunions. I remember one night my dad came home so late that my Mom would not let me play with him. I was so angry at my mother. She was angry at my father, and my father was angry at my mother. Everybody was angry. Bonnie needs to know I'm happy to see her Dad and happy that he has a good job. We could run to the door together when he comes home. Maybe I never did it before because I was stuck in my childhood memories without even knowing it. I am different from my mother. It is my decision not to work now. My mother never had the choice."

Peggy became aware of childhood memories that were related to family reunions and acknowledged the ways in which she was different from her own mother. Although she had ambivalent feelings, she had decided not to return to work after Bonnie was born and was pleased with her decision. She did not resent her husband as her mother had resented her husband. Peggy's self-reflection and insights about her own mother and childhood helped to affirm the choices she was making as a mother and to support her daughter's reunions with her father.

Conflicts between Work and Family

Integrating a career with family life can be a challenge. Not only are the logistics complicated, but if a mother is ambivalent, difficulties increase. Corinda was passionate about her work and about being a mother; however, like many women, she struggled with both roles. Corinda's conflicts between work and motherhood were rooted in childhood memories. Her combined devaluation and over-idealization of her own mother intensified her difficulties managing the integration of work and care of 20-month-old Burgundy. Corinda explained:

"My Mom was always the perfect mother, but she never did anything else with her life. I was always determined that when I grew up I would take care of my children and have a career. My mother only took care of my father, me, and my siblings. She was one hundred percent old fashioned tradwife. I remember the smell of freshly baked cookies every day when I came home after school. They were perfect! Now, on my way home from work, I stop in the bakery for cookies to bring home to Burgundy, but it's not the same. Store bought is not the same as home-baked and it makes me get home too late. Sometimes she's already asleep. I want to have a career and I want to be with Burgundy. A woman without a career is nothing."

Corinda's extreme split characterization of her mother's perfections as a mother and denigrating devaluations of the rest of her mother's life made it difficult for

Corinda to integrate work and motherhood. Corinda had a full-time demanding job that she loved, but believed that working meant that she was not the "perfect mother" that her mother was. Corinda was trapped in her conflict between work and family until she had an insight:

> "I just realized, I'm trying to be some fantasy of a perfect mother and a perfect executive to avoid being a devalued woman like I see my mother. Maybe if I didn't devalue her so much, I wouldn't need to see her as such a perfect mother. Intellectually, I believe that women have equally valid choices, but emotionally I guess I don't."

With this insight, gradually Corinda was able to find better solutions to integrating work and family life. Freshly baked cookies every day were no longer a self-imposed requirement. In addition, she changed her work schedule to four days a week.

During Mother-Toddler Separations

Babysitters and other caregivers can ease the stress of separation by creating shared narratives that support a toddler's internal sense of her mother when separated. Winnie described some of her suggestions to the babysitter about what to say while she was at work:

> "Mommy is at work. I think she is sitting at her desk typing on her computer. Remember we said bye-bye after breakfast. Mommy kissed you. Mommy will be home after we play, have lunch, go to the park, and have a bath. Let's draw a picture for Mommy. You can give it to her when she comes home. I will tell Mommy we talked about her when she was at work."

These communications include a specific way to envision her mother at work, a shared memory of their goodbye kiss, the specific sequence of activities after which her mother will come home, and some details and preparations for their reunion; feeling emotionally close to her mother is supported while separated.

Play Alone in the Presence of Mommy

A toddler's experiences of playing alone in the presence of her mother promote the developing capacity to cope with separation (Winnicott, D. W. 1990). As described earlier, "alone in the presence of" describes when a mother and her child are physically together, intermittently interactive, and emotionally connected while each is focused, with pleasure, on her own activity. They are aware of each other's focus, but alone in their own focus of attention. For example, every morning when Cameron took a shower, Mazie played with her blocks in the bathroom. Mazie and her mother could not see or talk to each other; the shower noise was too loud and the glass was opaque. Mazie felt emotionally with her mother, while also alone. Her internal sense of being with her mother was more salient than their interactive being with each other. This routine experience not only enabled Cameron to take a shower while Mazie played contently, but also promoted Mazie's capacity to be alone.

Separation and Sleep

Typical toddler worries related to separation can disturb sleep. Stressful experiences during the day and frightening dreams at night can disrupt sleep. Toddlers and parents need sleep, and sleep difficulties are stressful. In order to resolve sleep problems, it can be useful to understand the details of thoughts, feelings, and memories that are associated with sleep. The following example illustrates the impact of a mother's traumatic separation from her newborn that reactivated the mother's childhood trauma and disturbed both the mother's and her daughter's sleep.

Annie was in the NICU for ten days after birth. She was a strong, full-term newborn who was treated in the hospital for an infection with intravenous antibiotics. Her mother, Florence, was discharged from the hospital when Annie was two days old. Every day from 5:00 a.m. to midnight, Florence took care of Annie in the NICU; she breastfed, played with her all day, and returned home each night to sleep while her husband stayed with Annie in the hospital. When Annie awoke in the middle of the night, her father gave a bottle of breast milk to her. Annie adapted well to nursing during the day and a bottle in the middle of the night. However, Florence was not able to sleep. She tossed and turned for a few hours, then returned to the hospital. This early stressful separation from Annie and the anxiety it triggered lingered. Both mother and daughter continued to wake throughout the night and have difficulty falling back to sleep until Annie was 17 months old, and Florence connected a childhood memory to both of their sleep difficulties:

> "I just remembered, when I was 8 years old I had meningitis and was in the hospital for about a month. My Mom visited me during the day, but at night I was alone. All through the night the nurses woke me to take my temperature, listen to my heart, and check my IV. My Mom always says that I almost died. I think when Annie was in the NICU in some ways I was reliving my own childhood trauma. I didn't realize it."

After Florence's insight about the connections between her childhood memory, the NICU, and her and Annie's current sleep difficulties, both Annie and Florence gradually began to sleep with fewer disruptions. Separations during the day also became easier for them both.

Sleeping through the Night

There are two complex developmental milestones that are popularly called "training." For decades, teaching and learning to use the toilet, in English, has been called "toilet-training." Up until more recently, it was the only teaching-learning developmental milestone that was referred to as training. In recent years, another developmental milestone has been popularly described as training: "sleep-training."

The word "training" suggests that the process consists of the mother instructing or demanding, and the child obeying. The term training further suggests that the internal world – thoughts, feelings, temperament, or life experiences of both the mother and her child do not matter in these teaching-learning, mutual regulation interactions; but of course they do. Although the term "toilet training" has persisted in the United States, parents and child development books include the emotional responses of toddlers to learning to use the toilet. The emotional meanings of sleep to parents, babies, and toddlers are also getting some attention.

Transition from Crib to Bed

A main aspect of the transition from crib to bed is that both the toddler and her mother transfer their feelings of coziness and security that were established in the crib to the bed. If such feelings were not established in the crib, they can be established in the bed. The transition from crib to bed is facilitated by a child securely knowing that *Mommy is close while I am sleeping, and separation from Mommy during sleep is followed by reunion upon awakening.*

Reunion routines when a baby sleeps in a crib require the mother coming to the baby. When a toddler sleeps in a bed, morning reunions often transition to the toddler coming to her mother. Morning reunion routines help to ensure that when a toddler wakes and gets out of bed, either in the morning, afternoon, or middle of the night, she comes directly to her mother. At whatever age between around 1½ and 3 years the transition from crib to bed is made, these elements are useful to consider. Once the decision about a bed is made, it can be helpful to disassemble the crib in front of a toddler and store it, even if for a short time until another baby uses it. A mother's communication to her daughter that she knows this is the right time for a bed can be clear and can be a comfort. What her mother thinks and feels about a bed has more influence on her daughter than an extraordinary bed design or fancy sheets.

The meaning to a mother of her little girl sleeping in a bed can be significant. The bed can be a symbol of loss, "It's so sad, I no longer have a baby." If the crib is viewed as a physical restraint, fears can be triggered by the freedom of a bed. A toddler's bed can evoke a variety of thoughts, feelings, and memories consciously and unconsciously – pleasurable and frightening, shameful and cozy memories – about a mother's own childhood bed.

Dreams

Little girls approaching two years have had significant experience regulating emotions. They have had rages, meltdowns, and temper tantrums, and they have recovered. They have felt enraged, sad, and terrified, and they have been comforted. They have become out-of-control excited and calmed. They have felt embarrassed and jealous. Toddlers have been helped to identify emotions and re-regulate. During nighttime dreams, the resources that are available while awake to cope with intense feelings and impulses are not available. While awake, a fierce tiger may lurk under the bed and be feared, but is manageable with her mother's help; during a dream, it feels like the tiger is going to attack and there is no one to help. A mother's explanations of dreams can comfort her daughter. Such an explanation includes:

> "Dreams are stories you tell yourself while you are sleeping. Dreams can be happy, sad, scary, and sometimes silly stories. Everyone makes up their own dreams. Thoughts and feelings during the day may be hidden in your dreams at night. Your wishes and fears during the day are part of the stories you tell yourself in your dreams. We can talk about dreams."

The empowering core of these ideas is that the dreamer creates the dream.

Internal Conflict and Play with Friends

A toddler's ability to tolerate ambivalent feelings and to resolve internal conflicts among wishes is part of her increasing capacity for emotion regulation. As has been described, one way in which a little girl resolves her conflicts between following her mother's rules and doing what she wants is to signal her intention to her mother before acting. Another internal conflict that intensifies during this phase of development is the pleasure of playing with a friend and the desire not to have a friend touch her toys. Elaine was almost two years old and wanted playdates with Lexis, but did not want Lexis to touch any of her toys. Games together that did not involve her toys and a snack together were fun. Before Lexis arrived, her mother told Elaine:

> "Lexis is coming to visit. Choose a few toys you do not want her to touch and I will put them in the closet. The rest of the toys will be for sharing."

Gradually, internal conflicts can be managed mentally. Opposing wishes to possess all the toys and to play with a friend can be reconciled internally. At this phase of development, before playdates, some external help may be useful.

Summary: Emotion Regulation

A mother's emotion regulation and her daughter's developing emotion regulation are intricately entwined. Mother-toddler interactions, both non-verbal and verbal, are a primary way in which a little girl's emotions are regulated during the second year of life. Mother-daughter talking about thoughts and feelings becomes increasingly useful: words are used to identify and communicate feelings and to co-construct memory narratives in order to process thoughts and feelings together. Children need to be protected from emotional pain and need to learn to cope with emotional pain. A toddler's attachment to a treasured toy and mental capacities to think about thoughts and feelings are part of developing emotion regulation. Emotion regulation is the ability to maintain, and when disrupted, to return to a state of well-being.

Meeting of Minds and Separateness of Minds

During this phase of development, mothers and daughters have new pleasurable experiences of their meeting of minds, intensified conflicts derived from their separateness of minds, and complex combinations of both. Mother-daughter moments of intersubjectivity intensify. A little girl is discovering the pleasures of emotional intimacy – feeling deeply known and knowing the other. Mother and daughter co-construction of memory narratives about stressful experiences creates shared moments of their minds in sync and provides comfort. Although mothers and their daughters having strong feelings about their different ideas can create conflict, these interactions can also provide the opportunity to discover alternative ways of looking at the world and each other. Little girls continue to signal their intentions to do things that they know their mothers will disapprove of. However, these interactions also provide opportunities for moments of intersubjectivity that include both the meeting of minds and the assertion and substantiation of their separateness of minds. A little girl is discovering her own mind.

Christina was trying to teach 15-month-old Melissa not to touch the garbage can. But every day they had the same angry interaction until Christina realized that Melissa was communicating her intention to touch the garbage can before she touched it. Melissa was letting her mother know that she remembered the rule, and for a few moments, she was stopping herself. In addition, Christina realized that Melissa was imitating her: that is, she realized that Melissa wanted to do the same thing that she watched her mother do, throw things into the garbage can by pressing the pedal that popped open the lid. Melissa walked toward the garbage, put her foot on the pedal, paused, got her mother's attention, and smiled. Christina smiled and said:

> "I see you remember there is no touching the garbage, but it looks like you want to do what I do. I will help you to open the garbage-can and throw something in. You can be Mommy's helper."

Melissa learned to signal her mother when she had something to throw into the garbage so her mother could help her open the lid. In addition, Christina created a "job" for Melissa: to help her mother dump the garbage after dinner. What had been repeated mother-daughter angry interactions about their separateness of minds became pleasurable moments of their meeting of minds that recognized their separateness of minds.

Likes and Dislikes – Food

Little girls may begin to have strong food preferences. Self-feeding and the mess that accompanies it increase. Food can be extraordinarily pleasurable and delicious, or unpleasant and disgusting. Food is necessary for survival, is a symbol of love, and is negotiated for autonomy. Meals can become fertile ground for mother-daughter power struggles. A mother's responses to her daughter's food likes, dislikes, and eating messiness may be influenced by her ideas about nutrition, table manners, her own food preferences, and childhood memories. Women who have currently or have had eating problems are vulnerable to food struggles with their daughters.

In the middle of a mothers' group discussion about food, Meri described family meals:

"JoEllen is 15 months and a very picky eater. Calling it likes and dislikes doesn't capture it; she hardly eats anything. My husband always eats food off my plate; it's disgusting. I tell him not to, but he can't keep his hands to himself. JoEllen always tries to feed me; I want to feed myself. She won't let me feed her, and she won't eat by herself. She eats so little; I'm worried. I was a picky eater also. Maybe I still am."

Family meals had become fraught with power struggles, disgust, worry, and anger. After a momentary pause, Meri blurted out how her mother and father always eat off each other's plates and feed each other:

"It's like they are having sex at the table in front of everybody. They actually lick each other's fingers; it's really disgusting."

Another mother in the group asked Meri how these thoughts about her parents that popped into her mind were connected to her reaction to her husband eating off her plate and to her reaction to JoEllen trying to feed her. Meri answered:

"I just realized that my disgust reaction to my husband is really about how I have always felt watching my parents eat since I was a little girl. Maybe my reactions to my parents also influence how I react to JoEllen and food."

Meri's reflections led to a change. She began to share some foods at the table with her husband and to let JoEllen feed her. JoEllen began to taste the food that she was feeding to her mother; her repertoire of liked foods expanded. Meal-time pleasure increased for all. A mother discovers new facets of her own mind. Her childhood memories ignite the process. In the poignant words of one mother, "I'm remembering things that I never knew." In other words, she was remembering things that in the past she did not allow herself to know.

Discovery of a Toddler's Mind

A mother-toddler group was meeting for the first time. Darcy described her 22-month-old daughter Millie:

"She's just a happy baby. She doesn't understand anything. I don't think she has any thoughts or feelings yet."

Darcy's description of Millie was strikingly different than the other mothers' descriptions of their children, who had passionate thoughts, feelings, and intentions. Week after week, Darcy was highly motivated to assert Millie's happiness and deny her developing mind, but it was not clear why. It was as though for Darcy, to be happy meant not having any thoughts or feelings.

Millie had two mothers. Her other mother did not participate in the mothers' group and Darcy rarely talked about her. She was a lawyer at a large firm that Darcy had also worked at before maternity leave. She had given birth to Millie and took primary care of her. Darcy continued to insist:

> "Millie doesn't know anything. I'm going away next month. She won't even notice that I'm gone. I don't think she's that aware of anything; she's just a happy baby."

I wondered whether Darcy also believed that Millie did not notice that she had two mothers and the other children that she knew had a mother and a father. A few weeks later, when the other women were describing their daughters' typical oppositional behavior, Darcy's description of Millie slightly but meaningfully changed:

> "Millie never opposes me. She always wants what I want. She never has her own thoughts or feelings."

Darcy was highlighting that Millie had the same thoughts and feelings that she had, not that Millie did not have any thoughts or feelings. Darcy indicated how she and Millie were different from the other mothers and children – that Millie was not oppositional – but that she and Millie had the same thoughts and feelings. Her ideas about similarities and differences were shifting. Mothers' group support paved the way for Darcy's self-questioning and interest in what motivated her conviction that Millie was unaware of everything and did not have her own thoughts and feelings. Two weeks later, Darcy began:

> "I don't know why I think Millie doesn't know anything and only thinks what I think. Why do I think she's just a baby?"

I responded: "That is an important question. Who was the baby in your family?" Darcy quickly remembered:

> "My self-esteem is from my dad. He always said that I could do anything, be anything, and have anything I wanted. My mother always said that what I wanted didn't count. What I thought didn't matter. I was too young for everything. I was just dismissed."

In order to connect Darcy's childhood memory to her view of Millie, I said, "Maybe your mother saw you as just a baby." The following week, Darcy told us that her view had changed:

> "Millie knows more than I thought. I realize she's more like the other children. She needs me to tell her more about what's happening and what I think. I can influence her thoughts, but she also has her own thoughts."

Darcy realized that while she and Millie were different from the other mothers and children in some ways, in other important ways they were the same. Darcy had her own thoughts, but she was being influenced by their thoughts. Darcy now believed that Millie might miss her while she was away on vacation and planned to FaceTime with her. She realized that she had been treating Millie the same dismissing way she described her mother treating her.

If Millie was dismissed as "just a baby," Darcy could more easily defer thinking about and talking to Millie about having two mothers. Darcy's awareness that Millie had her own thoughts and feelings, but that she could influence what Millie thought, made thinking and talking about having two mothers possible. Darcy began to notice Millie's curiosity about fathers. They began to talk about the different kinds of families they encountered in their everyday lives and were portrayed in the picture books that they began to read. Millie's awareness of having two mothers was now clear to Darcy:

> "I was afraid to talk to Millie about so many things; I was afraid about what she would think and feel. We are much closer now."

Darcy and Millie's story dramatically illustrates the discovery of each other's minds – their meeting of minds, separateness of minds, and the deepening of their relationship. Although Darcy was unaware of her fear of her daughter's thoughts and feelings about having two mothers, her fears prevented her from acknowledging Millie's needs for her mother to recognize her emerging perceptions, thoughts, and feelings. As Darcy became able to be more aware of Millie's mind – her inner world of thoughts and feelings – Millie became able to see more of herself, and mother and daughter were able to connect emotionally more fully.

A Mother's Childhood Memories and Her Daughter's Hearing Loss

Colette and two-year-old Kenzie were in a mother-toddler group and Kenzie had just completed a speech evaluation. Colette explained:

> "I'm very worried. Kenzie has a slight hearing loss that might be the reason she is not talking. She may need tubes surgically implanted in her ears. Maybe she will need hearing aids. I know other kids will tease her; they can be so mean."

Grasping for reassurance that Kenzie would be okay, some of the other mothers jumped in quickly:

> "I know many children who needed tubes and they're fine. It's not such a big deal; lots of kids have them."

The distress in the room was palpable. When mothers hear about a child's possible disability, their own anxiety escalates. They may even react as if the disability is contagious. I said:

> "Colette has serious worries. Colette's concerns seem to trigger so much anxiety in everyone and maybe memories. It sounds like you are all trying to reassure yourselves and Colette, but I'm not sure she feels reassured."

Colette added:

"When I was 10, I had a bad lisp and needed to see a speech therapist. I was so embarrassed, it was awful. I was always teased. The worst part was that my mother was embarrassed and thought I wasn't trying hard enough to talk better. She kept correcting me. She kept telling me to talk slower. I think she didn't want me to talk at all."

Several of the mothers in the group described related memories. Emery reminisced:

"When I was about 8, I had eye-surgery and needed to wear a patch. Everyone called me Captain Hook until my mother got me a pink eye-patch."

Lysandra added:

"My 5-year-old stuttered for a while when she was 2. It was very stressful and embarrassing. The doctor tried to reassure me that it would most likely self-correct in about 3 months, but it did not reassure me. Luckily her stuttering stopped."

Colette responded:

"I never realized that so many other people had the same kinds of experiences that I had, and that as bad as they were, each one was different. Maybe it doesn't need to be as terrible for Kenzie as I've been imagining."

Colette's childhood memories about her own lisp, including her mother's reaction, had contributed to her feelings of catastrophe and hopelessness about Kenzie's speech delay and hearing loss. Understanding the impact of her own childhood memories on her current reaction to her daughter's hearing evaluation, and talking to other women who had similar experiences, lessened Colette's despair and certainty that everything would be terrible. Colette's reflections led to her new conviction about helping Kenzie, whatever the outcome of her hearing. This change in the meaning to Colette of Kenzie's language delay and hearing loss, and her new, more positive attitude about helping Kenzie, influenced her interactions with Kenzie and promoted their minds in sync with positivity that predicted a better overall outcome for Kenzie regardless of her medical future.

Memories of the "Silent Treatment"

The "silent treatment" – refusing to talk and remaining silent when someone talks to you – is stressful because it prevents needed emotional connecting. Childhood memories of receiving and giving the "silent treatment" are often vivid. Devlynn described what happened when she prevented 22-month-old Kindra from running into the street:

"Kindra got angry and started to hit me. I held her hands tighter and then she bit me. I was very angry; I grabbed her arm and yelled at her. She started to cry and then wanted me to hold her. I was too angry. I didn't even want to talk to her."

At this moment, Devlynn remembered:

"Whenever my mother is angry, she gives me the silent treatment."

The link between Devlynn's memories about her mother's silent treatment and her thought, "I didn't even want to talk to her," was easily recognizable. The idea that children sometimes learn the silent treatment from their own mothers helped to temper Devlynn's rage at her mother and to modify her interactions with her daughter. Devlynn became curious about how her mother had learned the silent treatment and became less self-critical of her own impulse to give the silent treatment to her daughter. Her expectations of rupture and repair cycles of loving feelings without the silent treatment helped recovery from angry feelings with Kindra to go more smoothly.

Painful childhood memories about the silent treatment from parents and siblings were described by other group mothers. Vera remembered:

"I don't know how I learned to give the silent treatment to my little sister. I was so mean. I just ignored her and pretended I didn't hear her. She cried, but I kept doing it. I still feel guilty about it."

Linking childhood memories to current interactions with their daughters, when their separateness of minds triggered the mothers' memories of the silent treatment promoted mother-daughter meeting of minds about needs for the repair of loving feelings.

Doctor Visits and Feelings of Safety

There may be times when a mother intends to communicate to her daughter that she is safe, but she herself feels uncertain and her toddler reacts to her mother's underlying feelings of anxiety. For example, Audrey had a lifelong fear of doctors that she did not want Lylah to have. Audrey believed that her traumatic experience being hospitalized and having her appendix removed when she was nine years old had created her fear of doctors. She had thought that she was being taken to the doctor for a check-up, but she was taken to the hospital for surgery and a week-long recuperation. Unlike the total surprise that her hospitalization and appendix surgery had been, she decided always to prepare Lylah for doctor visits so she would know what to expect. However, each time they entered the doctor's office, Lylah

cried and clung to her mother. Audrey was not aware that even though the prepara-
tory "going to the doctor" play with 23-month-old Lylah allowed her daughter to
become familiar with a blood pressure cuff, tongue depressors, a syringe, and a
stethoscope, she was communicating her own reactivated fear to Lylah. After a
mothers' group discussion of similar experiences, the next time Lylah had a doctor
appointment, Audrey tried a different approach. Before they played "going to the
doctor for a check-up," Audrey said:

> "I feel a little scared whenever we go to the doctor for a check-up because it
> reminds me about my surgery that was a long time ago. The surgery was scary,
> but the doctor helped me feel better. You will have a check-up, no surgery."

Exquisitely attuned mother-daughter relationships and a little girl's emerging
empathy, enable daughters to be sensitive to their mothers' authentic feelings. In
the above example, Lylah most likely was unable to understand all of her mother's
words. However, Audrey's words helped her to separate her own reactivated fears
and memories about her traumatic childhood experience of surgery from the present doctor visits for her daughter. Mother and daughter could have a meeting of
minds about a check-up. Her daughter became able to benefit from her mother's
adult perspective on well-baby-care doctor check-ups and their doctor play. Lylah's
panicky crying in anticipation of and during doctor visits subsided.

Summary: Meeting of Minds and Separateness of Minds

During the second year of life, a mother and her daughter's awareness of
their meeting of minds and separateness of minds increase. There are many
moments when mothers and their daughter's disagree and have angry interactions, when they have different ideas in mind. Toddlers communicate their
ideas about doing things that they know their mothers disapprove and in
this way assert and substantiate their separateness of minds, as well as their
motivation to please their mothers – *I am thinking about doing something I
know you don't want me to do. My thoughts are mine; my wish to please you
is strong.* Differences in what a mother and her daughter like and dislike can
be striking and highlight their different temperaments and their separateness
of minds. Nevertheless, the influence a mother has on her daughter's developing mind is enormous. A little girl both identifies with and individuates
from her mother. A mother's ability to see the world through her daughter's
eyes unfolds. Through their separateness of minds, both mothers and their
daughters discover alternative ways of looking at the world and themselves.
In addition to the discoveries that emanate from their separateness of minds,
the pleasures of their meeting of minds intensify. Mother-daughter experiences of their separateness of minds and the sweetness of their minds in sync
combine to build a powerful relationship.

Play

The most distinctive characteristic of play is pleasure – engaging, captivating, pleasure. Play is a self-motivated way in which children learn cognitively, socially, physically, and emotionally – about the world and about themselves. Children can "say" things in play, that is, they can experience things and act things out in play, that they cannot say in words. All play has meaning.

Block Play

Block play is classic. Often, the earliest pleasure that a toddler has playing with blocks is knocking down a tower that her mother has built. A little girl gleefully knocks it down and her mother re-builds it. A toddler's excitement and urgency to knock a block tower down again and again, and to see it restored each time by her mother may capture the valued reassurance of the fundamental permanence of the structure: it can always be rebuilt. The meaning of this play that delights a little girl may be related to the rupture and repair of loving interactions – *No matter how angry I make Mommy, she loves me.* During a game of "I build it up, you knock it down," the mother's focus of attention and action is mainly on building the tower, the toddler's focus is on knocking it down. However, they both are aware of and enjoy each other's focus and identify with each other's pleasure. Awareness of their separateness of minds is activated. Their mutual pleasure is shared. Their minds are in sync about playing the game. There is a simultaneous awareness of their meeting of minds and their separateness of minds.

Filling, Emptying, and Nesting – Holding on and Letting Go

Toddlers are intrigued by filling and emptying. Whether water in a cup, sand in a pail, or dried pasta in a pot, the appeal of filling and emptying is widespread and may be connected to the body experiences of eating, peeing, and pooping. Things that are outside the body can get inside, and things that are inside can get out. Another body experience related to filling and emptying is, holding on and letting go. Sigmund Freud described his grandson's play of holding on and letting go to cope with the stress of separation from his mother. While holding the piece of string that was attached to a wooden spool, the 18 month old threw the spool and pulled it back close, repeating the words fort-da, which mean "gone" and "there" (Freud, S. 1920).

During the second year of life, a little girl's abilities to hold on and to let go increase. Catching a ball and throwing or rolling it are pleasurable first games of holding on and letting go. In addition to meanings about separation from and re-union with her mother, holding on and letting go play has body meanings. A little girl gradually becomes able to hold on to pee and poop, and to let them go. She learns to blow her nose and sniff mucous in. She discovers the power and pleasure of starting and stopping a urine stream or going to a special place to make a poop – holding the poop in her body and letting it go where she chooses.

Nesting toys that include dolls and eggs are also about filling and emptying, insides and outsides. Nesting toys add the dimension of size and repeated coming into being. Nested inside the outer, largest doll or egg are smaller and smaller ones: one by one, each that is nested inside the larger one is revealed. The interest in this toy may be its portrayal of pregnancy, birth, and a small beginning self that grows bigger and bigger. While both boys and girls enjoy filling, emptying, and nesting play, this play may have special meaning to a little girl that is related to her dawning awareness of her own body's potential for pregnancy and childbirth. The appeal to little girls of play that includes filling, emptying, nesting, holding on, and letting go may be the meaning that the play has to a young girl who is developing an awareness of and investment in the power of her female bodily sense of self.

Belly Button Play

In many families, belly buttons get attention. Not incidental to an interest in belly buttons is that they are close to the genitals, are often concealed, both females and males have them, and they are sensitive to the touch. An aspect of the attention belly buttons get is the fun of designating a belly button either an innie or an outie. While both females and males have belly buttons, and both males and females have innies and outies, innie or outie may be a slightly disguised reference to genital female-male differences and part of the excitement of belly button attention.

It is noteworthy that adults in many situations continue to use the word belly button rather than navel. This may be related to the power of childhood experiences, meanings, and memories of the belly button. In addition, the belly button is a remnant of the biological mother-fetus attachment and continuing to use the word from childhood may evoke early memories of mother-child attachment and the continuing bond.

Toys and Cultural Change

During the 1950s, toy guns were part of everyday play for many children. Gun play, however, has different meanings today than it did in the past, so toy guns are no longer as common. Nevertheless, children create other kinds of hostile, aggressive play – actions in play that are otherwise prohibited – from which they benefit. Political, economic, and cultural changes influence the manufacturing, marketing, and purchasing of toys. Although children's play occurs in the context of the larger society, a child's developmental process and life experience determine the themes and meaning of her play. The individual play preferences and pretend play themes of a little girl indicate the thoughts and feelings that are on her mind, the adaptations and solutions she is considering, and the cognitive advances she is making.

In the past, distinctions between toys for girls and toys for boys were common: dolls were for girls; trucks and cars were for boys. Tea sets were for girls and cash registers were for boys. Today, a wide range of toys for boys and girls is appreciated and reflects the current greater range of jobs for and activities of men and women. Past and current ideas about gender, including discrimination against women, sexism, and male chauvinism, can evoke a woman's strong feelings when watching her daughter play with a baby doll. The meaning to a little girl of her play may be different than it is to her mother. To a little girl, the meaning of her play is derived from her own experiences being a baby cared for by her mother. Her doll-play reflects the vital developmental processes of identifying with and individuating from her mother.

The toys that become popular at a particular time in history, within a specific sub-culture, and within each individual family are determined by many factors: developmental, political, economic, and personal. As there are fashion trends, food fads, and music crazes, there are also changing toy favorites. A mother's child-hood memories may influence the toy choices she makes for her daughter and her responses to her daughter's play preferences.

Books for Toddlers and Diversity

Cultural changes influence the themes and illustration of books. During the last three decades, diversity within families and differences among families have rapidly increased; toys and picture books for toddlers reflect these changes. A toddler's growing awareness of differences and similarities within her family and among people in her community, and what the differences mean, is influenced by many factors.

During their first three years, children learn a great deal explicitly and implicitly about differences and similarities among people. They learn from their own observations and from what they are told. Just as all human beings are unique, each family member has traits that are different from the others. Each has some traits that are similar to the others. Families may observe and talk about the similarities and differences. The similarities highlight familial connectedness, whether genetically determined or not. The ways in which a family assimilates differences into or alienates them from the family culture can be a complex process and can extend to attitudes about differences among people outside the family. Families may talk about facial features, handedness, and eye color similarities and differences. Specific traits such as birthmarks may be identified. How people feel about the similarities and differences may be talked about less. Some striking similarities and differences may not be talked about at all. Understanding why they are not talked about may be important.

Reading to Toddlers

Reading picture books to toddlers creates a joint focus of attention to the pictures and the story, to their meanings, and the feelings evoked. Picture books are frequently read and re-read because their themes are not only important during early development but are relevant throughout life. The shared mother-toddler attention to these themes can be enriching for both the mother and her little girl.

Rose and 20-month-old Melanie provide a dramatic example. Melanie's play and language development were significantly delayed and Rose was concerned. Although Rose was not aware of it, she was keeping her distance from Melanie both physically and emotionally because Melanie's skin was darker than her own. While growing up, Rose had the lightest skin in her family and among her friends. Because of her light skin, she escaped much of the racist discrimination that they experienced. Melanie's darker skin activated Rose's long held feelings of fear, shame, and guilt about the color of her own light skin. Although she was not aware of it, Rose felt safer being distant from Melanie, but was missing the kind of relationship with Melanie that she wanted and that Melanie needed. Mother and daughter were struggling to find each other; in other words to connect emotionally.

With the help of developmental consultations and Rose's insight, Melanie and Rose began to connect emotionally. Reading *Mommy, Where Are You?*, a picture book for toddlers, became captivating to them both. Though sitting on separate chairs, but next to each other, they read the book many times a day. The reading routine brought them closer physically and emotionally. The story resonated with their struggle and reflected their gradual success emotionally connecting with each other. While reading the book, Melanie could always find the hidden Mommy by lifting the flap, and Rose could always enjoy the pleasure of the Mommy being found.

Once Rose and Melanie were able to play together, talk to each other, and be physically affectionate with each other, Melanie listened to *Mommy, Where Are You?* cuddled on her mother's lap. Reading *Mommy, Where Are You?* had acquired new meaning. In Rose's words, "When Melanie found me, she found herself." I think Rose's words also meant that when Rose found part of herself that she had rejected, she was able to find Melanie.

Competition, Winning, and Losing

Toddlers experience various forms of competition: some in play, some in everyday life. Toddlers with siblings may be inundated throughout their daily lives with fierce competitions for space on Mommy's lap or for their parents' attention and love. There is evidence that competition is an inborn human trait that can be promoted, squelched, or shaped by the environment. Whereas some aspects of competition are adaptive and promote achievement, others are defeating. As play with friends increases, various kinds of competition arise including who goes first, and whose choice of book is read. When cupcakes are served, competition may arise to determine who gets the chocolate, or who gets the strawberry; sometimes, all cupcakes are kept the same in an attempt to avoid competition. A mother's thoughts about competition, winning, and losing are related to a combination of her own childhood experiences, her ideas about psychology, and her philosophies about societies. Her ideas may change as she watches her daughter develop.

During first mother-toddler winning and losing games, such as a race, a mother may have the impulse to either let her daughter win all of the time, some of the time, or never. The reasons for her decisions may be of interest. A mother may want to teach her daughter about the pleasures of winning and the value of trying hard. She may want to help her daughter adapt to losing. A mother's own memories of winning and losing may be activated.

Pretend Play

Activities of daily life are repeated in beginning pretend play. When a little girl repeats familiar activities, such as mixing pretend food in a bowl and feeding a doll, she is in complete control. Her autonomous sense of self is activated. We can wonder: when a toddler pushes a teddy bear in a stroller, is she imagining what the teddy bear feels being pushed in the stroller, or is she imagining what it feels like to be a Mommy and push her little girl in a stroller – or some of both? Such scenarios may have rudimentary elements of role-play.

In addition to everyday experiences, pretend play includes scenarios about events such as doctor visits, haircuts, and a family move; pretend play can reduce stress and promote coping. When a little girl pretends to give an injection to her doll or washes her doll's hair, she is turning the passive experience of getting an injection and a shampoo into an active one. With play that turns passive into active, she builds resilience to the stress that she may experience during the activities. Pretend play also helps toddlers cope with traumatic experiences including accidents and painful and frightening medical procedures.

Pretend Play and Body Integrity

The adaptive creativity of a little girl's pretend play is captured in the following example. Savannah was 24 months. While ice-skating with her family, her mother, Eve, accidentally stepped on Savannah's finger in a way that ripped off her nail. After a dash to the emergency room, several painful injections to numb her finger, and an x-ray, the doctor bandaged her entire hand and told them that her nail might not grow back. While Eve felt very guilty about the accident, she included in their memory narrative about the accident that she had stepped on Savannah's finger by mistake and caused her injury. Eve explained:

"I wanted Savannah to know how the accident happened. Her pain, our fear, and my guilt had reasons. Everything that happened could be known and talked about. Even though I was running the risk of being blamed, I told her that at the very moment she tried to touch my skate, I took a step and stepped on her finger by mistake – a big mistake that I felt terrible about. The ice-skate was very sharp and cut her finger. We rushed to the hospital to see the doctor who numbed her finger with a needle, took a special picture of her hand called an x-ray, and put on medicine and a big bandage that covered her hand. I told Savannah that she can't see her hand because of the bandage and when the bandage is taken off, she will see her hand and all her fingers. It will get better. I felt that even if her nail did not grow back, her finger would heal and be okay."

A week later, after the bandage was removed, her finger was healing and the nail was growing back, Savannah's main play activity for several weeks was shredding pieces of paper, crumpling the pieces together into a ball the same size that her bandaged hand had been, and binding the clumps together with tape. This activity was repeated many times a day. The corners of the living room floor were piled high with these put-together body repair constructions. Savannah's play represented the accident (shredding pieces of paper), bandaging her hand (crumpling the shredded pieces together into a ball), and most importantly, the healing (taping the shredded pieces of paper together). Savannah created the play to cope with her feelings about damage to her body. When her feelings of body integrity were restored, she no longer needed the play. For Savannah, the damage to her body and its healing were most salient. For Eve, having caused the injury and her feelings of guilt were central to the experience. Savannah's repeated damage and repair play to cope with the accident reassured Eve that Savannah was coping. For Eve, acknowledging in the memory narrative, her role in the accident helped to assuage her guilt. For Savannah, both her play and the mother-daughter shared memory narrative that contributed to her play helped her recover from the accident.

Fears and Pretend Play

At 16 months old, Kimberly was terrified of dogs. She was so frightened in a dog's presence that she kept her distance and demanded to be held by her mother while vigilantly keeping her eyes on the dog. Her mother, Tara, did not understand Kimberly's "hysterical" reaction:

> "I don't know why she's so scared. Most of the dogs are small and quite calm. Tara has never been bitten; but I was bitten on my face when I was 10. I guess I'm still scared of dogs."

Tara decided to buy a toy dog to help Kimberly. The handle of the leash had two buttons: one made the dog walk and the other made the dog flip-over. Tara and Kimberly created a variety of start and stop games with the toy. At first, Kimberly controlled the dog's walking and flipping with her words and her mother pressing the buttons, and then by herself. Her fear of dogs diminished, but never went away. Some fears become intergenerational, that is, they are passed from mother to daughter.

Pretend Play and Shared Expectations

In anticipation of a potentially stressful family event, pretend play to create shared expectations can promote a toddler's ability to cope. A family move, for instance, is a major event with inherent stresses. As moving day approached, Zadie and her husband began to pack up the apartment. Zadie felt increasingly agitated and 22-month-old Cate became increasingly clingy, not only to her mother but also to the family cat. Zadie bought a toy family set including a mother, father, and a little girl, some doll-house furniture, and a toy truck. She also included a cat. Zadie and Cate loaded the truck with the furniture, the family, and the cat. They pushed the truck to another room, unloaded it, and set everything up. Zadie also bought Cate a small suitcase that Cate could carry herself on moving day. They filled it with several of Cate's special items of clothes, a pair of pajamas, two toys, and her favorite book. Cate kept the suitcase close until they moved. Zadie and Cate were able to enact in play far more than could be explained with words. Cate understood through play that all the items of their home could be moved to another place, and the entire family, including the cat, would stay together. On moving day, Cate carried her own suitcase and helped to unpack it in her new room. Everything was there and everything had a new place.

Play and Learning to Use the Potty

Before little girls learn to use the potty, they have learned a great deal about peeing and pooping. Most important, toddlers have learned about the body sensations before and while peeing and pooping. They have learned that pooping gets their mothers' attention and that they have a series of interactions with each other related to pooping that include words, shared attention, and body-care. Poop is highly valued, yet it is discarded. It produces a pleasurable body sensation, and a recognizable odor. It is the toddler's poop, it comes out of her body, but it is not to be touched, although sometimes a toddler is curious and may try to do so. While there are some hazards for babies and toddlers in bathrooms, the bathrooms are established as safe. A multitude of contradictions are attached to poop and learning about the potty; play can help.

Clara was 22 months old and always went to the same place when she was about to poop – under the table. This meant that she knew when she was about to poop and could hold it until she got under the table. When her mother, Wynn, saw Clara go under the table, she said, "poop is coming" as she remembered her own mother saying to her. Clara began to say the same words before she went under the table. Wynn thought it was the right time to buy a potty for Clara; there were many to choose from. Some potties had elaborate decoration and gimmicks, but Wynn decided to keep the focus on the poop, their interactions with each other, and Clara's accomplishments. She recognized that potties on the floor enable toddlers to get on and off safely without assistance, and while seated on the potty, their feet are positioned securely on the floor. Feelings of safety and autonomy are both activated. Wynn chose a plain white potty. They unwrapped it together and placed it in the bathroom next to the tub. As Wynn was filling the tub with water, she suggested that Clara sit on the potty before her bath. Clara wanted a different first step to learn about her potty. With uncertainty about the new contraption and an assertion of autonomy, she said, "No Mommy! Kitty Cat sit on the potty." Both Wynn and Clara praised Kitty Cat.

Sitting on the potty, holding on to poop and pee, and letting them go into the potty are up to the toddler. The primary motivations are curiosity, a sense of mastery, and the wish to please Mommy. The first step is to feel comfortable on the potty. For Clara, Kitty Cat needed to be comfortable first. Pretend play with dolls or stuffed animals on the potty or with toy figures and toy potties can become part of each phase of learning to use the potty.

The specific interactions of each mother and her toddler that lead to learning to use the potty are unique but share basic principles. Many things contribute to the details: cultural standards, the physiologic rhythms of the toddler, ages and sex of siblings, the toddler's medical history, past and present emotional stresses, and mothers' thoughts and feelings about the process; ultimately, the teaching-learning interactions between mother and toddler are paramount. A mother's wish for her daughter to poop and pee in the potty and a little girl's wish to please her mother are central to the process. If gold stars or other rewards are used and are successful, it is because they represent a mother's praise. For a little girl, her mother's praise and admiration are the greatest rewards.

Learning to use the potty is a meaningful developmental achievement. The achievement includes awareness of the body sensations that signal that poop is coming, and the autonomous body control the toddler acquires. Learning to use the potty is a step-by-step collaborative process filled with a mother's support and congratulations, and a little girl's autonomy and pride in her body and all that she can do with it. The beginning phase has been described: the following chapter will have examples of the ways in which the process progresses.

Separation and Reunion Play

During this phase of development, separation protests may intensify. Waving and saying goodbye enable toddlers to expect the separation and how it will feel, to be active rather than passive when separating, and to ease the distress. Separation play, including peek-a-boo, hide-and-seek, and imaginative scenarios, increases.

When it was time for Alyx to leave for work, her 18-month-old daughter, Denise, combined play and saying goodbye. Their usual routine had included Denise and her babysitter walking Mommy to the elevator and Denise pressing the elevator button. As usual, Alyx stood next to the front door and called for Denise, "It's time to say bye-bye, I'm going to work." Denise ran in the other direction and hid behind the curtains. In this way, Denise achieved two things: she delayed her mother's leaving and she actively did the leaving rather than passively being left. Together, Alyx and Denise turned hiding behind the curtains into a game of hide-and-seek that created a joyful separation and reunion game of mastery before an actual separation. For a short while, Denise hiding behind the curtains, and the happy reunion with her mother became part of their goodbye routine.

Summary: Play

Pleasure and self-motivation are the most distinctive characteristics of play. Play is all-consuming and intensifies self-awareness. A little girl's play from one to two years old includes pretend play, manipulative toys, and physical activities. Play is a primary way in which she learns cognitively, emotionally, physically, and socially. She learns how to do things and to be successful. She learns from mistakes, successes, and perseverance. She learns to cope with past experiences that were frightening or disturbing by controlling them in play, and she plans for the future. The pleasure and captivating attention of a little girl's play is derived from the meaning of her play and her empowered sense of self, where endless achievement is possible. All play has meaning.

Codes of Behavior

During the second year of life, toddlers learn basic codes of behavior. Gradually, a mother's do's and don'ts that she explicitly teaches to her daughter mostly become her daughter's own codes of behavior. A little girl also watches her mother closely and learns many things from her mother that she is not explicitly taught. Importantly, she learns the underlying values of what she is being taught and the ways in which she is being taught. Underlying values, which are the main elements of social order, include safety, empathy, concern for others, and consideration of the things that surround her. In addition to all the things her mother wants her daughter to learn, a little girl may also learn things from her mother that her mother does not want her daughter to learn. The well-known proverb, "Do as I say, not as I do," refers to this dynamic.

Because toddlers are watched closely, and because they want and need their mother's approval, they become increasingly self-observant. As described earlier, during repeated mother-daughter conflicts about behavior, a little girl develops internal conflicts between wishes to please her mother and her own wishes that are unacceptable to her mother. The resolution of these internal conflicts paves the way to developing a conscience. It may be easier for a mother to identify rules that have not yet been learned by her daughter than all those that have. The ones that have been learned may be so incorporated into everyday life that they go unnoticed.

Learning codes of behavior – the dos and don'ts of everyday life – is a gradual process. To emphasize again, in addition to learning ways to behave, an essential part of the process is the development of mental and emotional capacities including frustration tolerance, impulse control, the ability to manage ambivalence, empathy, and a value system of right and wrong – a conscience. The goal of teaching socialized behavior is that a child begins to develop standards of behavior for herself and acquires the emotional development needed to implement and maintain the behaviors in multiple contexts and variable emotional states. A mother's attention to both the external behavior of her little girl, and to her daughter's thoughts and feelings during limit-setting interactions can result in her daughter's complementary behavioral learning and emotional development.

Mother's Disapproval

We can assume that when a toddler's behavior is disapproved of, her feelings of self-worth may momentarily be diminished. We can also assume that mother-toddler attachment with its ongoing feelings of security and expectations that loving feelings will return after disapproval and angry feelings dissolve, protects toddlers from becoming overwhelmed by disapproval. A mother's disapproval of a specific behavior, rather than a criticism of the total child, helps a toddler maintain a positive sense of self when confronted with disapproval about behavior. A toddler's experience might be, *I am a good lovable person, who did the wrong thing.* Throughout the first three years, teaching-learning mother-toddler interactions about behavior increasingly evoke feelings of frustration, anger, shame, and fear for both mothers and toddlers. The intense feelings that are part of this process can awaken mothers' childhood memories. Recognizing feelings from the past that are activated during these moments can lessen the distress.

Mothers' Conflicts about Setting Limits

The instruction, "Don't do it again," followed by the warning, "If you do it again," may reflect the mother's internal conflict about setting the limit. The expectation and plan for her daughter to do something that she has just prohibited her from doing may influence her toddler to do it again. A mother preventing her little girl from doing what she has prohibited can reinforce the limit. During a mothers' group discussion about setting limits, Laurel talked about her frustration with Judie:

"I told Judie three times there is no drawing on the wall. If you draw on the wall one more time, I will take the crayons away. Just as I expected, she did it again."

I proposed an alternative to consider:

"While taking the crayons away saying a version of the following might be clearer: 'There is no drawing on the wall. I am not going to let you draw on the wall; I will help you stop. You can have the crayons back when you are ready to draw on the paper.'"

Laurel disagreed:

"It would not be fair if I didn't tell her before I took the crayons away."

I said:

"Maybe you think the limit is unfair. Maybe you think it is unfair that you have more power than Judie or you are reminded of unfair limits when you were a little girl. Or it seemed unfair that your mother had more power than you."

Laurel felt that many things were unfair to children:

"I get to sleep with my husband, Judie needs to sleep alone. I get to drink wine, Judie doesn't. I can eat what I want and do what I want. It isn't fair. I guess I am remembering many feelings I had as a child. My little girl feelings are making it hard for me to say 'no' to Judie. It's not easy to be a child. There is so much you can't control. My mother never appreciated how I felt."

Laurel realized that her childhood memories were making it difficult for her to teach Judie the things that she needed to learn. She discovered that she could acknowledge Judie's feelings, she could be empathic and considerate, and still set limits clearly and firmly. Laurel decided to buy an easel for Judie to draw on.

Mother-toddler teaching-learning interactions are part of the process whereby a mother's prevention and disapproval of a behavior become a toddler's own disapproval of the behavior and a means of self-control. When a little girl feels understood, when a toddler's thoughts and feelings are recognized and accepted as understandable, it is easier to learn her mother's codes of behavior. A mother's approval, support, and validation become part of a toddler's self-approval, feelings of self-worth, personal standards of behavior, and development of a conscience.

Lillie was 20 months old and desperately wanted to make her own ponytail. She was unable to do it, but she persisted. In a rush to meet friends at the park, her mother Pamela gently tried to offer some assistance. Angry and asserting her autonomy, Lillie smacked her mother in the face. Startled and angry, her mother yelled at her, "No hitting." In that moment, for Lillie, it was as though her loving Mommy had disappeared or turned into a frightening monster. Lillie did not want to hurt her mother, she loved her. Her mother's angry response was understandable but terrifying to Lillie. She started to cry; her attachment needs felt threatened. She may have also felt some remorse. Pamela was startled by her angry response and moved by Lillie's distress. Gazing lovingly into each other's eyes, Pamela said:

> "I know you want to make your ponytail all by yourself. It takes a long time to learn to make a ponytail. You were very angry when I tried to help you, but there is no hitting even when you are very angry. I got startled and yelled at you so loud. You got scared."

Moments of deeply knowing each other's subjective experience and one's own are a part of everyday life for mothers, babies, and toddlers. Lillie knew she was a lovable person who did the wrong thing.

Learning Codes of Behavior and Making Mistakes

The do's and don'ts of everyday life need to be learned in a way that a toddler can apply them, and when uncertain, can check back with her mother as a secure base. A startle in response to a mother's prohibition may indicate a degree of hyperarousal that may interfere with processing the limit and its flexible parameters. Topaz, another group mother, remembered the first time 18-month-old Sally entered the playroom:

> "She pointed at the toys, froze, and said, 'No touch, no touch.' I was so surprised. I realized that I often tell her, or shout, 'No touch.' She always startles and then freezes."

Sally was unable to check back with her mother and rigidly applied the "No touch rule" to toys in a new playroom. Topaz realized:

> "There are so many things I don't want her to touch. But I don't want her to think she can't touch anything. I need to change my frightening no touch rule to gentler, more specific teaching-learning interactions and find ways to

say yes. For example, yes the flowers are beautiful. We can look at them and smell them together. Let me help you."

Topaz discovered that many things that Sally wanted to touch and to do were good ideas, but she needed to learn how, when, and where to do them. Playing with food was changed into learning to decorate a bowl of yogurt with fruit; jumping on the bed was not okay, but jumping on a bouncing platform was, and spilling cups of water at the sink replaced spilling water at lunch.

Part of the long-range goal when teaching the do's and don'ts of everyday life is to allow some space for conflict, mistakes, and the inconsistencies, complexities, and nuances of the things being taught. This complexity starts in the mother's mind and will be evidenced in her daughter's growing adaptation to the changing demands of the environment. When mothers' limit-setting or disapproval of behavior evokes excessive amounts of fear, shame, or anger, a little girl's self-disapproval may become too harsh. She may inhibit exploration and initiative. A toddler's frightened crying when reprimanded may indicate the need for the return of loving mother-daughter interactions.

During a mother's discussion group about the rupture and repair of loving interactions with their daughters, Emmy described an interaction with 17-month-old Mindy:

"I've told Mindy a hundred times, no climbing on the coffee table. Yesterday she climbed on the coffee table and lunged towards a bouquet of flowers in a fragile glass vase. I got frightened and yelled. Mindy startled, got terrified, and scrambling to get off the table she knocked-over the vase and shattered it. I realized what had happened and how scared Mindy was and said, 'I yelled so loud, you got scared. Breaking the vase was an accident. I got scared too. I am going to say it softly; I know you like to climb, there is no climbing on the coffee table. You can climb onto the sofa.' Mindy stopped crying and had fun climbing on the sofa."

Daphne, another mother in the group, had a strong reaction to Emmy's story:

"Saying things like that in the heat of the moment can sound fake even when the feelings are genuine. My mother often mocks me when I say things like that. But of course, she's very critical of me. Empathy is not her strength."

After many teaching-learning interactions about behavior that also promote emotional development, toddlers gradually internalize the codes of behavior and make them their own. This process is different from obedience. With obedience, behavior is controlled by submission to authority in order to avoid punishment or her mother's anger or disapproval. Submission to authority does not promote emotional development or integrity. Submission does not lead to the development of a conscience – a personal sense of right and wrong.

Summary: Codes of Behavior

From one to two years old, a mother teaches her daughter many do's and don'ts of everyday life. A little girl's growing foundation of sturdy emotional development, combined with the codes of behavior that she is being taught, leads to her autonomous and reliable socialized behavior. Emotional development includes mother-daughter attachment, and a little girl's increasing ability to inhibit behavior when impulses are strong, to tolerate frustration, resolve ambivalent feelings, and to develop a personal sense of right and wrong. Underlying the codes of behavior that a mother explicitly teaches to her daughter are implicit values that include safety, concern for others, and empathy for her daughter's thoughts and feelings when the learning is difficult. When these values guide the mother-child teaching-learning interactions about behavior, both emotional development and learning codes of behavior are promoted.

Sense of Self

During the second year of life, the sparkle of self-awareness that lights up a little girl's eyes, and her strong determination are indications of her emerging sense of self. Her attention to her body, and her investment and pleasure in cognitive and physical learning, reveal facets of her developing sense of self – body and mind. Her strong protests are also indications of her developing self. Her likes and dislikes, desires and rejections are passionate. Her emotions are part of her sense of self. Her sense of self is blossoming.

Mother-daughter interactions are an intricate part of a little girl's emerging sense of self. As she explores the world around her with all its pleasures, uncertainties, and difficulties, secure base interactions with her mother gradually become part of her sense of self: *Mommy sees me, I see myself; Mommy knows me, I know myself.* Her awareness of body and mind develops and influences each other. Learning the names of body parts, experiencing body pleasures and body pains, and the achievement of physical abilities all have mental components. Both a bodily sense of self and a mental or psychological sense of self develop. Special interests and abilities are aspects of an emerging sense of self. A little girl is learning, *All of these are part of me.*

Relationship Themes and Developing Sense of Self

The mother-daughter relationship themes outlined in Chapter 1 – being the same and being different, attachment needs and autonomy strivings, identifying and individuating, pleasing oneself and pleasing others – describe a little girl's experiences that coalesce and contribute to her developing sense of self.

Attachment and Autonomy

The mother-daughter attachment relationship creates the foundation for a little girl's sense of self. She sees herself reflected in her mother's eyes, which is a combination of what her mother sees and her mother's reactions to what she sees. A little girl's autonomy strivings help to elaborate facets of her developing sense of self. In addition, the ways in which she resolves internal conflicts between her attachment needs and autonomy strivings are a part of her developing sense of self.

As described earlier, Christina was trying to teach 15-month-old Melissa not to touch the garbage. Melissa's conflict between her attachment needs and her autonomy strivings was activated. Melissa satisfied both by signaling her intention to touch the garbage before touching it. Christina's awareness that part of Melissa's motivation to touch the garbage was in order to be the same as her mother led to teaching Melissa how to open the garbage can with her foot, and designating Melissa "Mommy's helper." Melissa's sense of self in the moment included, *I have my own ideas about touching and not touching the garbage, I can open the garbage can with my foot, I am doing what Mommy wants, and I am Mommy's helper.*

Being the Same and Being Different

A little girl's discovery that she and her mother are both female is a gradual yet significant realization with evolving meanings and implications. Mother and daughter being the same sex is accompanied by multiple mother-daughter body differences. Based on similarities and differences, children begin to create categories to mentally organize their observations. Girl and boy, and mommy, daddy, and baby, big and little, are among the first categories. Within these categories are the ideas that mothers were little girls before they grew up and became women and mommies, and fathers were little boys before they grew up and became men and daddies. A little girl actively designates who belongs in each category and in which category she belongs. *I am a girl* is part of her developing sense of self with the potential to grow up and be a mother. A toddler becomes aware of other physical similarities and differences within her family, in addition to sex, for example, eye color. Her sense of self will begin to include categories of the same and different, *I am a girl like Mommy. Daddy is not a girl. Mommy has brown eyes. My eyes are different. I have blue eyes like Daddy and Grandma.* Other categories include disabilities, race, religion, and language. Differences and similarities contribute to a little girl's developing sense of self.

Camille spoke exclusively French to two-year-old Antoinette. When in English-speaking social situations with other children, this created a bubble around Antoinette and Camille that interfered with Antoinette's social interactions with the other children and adults. We can imagine that Antoinette's developing sense of self included some version of, *Mommy and I talk French. I can only talk to Mommy. Mommy talks to me and to other people. I am different. I only talk to Mommy.* Camille recognized Antoinette's isolation in social situations, but had been unable to integrate English into their interactions when they were with English-speaking people until she became aware of her own sad feelings when she spoke English to Antoinette. Camille explained:

"My mother lives in France and does not speak any English. She felt totally abandoned by me when I moved to New York. When I speak English to Antoinette, I feel so far away from my mother and that I am excluding her. When I speak French to Antoinette I feel close to her and to my mother, but Antoinette is being isolated from everyone."

Camille's insight enabled her to expand Antoinette's social interactions in English. We can imagine that Antoinette's sense of self began to include some version of *Mommy talks French and I talk French. Mommy talks to other people in English. I can talk to other people in English also. I can have friends. Mommy wants me to have friends.*

Identifying with and Individuating from

A little girl's developing sense of self is an integration of both her identification with her mother and individuation from her mother. As discussed in Chapter 1, a little girl takes some of her mother's thoughts, feelings, and behaviors that make up her mother's personality and are expressed in their interactions with each other to be part of herself, and simultaneously becomes a distinct individual with her own thoughts, feelings, and ways of being. Her developing sense of self reflects both. When she signals an intention to do something that she knows her mother will disapprove, she reveals the tensions between her identifying with and individuating from her mother.

Mothers and daughters both being female influences the identifying and the individuating process. Carrie was two years old and refused to wear the new bathing suit that her mother bought. Her mother, Zinnia, did not understand what was going on until she remembered:

"When I was buying Carrie the bathing suit, I couldn't decide whether to get the bikini or the one-piece. Then I remembered that when I was about 9 years old and my sister was 12, we were at the beach. We always wore bikini bottoms. Never the tops. This time my mother said that my sister needed to wear a top but I didn't. I felt awful. It was as if I didn't qualify as a girl. I guess my indecision about a one-piece for Carrie or a bikini was linked to that memory. Bikini tops look silly on 2-year-olds and a one-piece bathing suit makes it clear that she is a girl. I really liked the bikini better, but I bought her the one-piece. I always wear a bikini. Maybe that's why Carrie refused to wear the one-piece. She wanted a bikini like I wear. Maybe for Carrie, wearing a bikini is what girls do."

Being seen as a girl starts at the beginning of a girl's life. Self-identifying as a girl evolves. For Carrie, wanting to wear a girl bikini like her mother was an indication that her developing sense of self included, *I am a girl like Mommy. I want to wear the same kind of bathing suit that Mommy wears.*

Pleasing Oneself and Pleasing Others

As discussed in Chapter 1, the mother-daughter relationship theme "pleasing one-self and pleasing others" can influence many behaviors. Whining, as described earlier, can be a compromise between pleasing oneself and pleasing the other. Pleasing the other can be enriching to the sense of self. However, sharing precious possessions or accepting unwanted hugs to please the other can diminish the sense of self. In many settings, there are social pressures on little girls and their mothers to please others. Complying with or defying the pressures can have an impact on their sense of self. Mothers make decisions about when to support their little girls pleasing themselves and when to require them to please others. Their decisions are based on cultural standards, the immediate context, and their own childhood memories.

Cricket, Bobbie's mother, had a twin sister and three younger sisters, all very close in age. When she was a child, their toys were all "shared property." Their clothes were hand-me-downs and belonged to all of them. A regular seat around the kitchen table could not be claimed. The sisters shared a bedroom, but each had her own bed with a connected desk. Cricket's desk and bed were her only exclusive possessions. Cricket explained:

> "For my mother, sharing everything meant you were a good person. If my sisters and I had a fight about a toy, my mother took it away. If we fought about clothes, she took them away. Pleasing your sister was a priority. I'm sorry to say it, but I learned the lesson well. It's very hard for me to do any-thing to please myself; it makes me feel that I am selfish and mean. Bobbie is almost 2 years old and every time she says, 'It's mine', whether it's her special blanket, my lap when I'm holding my niece, or a bunch of grapes we take to the playground to share, I cringe and insist that she share. I don't say it, but I think she's being mean and selfish. I don't want her to have the same problem I have pleasing myself. I always please the other person rather than myself. If there are three plums in the fruit bowl and one of them is bruised, I take the bruised one. If I pleased myself and took the best one, I would feel like a bad person."

Cricket was aware that her sense of self as mean and selfish if she pleased or wanted to please herself was being perpetuated with her daughter. Cricket decided:

> "When Bobbie says, "My Mommy" and tries to push my niece off my lap, I realize she is asserting her sense of self. I want to support her developing sense of self by saying, 'Yes I am only your Mommy; I can hold you and your cousin'. But it's hard for me. I think that one of the reasons I became a writer is because the only time I truly felt like myself growing up was when I was sitting at my desk, writing – my only possessions were my desk and my words on paper."

Cricket realized that when her daughter said, "My Mommy" and tried to push her cousin away, not only was she asserting her feelings of love and attachment to her mother, but also her sense of self.

It's Mine

The emergence of saying, "It's mine" about people, objects, and then ideas, is a clear indication of a developing sense of self. For many toddlers, "My Mommy" is the first possession. Among the first objects that are claimed as "mine" are treasured toys. When a toddler asserts "It's mine" it can mean I want it, I want a turn, I like it, etc. "It's mine" embodies a girl's sense of self.

Body-Care and Pooping

Toddlers begin to participate in their own body-care, which contributes to their developing sense of self and paves the way to learning to use the potty. Beginning self-body-care includes washing their tummies during baths, hand washing at the sink, a turn at teeth brushing, nose blowing, and maybe shampoo lathering. As she approaches two years old, a toddler has learned a great deal about peeing and pooping; she knows how it feels and recognizes that it gets her mother's attention and leads to affectionate body-care – all of which contribute to a little girl's developing sense of self.

Mothers usually do not have childhood memories about learning to use the potty, but they may have related memories. Flora had a vivid teenage memory that she described during a mothers' group:

> "I was walking home from school with my best friend Patsy and we were hysterical laughing. I had my period and needed to pee. By the time I got home my panties and dress were a mess. I had pee and blood all over them. Patsy and I were still laughing when we walked in the door; my mother was furious. She thought it was disgusting that we were laughing. The more she yelled, the more we laughed. Now I think it's disgusting when Alexa poops in the bath and she thinks it's funny and tries to catch the floating poop. I guess she's curious and feels good about it. It's her poop. I used to say, 'that's disgusting.' which really meant, 'you're disgusting.' Now instead of saying 'that's disgusting,' I have started to say, 'Yes, you made a big poop. I am going to put it in the potty. That's where it goes. Next time you can make it in the potty.' She doesn't use the potty yet, but she has not pooped in the bathtub again."

When a toddler poops and what is happening is identified, she learns that her mother is interested in pooping and poop, and it is something that can be talked about together. A foundation for future learning to use the potty is being created. Children are interested in the things that their mothers are interested in. Defecating is a pleasurable body experience that triggers mother-daughter interactions – a joint focus of attention, a word, and body-care interactions. A little girl is experiencing, *Pooping feels good. Mommy cares about my poop. It must be important.*

Genital Curiosity, Sensations, and What Gets Talked about

Being naked is exhilarating. Part of the pleasure is from gentle skin sensations unincumbered by clothes. Part of the excitement is from feelings of unrestrained body freedom and the exposure of body parts that are usually covered. Toddler girls are proud to show their naked bodies and to have them appreciated and admired by their parents. There are innate and acquired individual differences of a little girl's body explorations, and the amount and kind of genital pleasure each girl seeks. A toddler may be curious about all parts of her genitals: how they look, smell, and feel. There is enormous individual variation in genital curiosity and exploration. Mothers' stories about their toddlers' genital touching may include mothers' own feelings aroused and childhood memories activated. A toddler's body excitement can be contagious or barely noticed. A little girl's body sensations and her mother's reactions contribute to her developing sense of self.

A mother has intimate contact, both visual and physical, with her daughter's body. Her own early fantasies and body experiences can be aroused and may be repeated. For example, Beatrix told a mothers' group about a nighttime ritual of gently fingertip tickling her daughter's arm, back, and tummy before sleep, as she had been tickled when she was a little girl and fondly remembered. One night, pointing to her genitals, her two-year-old daughter said, "Mommy, tickle me there." Beatrix was startled. She had not remembered or realized that the tickling had been arousing, "in that way," when she was a girl. During the present moment, while tickling her daughter, a reliving of the past had replaced remembering.

During another mothers' group, Elianna described Louisa's discovery at 18 months:

> "Louisa's older brother was taking a bath and she was sitting on the floor naked with her legs spread, exploring her genitals with her fingers. I was so surprised when pointing to her clitoris she said, 'this is my little penis.' I was happy about her discovery and told her that's her clitoris. I wanted her to know the word and to know that it's great to have a clitoris. She said, No Mommy, that's my little penis. It seemed important to Louisa in the moment to think about it that way, I don't know why, but I stopped myself from insisting it's her clitoris."

Further discussion highlighted that Louisa's brother was four years older and everything about him was bigger. And while it was important to her mother that her daughter learn the word clitoris and not compare a clitoris in a diminished way to a penis, she was confident that her daughter valued her clitoris. She believed Louisa's statement had different meaning to her daughter than it had to her. It was important to Elianna that her daughter knew her own mind, especially her thoughts and feelings about her body.

Mothers make different decisions about what gets talked about with their toddlers. Girls are aware of their vulva, and may have discovered their clitoris, vagina, and the scent of their vaginal secretions. They may want to know what their mothers' think. The genital pleasure toddler girls experience may be apparent. Their pride may be palpable; inhibition may be absent. Individual variation is huge. While the aim of toddlers' pleasure in touching their genitals may not be orgasm and the specifics of their fantasies may not be known, we can think about toddler genital pleasure as sexual because it involves the sex organs.

We might say that each mother simultaneously celebrates her daughter's body and all it can feel and do, while she also teaches her the sexual norms of her culture and family codes of behavior. In other words, mothers communicate that genital pleasure feels good but is not something to do at the dinner table or while playing with friends, etc. It is good to be curious and explore your body in private, but not okay to explore Mommy's body. There are parts of genital pleasure that get talked about and parts that are private. In general, toddlers quickly learn both the approval of body pleasure and curiosity, and the limits to pursuing them.

Summary: Sense of Self

Relationship themes that characterize mother-daughter interactions: being the same and being different, attachment needs and autonomy strivings, identifying and individuating, and pleasing oneself and pleasing others coalesce and contribute to a little girl's developing body-mind sense of self. Intimate and tender body-care, pleasurable body sensations, and moments of mother-daughter intersubjectivity create the foundation. Discoveries about the separateness of minds contribute. The assertion, "It's mine," during the second year of life indicates that a sense of self is coming into being.

---

7 Two to Three Years

During development from two to three years old, mother-daughter relationship themes: being the same and being different, attachment needs and autonomy strivings, identifying with and individuating from, pleasing oneself and pleasing others become more identifiable. Major cognitive and emotional developmental milestones are achieved. Gender identity continues to develop. The sex of a child is biologically determined at birth; gender is socially constructed. The individuals that make up a culture determine the behavior, roles, responsibilities, and privileges that are attributed to women, men, girls, and boys. Since definitions of feminine and masculine are socially constructed, gender specifics vary from culture to culture, and over time within each culture. The details are determined consciously and unconsciously, and communicated to children explicitly and implicitly. Gradually, little girls absorb many of the expectations related to gender that surround them and reject others. The activities, dress, and hairstyles that signify female and male are noticed. What it means to a little girl to be female evolves.

Isabella was almost three years old and had very short hair. Both her mother and sister had long hair, her father and brother had short hair. Isabella desperately wanted long hair like her sister, "I want long hair like Emmy. I'm not a boy." She hated being mistaken for a boy and clung to her mother and cried each time it happened. She thought that if she had long hair it would be a sign to the world, *I am a girl*. Isabella chose another sign – a sparkling tiara. She insisted on wearing the tiara that had been among the dress-up clothes for Halloween in a neighborhood store. Over the next many months, her mother helped her acquire a collection of tiaras and princess style dresses. Every day she insisted on wearing a dress and a tiara. Her mother helped her to make it clear to the world that she was a girl. Isabella was no longer mistaken for a boy even though her hair was still short. When her own female gender identity was more firmly established, Isabella shed the tiara and princess dresses. Her hair had grown a little bit longer, but it was still short. She continued to wear dresses, but not princess style dresses. In time, she added jeans to her wardrobe.

The gender symbols that a little girl embraces may be exaggerations of everyday norms, as were Isabella's tiaras and frilly dresses. Sparkling tiaras were not

DOI: 10.4324/9781003687603-8

the usual dress for girls or women in New York City in 2012, but for Isabella and the world around her, wearing a tiara identified her as a girl. It is interesting to note that Isabella's mother usually wore pants, as did most of the women they knew. As women were gaining more economic and political power, and began to wear pants not only for leisure activities, but also for work and formal occasions, at the same time, little girls began to wear more "princess" style dresses, not only as costumes for Halloween, but for everyday activities as well as for parties. Also around the same time, Victoria's Secret lingerie, including bras and panties for teens and young women, was featured in their catalogues. By 1997, 450 million catalogues a year were distributed across the United States – clean pornography at your doorstep. The Victoria's Secret models were called Angels. A halo is a symbol of holiness for an angel as is a tiara a symbol of purity for a princess and a bride. As Naomi Fry observed in The New Yorker Magazine in 2022, Victoria's Secret was a brand created to "… shape our collective imagination of what a woman can and should be" – a sexy angel. Victoria's Secret highly air-brushed photos of almost naked young women (many of whom were college students in their late teens) on billboards and buses changed city landscapes and the daily images seen by little girls. Sexy co-eds and "princesses" decked the city streets.

Cultural shifts and mother-daughter relationship themes intertwine. Personal and cultural meanings can collide. Carla described herself as a woman who rejected female gender stereotypes and found her three-year-old daughter's exclusive choice of sparkling party dresses disturbing:

> "I do not want Mila to be a girly-girl. She only wants to wear her party shoes and dresses, even to the playground. For Halloween she only wants to wear a princess costume. An airplane pilot or a doctor would be out of the question. We fight all the time about what she wears and what she plays with. She got a Barbie for her birthday and that's all she plays with now. She even wants to wear bikini lace panties like her friend. She's only 3."

Suddenly, Carla remembered that when she was a little girl, her mother had wanted her to wear bikini panties, bows in her hair, and uncomfortable dresses with tights:

> "My mother always wanted me to be a different kind of girl than I wanted to be. She still does. She always says things like, 'get a hairstyle, wear some makeup. You still look like a ragamuffin tomboy.' The other day we went shopping and she criticized my underwear; I don't wear bikini underpants. I can't believe it, I'm almost 40 and she's still trying to dress me. I'm doing a different version of the same thing with Mila that my mother does with me. I'm trying to get her to be more like I am. She's the kind of girl my mother wanted me to be."

With her new awareness of the connections between her childhood memories and current interactions with her mother and daughter, Carla was able to allow her daughter to be the kind of that girl she wanted to be – a different kind of girl than her mother. In addition, Carla began to enjoy her daughter's pleasure in being a girl even though the gender symbols she chose were not the same as the ones that Carla chose for herself.

Carla filled Mila's underwear drawer with a collection of lace panties, and in time, Mila chose to wear jeans and sneakers to the playground like her mother and the other little girls. Carla was able to recognize the activation of mother-daughter relationship themes that contributed to their angry interactions. Carla now believed that their fights about lace panties had to do with Mila's autonomy strivings. Carla and her own mother attributed the same meaning to lace panties – the sexual pleasure of men – but had different reactions to the meaning. Carla and her daughter attributed different meanings to lace panties. For Mila, wearing lace panties meant wearing different kinds of panties than her mother wore, but the same kind of panties that her friend wore. For Mila, lace panties had nothing to do with men and sex.

Mother-daughter relationship themes: being the same and being different, attachment needs and autonomy strivings, identifying and individuating, and pleasing oneself and pleasing others could now have the space to exist in Carla and Mila's relationship, and be resolved without mother-daughter clashes. Typical mother-daughter teenage conflicts about skirt lengths and bare midriffs, in addition to having new teenage sexual meanings, reflect the activation of mother-daughter relationship themes that originate during the first three years.

I Am A Girl

As her father stepped out of the shower, 34-month-old Candice said: "Daddy you have a tail!" Although Candice had known about male-female genital differences for some time, knew the words penis and vagina, and could identify who was a girl and who was a boy, who was a woman and who was a man based on appearance when clothed, her words reflect her feelings of excitement, curiosity, and ongoing efforts to integrate the image of her father's penis with her own experience. Candice added, "I have a secret garden like Mommy with many hidden treasures." Maybe these words that Candice spoke had different meaning to her than they have to adults, but she did understand that her mother, from whom she had learned these words, thought that she had something special. Candice also understood that her "something special" was connected to her pleasurable genital sensations of which she was aware.

The following day, Candice, her mother, and father were all going to a party. Wearing a new dress, sparkling shoes, and a barrette that glittered, Candice asked her mother, Lori, "Do I look pretty?" Her mother was disturbed by the question and angry at the world that her not-yet-three-year-old daughter was concerned about looking pretty:

> "There is so much pressure on girls and women to be pretty. Boys don't worry about being pretty or being handsome. The only time in my life that I didn't worry about being pretty was when I was pregnant. I just felt pretty."

Lori wondered what it meant to Candice to be pretty. She also wondered if there was any significance to the exact words of her daughter's question: "Do I look pretty?" Candice did not ask, Am I pretty? This distinction was important to Lori. She explained:

"The question that Candice asked, "Do I look pretty?" may mean that to her "pretty" is a description of the items she was wearing, not an evaluation of her innate physical traits. In contrast, the question, 'Am I pretty' would refer to an assessment of her. This way of thinking about Candice's question makes me feel better and gives me a chance to influence how she thinks about being pretty."

The women thought that the distinction was useful. The meaning of being pretty to a three year old may be more about mother-daughter attachment and party clothes than about the physical traits she possesses. These two vignettes highlight how mother-daughter interactions can influence feeling pretty. A foundation can be created that protects a little girl from the increasing social pressures to achieve an idealized standard or personal expectation of physical perfection.

Emotion Regulation

During this phase of development, using words to identify feelings, creating memory narratives, and symbolic play are primary ways to regulate emotion. Mother-daughter interactions that promote the development of these capacities are central to a little girl's emotion regulation. Out-of-control angry temper-tantrums, states of panic, and grief reactions are typical emotion regulation disruptions.

A little girl's communications that include exaggerations or that seem overly dramatic may be ways of asserting, *I feel strongly about this. It is important to me.* Leilani explained:

"Rosa is just like I was. She has a fake cry. When I tell her it's time to put the iPad away or no more bedtime stories she always does her loud, fake cry. I call her 'the drama queen.' That's what my Mom called me."

Leilani had identified with her own mother's critical and dismissing attitude, and even though she recognized that she had wanted understanding from her mother, she was behaving the same way with her daughter as her mother had behaved with her. Mother-daughter relationship themes continue and are intergenerational. I suggested:

"Maybe Rosa's cry sounds fake when she is angry. She wants something that she knows you won't give to her, she knows that you don't want her to even want it, and she knows that you don't want her to feel angry. Afterall, you are being completely reasonable; it's been a long day and it's bedtime. I wonder how Rosa would react if you said that you know how interesting the iPad is.

Maybe she would like to work on it for two more minutes, finish what she is doing, and then turn the iPad off all by herself. Before sleep, remembering together that you and Rosa had a wonderful day, listing the things you did, and the wonderful plans for tomorrow can help activate Rosa's cozy mother-daughter attachment feelings, and arouse her own sleepy feelings."

Leilani recognized that she had been ridiculing Rosa by calling her a "drama queen" and dismissing how she genuinely felt:

"Rosa has been doing exactly what I did as a child and I have been reacting to her exactly the same way that my mother reacted to me – not the way I wanted her to. Mostly, I wanted her to understand. She always said I was a great actor; I was not acting. If I was low-key she ignored me, if I was emphatic she ridiculed me. She never heard me. I hated French fries and she said nobody hates French fries. I still hate French fries."

A little girl's underlying feelings can be genuine even when her surface behavior looks melodramatic, defiant, or inauthentic. When the tensions between mother-daughter relationship themes are activated, feelings can be intense and behavior more oppositional and extreme. Both the feelings and the behavior can be understood in terms of relationship themes. Even hating French fries can be understandable if it means the assertion of an autonomous sense of self.

Body-Mind Regulations

Sensations of hunger and satiation, readiness to sleep and to be alert, urges to poop and to urinate are body experiences that from birth are autonomous. Throughout development, mother-daughter interactions have a different influence on a child's autonomous body regulations. Mothers, while considering the stage of development and individual needs, likes, and dislikes of their daughters, introduce schedules and expectations. An overarching principle during this phase of development from two to three years, is that little girls be supported in their awareness of and responsiveness to the signals that they get from their own bodies, while at the same time they increasingly learn to respond to external signals and expectations that are imposed on them. For example, external signals include daytime is for play and nighttime is for sleep, potties are to pee and poop in, dessert comes after the main course, and "Because Mommy says so." While a little girl is learning to respond to external signals that relate to her own internal body regulations, upholding the primacy of her awareness of and responsiveness to her body is valuable. Because a little girl's body regulations, emotion regulation, and mother-daughter interactions influence each other, identifying mommy-choices and toddler-choices can be useful. For example, bedtime is a mommy-choice – falling asleep is a toddler-choice. In other words, the mother designates bedtime, and the toddler's emotional state and body regulation induce sleep. Mealtime and the food prepared are mommy-choices – what is eaten and how much are toddler-choices: that is the toddler's body regulation of hunger and satiation, influenced by her emotional state determines what she eats and how much. Pooping is a toddler-choice: that is, pooping is a body regulation influenced by emotions and meaning. Pooping in the potty is a mother-toddler teaching-learning interaction. The mother provides the potty, the motivation, and the encouragement. The toddler does the pooping.

When toddlers protest, choices can be useful. For example, "It is bedtime; time to get into your bed. You decide when to fall asleep." Or "It's time for dinner. We have steak, potatoes, broccoli, and fruit tonight. I wonder what you will choose first." When learning to use the potty, "Tell me when poop is coming and I will help you go to the potty." While choices will not resolve every conflict, both mother and daughter knowing the toddler-choices that are linked to body regulation can promote a little girl's autonomous body-mind regulations and her responsiveness to external family routines and developmental expectations.

Exceptional Events

Television and the internet are ways in which world tragedies come into our homes. News programs with vivid visuals about school shootings, natural disasters, and war are frequently broadcast and seen at home. Overheard adult conversations may also have an impact even when it appears as if toddlers are not paying attention or that they do not understand. For example, while two-and-a-half-year-old Ruby was playing with her dollhouse, her parents were watching the news and were horrified by the destruction caused by an earthquake. Suddenly, Ruby started throwing the little dollhouse furniture and figures around the room. Her mother Ella realized that Ruby was reacting to the devastating images on the TV, as well as to her parents' horrified reactions. Ella said, "I think you saw the earthquake on television. It was scary. The earthquake knocked down a building. The earthquake is over now. Let's put all the furniture and dolls back in the dollhouse."

When a toddler has witnessed a disturbing event, words to identify her feelings, symbolic play, and a memory narrative can promote emotion regulation. Using technical language or unfamiliar words to explain what occurred can emphasize that it is a rare occurrence. The use of new words, special words rather than everyday language, highlights the unusualness of the event and can create distance from it.

Some topics that mothers would rather not talk to their daughters about may be relevant to their children, for example, donor egg or sperm, surrogacy, or adoption. Advice about what and when to tell children varies. It is generally accepted that children will eventually learn such information and that it is valuable for them to learn important information from parents.

A Mother's Miscarriage

During a mother-toddler group, Aria described her recent miscarriage:

> "It has been very difficult, but I'm okay now. Several weeks ago, my husband and I had told Leah that I was pregnant, her Dad and I are going to have a baby, and she would be the big sister. We've been talking about it for weeks. She

sometimes kisses my belly. I have not said anything to Leah about the miscarriage yet, she's not even 3 years old, but I think she knows something is going on. She hears me talking about it and I'm sure she knows how sad I feel, but she has not said anything. If I didn't talk about it, I would be totally depressed."

It seemed as if Leah did know that "something was going on." At the beginning of the group, she had given two dolls to her mother to hold and then ran off to play with a friend across the room at the sink. Leah giving two dolls to her mother suggests that her mother's pregnancy was on her mind. Leah seemed absorbed in her play at the sink; however, when her mother began to cry while talking about the miscarriage, Leah stopped playing, ran to her mother, and knocked the dolls off her mother's lap onto the floor. While Leah had been playing at the sink, she was emotionally tracking her mother and in some way she understood that her mother's crying had something to do with her babies. I said:

"I think Leah is trying to understand what has happened. Even before you started to talk about the miscarriage or to cry, your pregnancy was on her mind. When she walked in this morning she gave two dolls to you to hold. Maybe it would help to say something directly to her."

Aria held Leah tenderly and said:

"Remember Daddy and I told you that I was pregnant and was going to have a baby. I was wrong. I am sad about that, but I will feel better. I will have a baby another time and will tell you when it is time."

Leah picked up the two dolls she had thrown on the floor, put one of the dolls on her mother's lap, one doll back in the cradle on the shelf, and returned to the sink to play with her friend. How can we understand the meaning of what Leah did with the dolls? When she and her mother had arrived, before starting to play, Leah put two dolls on her mother's lap. This meant *Mommy has two babies.* When Leah heard her mother cry and talk about the miscarriage she knocked both dolls off her mother's lap. This meant, *I think Mommy is crying about her babies.* After Leah heard her mother's explanation of what had happened that included that she was not pregnant anymore, she would have a baby at another time, and she was sad but would feel better, Leah returned one of the dolls to her mother's lap and one to the cradle. This meant that in some way Leah understood, *My Mommy is not pregnant. She has one child, me.* Leah returning to play at the sink with her friend meant, *Mommy is sad, but she will feel better. I can play.* In addition, Leah understood that sad and complicated things can be talked about and happy feelings can return. It may be surprising to imagine that a little girls' actions can have these meanings.

Developing Sense of Humor

At the same time, toddlers are beginning to appreciate a joke, sarcasm, and illusion, they are also concrete. For example, Susan and her daughter Jolie were getting ready to go to the park. Susan as a joke put Jolie's hat on her own head and said, "I'm ready." The hat was lopsided, and half falling off. Jolie laughed, but then said in all seriousness as she grabbed her hat: "No Mommy. That's my hat. Don't do that."

Jolie both appreciated the joke and at the same time was disturbed by its possible reality and wanted to set the record straight.

Actions or words that are designed to be funny and cause laughter are unexpected or silly. Some humor may frighten or humiliate the listener. For example, the curiously common joke "I've got your nose" can be funny or terrifying and sometimes both. A two year old may laugh when grandpa playfully pretends to have severed his granddaughter's nose and is holding it peeking out between his index and middle fingers. For some toddlers, the adult's affectionate playfulness modulates the horror of the joke and the child giggles; for others, the terror of actually losing a body part, a heightened anxiety at this age, is triggered and the toddler rejects the joke.

Separations and Reunions

Stress reactions to separation for both mothers and their daughters can intensify at this stage of development. A new form of peek-a-boo may emerge. A toddler two to three years old may hide and trigger her mother's panic in an escalating combination of terror with the possibility of loss, and rage when reunited. A little girl may be evoking in her mother the fear that she herself experiences when her mother leaves her. She may also be enacting the wish to be found no matter what. This form of peek-a-boo that evokes a mother's genuine feelings of terror is not a game, but can be changed into a game.

Anya described what was happening with Penelope:

"She really hides. For a few minutes I can't find her. I actually get panicky. Maybe it triggers a memory. I just remembered; my mother told me that I once got lost in the supermarket when I was 4 years old. It took a while for her to find me and she was terrified that I had been kidnapped. When she found me, she spanked me. It was the only time she ever spanked me. Her terror changed to rage. I don't remember it at all. But it's a family story frequently told."

Natalie, another group mother suggested:

"Maybe you can change Penelope's hiding into a fun game. What if you tell Penelope when she wants to play the hiding game to tell you so you can get ready?"

The following week, Anya told us that Penelope now tells her when she wants to play the hiding game:

"I don't get panicky anymore. I also tell Penelope that I will always find her. If she hides in a closet, I will find her; if she hides under the bedcovers I will find her, if she hides behind the curtains I will find her. I will find her anywhere in the world. She now seems to like hearing this story more than hiding. She asks me to tell it to her many times a day. It's her favorite story."

When a child is lost for a few moments, or in other frightening situations, the mother's feelings of anxiety can be overwhelming. When safety is restored, emotion regulation can lag, and a mother's activated fear about her child can change into rage at her child for having triggered her feelings of terror.

Fear of Sexual Abuse

A mother-toddler group had been meeting for over two years. The women had shared many intimate details about their daughters, themselves, and their marriages. Claire mentioned a recent newspaper article about the sexual abuse of a young girl and declared her intention to teach Skylar how to protect herself: "I want to be sure that Skylar will never be sexually abused." Claire described how she was warning Skylar about potential dangers and teaching her self-protective strategies:

> "Never talk to strangers, never take candy from strangers, and never get into a car with strangers."

Since three-year-old children are rarely alone with strangers and the parents of a sexually abused child often know the abuser, Claire's rules about strangers seemed irrelevant. In addition, frightening warnings can make a three year old feel unsafe and unprotected. Furthermore, there are many opportunities to support babies' and young children's intuitive avoidant reactions to strangers. I wondered about the sexual experiences and the fears Claire may have had that triggered her anxiety. In the middle of reciting her instructions to Skylar, appearing startled, Claire remembered a kiss when she was 14 years old:

> "Right there in our living room, my father's friend put his hands on my bottom and kissed me in a way that tickled the inner edges of my lips with his tongue. I never told my parents or anyone. I've not thought about it for years."

I wondered what motivated Claire to keep the kiss secret. I wondered if Claire felt unprotected by her parents in other ways and whether she had been criticized for typical childhood body pleasures. I said:

> "It is the parents' responsibility to protect their children. Children cannot protect themselves. I wonder when else you felt unprotected."

Claire remembered:

> "When I was 10 years old, my little brother always spied on me when I was in the bathroom. When I told my parents, they accused me of teasing him and said that I liked the attention."

Claire's memory of her parents' accusations and disdain, and her feelings about sexually related pleasures may have motivated her to keep the kiss from her father's friend a secret and contributed to her anxiety about Skylar being sexually abused. I commented on Claire's memory:

> "Not only do you remember your parents not protecting you, but in addition you remember being blamed for your brother's peeping and being criticized for any excitement or pleasure you got from it."

Claire agreed and added that in some ways she had thought the kiss was her fault.

Little children cannot protect themselves. They learn to protect themselves when they have been protected by their parents. They also need to feel entitled to say "No" to unwanted touching and to be supported when they do say, "No." In addition, they need to know that their own childhood body pleasures and excitements are recognized and accepted by their parents; for example, running around their room naked. Rather than using frightening hypotheticals, there are many everyday opportunities to support toddlers saying "No" to unwanted touching and many childhood body pleasures to be validated and supported.

However, there are situations when children are required to be touched in ways that they do not want. Recognizing their discomfort and protests to being touched can be helpful. For example, when being examined by the doctor:

> "I know you don't like it when the doctor examines you, do you want me to hold you when you have your check-up."

Claire now recognized that a three year old is not able to protect herself. Skylar was no longer required to be touched when she protested doing high-fives with their neighbor, sitting on her uncle's lap, whom she saw rarely, or being kissed when she did not want to be. Claire began to hold Skylar during medical check-ups. In addition, Claire decided to discontinue using the babysitter with whom she had never felt comfortable, but was not quite sure why. Claire assumed her protective role.

Treasured Toys

Gradually, toddlers become increasingly capable of emotion regulation. As a little girl develops emotion-regulation mental capacities, she no longer needs her treasured toy in the same way as she had before. Mothers can notice these, sometimes subtle, developmental changes and support them. Anna described:

> "Since Peri was born we have kept her Pink Bunny close; first I did, then she did. When she was a baby, I snuggled it close to her when she nursed. It wasn't a treasured toy yet, but I thought it might become one. When she began to walk, she dragged it by the ears around the apartment. She kept it close during meals and she snuggled-up with it for her bedtime story. She slept with it every night. I kept it with her when we traveled – in the car and on airplanes. When Peri was about 2 years old, every day before leaving the

apartment to go to the playground she put Pink Bunny in her stroller. One day when she was a little over 3 years, as I was loading her scooter onto the stroller, Peri climbed in. She did not get Pink Bunny or ask for it. I was not sure if she forgot or decided she didn't need or want it. I decided not to suggest that she take it."

Peri was developing the mental capacities to tolerate feelings of frustration and anxiety; to cope with the grief of separation and loss; and to manage intense anger and terrifying fear. The meaning of and her attachment to Pink Bunny had changed. She still slept with Pink Bunny every night, but when she and her mother were going to the playground, she did not want to take it with her. The emotion regulation capacities she had attributed to Pink Bunny were becoming reliable, stable, internal mental processes.

While it has become popular in some communities for older girls to take a cuddly toy on sleepover dates and to sleepaway camp, their attachments to the object and its meaning are different than when they were younger. A younger toddler attributes to the treasured toy the emotion-regulating capacities and sense of self-feelings that she is developing internally. Adults have strong attachments to objects also and may even describe feelings of having "lost a part of myself" when they lose such objects; but they have not – early feelings, unstructured in language, have been activated. When a toddler loses her treasured toy, she has lost a piece in the process by which a part of herself is coming into being, and this developing process of emotion regulation needs to be, and can be restored even if the object is not found. Adult memories of treasured toys reflect the developmental process of emotion regulation (Lefcourt, I. 2021).

Some childhood treasured toys have been kept into adulthood. Special blankets, dolls, and soft, cuddly toys are carefully stored in memory trunks or tucked away in closets. Some remain in abandoned bedrooms and may be seen on occasion. Others have long vanished. The memories remain vivid. Adult memories of special teddy bears, blankets, bunnies, and other treasured toys maintain meanings similar to those that the cherished toys themselves had during early childhood. When the memories are recalled, feelings of comfort and pleasure are aroused. Even when the memories include a treasured toy's abrupt loss, or the toy was treasured in the context of threatening and difficult childhood experiences, the pleasurable memory of the object remains and tempers the surrounding pain. Alissa remembered:

"I had a special baby-doll. I slept with it every night and took it everywhere with me until I was about 4 years old. What I remember most is that my doll had a little bruise on her cheek. It's funny, I just realized, I have a bruise, it's really a birthmark on my cheek in the exact same place. Her name was Baby. I don't remember when or why I stopped taking her everywhere with me. My mother keeps my doll in her linen closet. I haven't seen it for a while, but every time I see it or think about it, I get a warm, cozy feeling. I just realized, sometimes when I'm comforting Halie I say, 'It's okay baby.' It's the only time I call her baby."

While comforting her daughter, Alissa's memories of comforting herself with her doll, Baby, are awakened. The realization that her vivid memory of the bruise on her doll's face is in the same place as the birthmark on her own face highlights the idea that a child's interactions with her treasured toy, and an adult's memory of a treasured toy, reflect the child's own developing mental capacities and sense of self.

Summary: Emotion Regulation

From two to three years old, mental capacities needed for emotion regulation develop further. These capacities include constancy and deepening of mother-daughter attachment, the ability to use words to identify and metabolize feelings, to participate in the co-construction of memory narratives, to tolerate frustration, and to be aware and responsive to body signals in addition to external signals. Little girls are sensitive to and reactive to the emotions of the people who surround them, especially their mothers. As emotion regulation develops, the meaning of and attachment to a treasured toy changes.

Meeting of Minds and Separateness of Minds

During this phase of development, mothers and daughters enjoy more moments of intersubjectivity. They are more aware of their meeting of minds and their separateness of minds. They are getting to know more about each other and are feeling more known by each other. While walking through the park, three-year-old Zara and her mother, Arden, passed a basketball court. Zara asked:

"Mommy, why are only the boys playing ball? The girls are just watching."

Arden was stunned and confessed to the mothers' group:

"I didn't even notice. I guess for me to see boys doing something that girls don't do is expected, part of everyday life. For Zara, it was striking. For me to see the male-female difference on the basketball court through her eyes triggered a pain that I wasn't even aware of."

Moments when mother-daughter separateness of minds surfaces provide the opportunity for the mother to see the world as her daughter does, discover new facets of her own mind, and of the mother-daughter relationship. This is part of a mother's expanding sense of self.

In contrast, mother-daughter interactions that highlight the separateness of minds can become increasingly angry. For example, the family was gathered for dinner. Lisbeth was 30 months old and did not want the bread that was on the table.

She had something else in mind and told her mother, "I want toast." Her mother, Sahara, was happy to toast some bread for her daughter and provided the additional choice of cutting the crust off or keeping it on. Making a choice requires having two things in mind. Lisbeth made a choice, "No crust."

When the toast was the light brown color Lisbeth liked, her mother presented her crustless toast to her. Lisbeth rejected it: "I want toast with crust. I don't like this toast." Frustrated, Sahara reasserted her intention to please Lisbeth, "You asked me for no crust." Lisbeth made it clear, "That's not what I want now." This is a typical two-to three-year-old version of asserting and substantiating the separateness of minds. Toast without crust was in her mother's mind. Toast without crust was not what was in Lisbeth's mind now. She changed her mind; minds are flexible. A little girl needs to feel understood and simultaneous needs to establish and maintain the separateness and complexity of her own mind may create challenges. Lisbeth was also learning about the limits of her ability to control her mother. Sahara told Lisbeth:

"You have two kinds of bread, toast without crust and bread with crust. You really know exactly what you want. You can choose."

A mother recognizing interactions with her daughter that assert and substantiate the separateness of their minds helps to mitigate angry feelings and can lead to interactions that promote a little girl's abilities to formulate her own thoughts and assert them in a constructive way. Lisbeth chose toast without crust.

Underlying Meanings of Behavior

When a mother and her daughter passionately disagree about a specific behavior, a meeting of minds about the underlying meanings of the behavior can be useful in resolving their conflict. In other words, a mother and her daughter may disagree about the behavior, but agree about the underlying meaning of the behavior. Maureen was jumping on the sofa. While lifting Maureen gently, but firmly off the sofa, her mother said:

"Yes, jumping is so much fun. You can jump on the floor or on the jumping-cushion, but there is no jumping on the sofa. Where do you want to jump? Where should I jump?"

Maureen and her mother's minds were in sync about the fun of jumping. Their separateness of minds was focused on where to jump. Maureen being able to choose whether to jump on the floor or the cushion shifted the conflict about "No jumping on the sofa" to an agreement about the fun of jumping and choices about where to jump. However, a mother may be critical of the underlying thoughts or feelings that motivate her daughter's behavior and in addition to wanting to change the behavior, she may want to change her daughter's thoughts or feelings. Changing someone's thoughts or feelings is different than changing behavior. For example, Georgia had begun to pick her nose. Her mother Dyanna was embarrassed, thought it was disgusting, and wanted Georgia to stop: "I keep telling her it's disgusting, but she keeps doing it." Becky, another mother in the group suggested: "Maybe it feels good to her; she doesn't want to think it's disgusting." Dyanna responded:

"I guess it feels good to Georgia to pick her nose, I did it when I was little and I was so ashamed. My mother always said that I was disgusting. Maybe I will tell Georgia she can do it in private."

Summer had a similar experience related to accepting feelings and explained:

"Shari loves to go to the playground. We go almost every day. Monday and Tuesday it rained, and yesterday I couldn't go; I was working. Shari kept asking and I kept saying, 'Don't ask me again;' but what I really meant was, 'I don't like to keep saying no, stop wanting to go.' Finally I said, 'I know you really like the playground and want to go every day. The playground is so much fun. You are very disappointed that we cannot go today.' I couldn't believe it, but once I acknowledged and accepted her feelings rather than trying to change them, she stopped asking."

When trying to change behavior, acknowledging and accepting a little girl's thoughts and feelings that motivate the behavior may be helpful. When trying to change thoughts and feelings, acknowledging and understanding the reasons for existing thoughts and feelings can be essential. For example, after witnessing a fight between her mother and father, Luna, who was two and a half years old told her mother: "I don't want to get married." Her mother said:

"I think you do not like it when Daddy and I fight. We had a loud, angry disagreement. Now it's over. We like being married."

Understanding the meaning of a toddler's behavior, her underlying feelings, and putting the meaning into words can be the first step toward influencing her thoughts, feelings, and behavior.

Memory Narrative Co-Construction

Co-constructed memory narratives of traumatic experiences may be particularly helpful in facilitating emotional recovery. Cody was almost three years old. While staying up late to wait for her father to come home, jumping on the living room sofa, she fell and cut her forehead on the corner of the coffee table. Cody's mother Joanna described the accident to me on the phone:

"I never should have let her jump on the sofa. Her face was covered with blood, but I could not see where it was coming from. I was overwhelmed and terrified. I shrieked helplessly frozen for several moments until I gained control and called an ambulance. I think I really frightened her. Cody's father met us at the hospital. He was shocked, silent, and frozen. I was so angry at him. I cried hysterically while trying to comfort Cody who was screaming as the nurses immobilized her for the sutures. I was so scared. The doctor told us that she expected the cut to heal well. Cody was given a lollipop."

Medical healing had begun; emotional healing would take more time. The next week, Joanna and Cody returned to the mother-toddler group. Cody, with a small Band-Aid on her forehead, eagerly entered and began to play with the dollhouse. She vigorously and repeatedly jumped the little girl doll on the small dollhouse sofa. Abruptly her play stopped. After a brief pause, she repeated the jumping, and then repeated it again, and again. She was unable to develop her play or to play with anything else. Cody had begun to use play to process the accident, but was unable to elaborate her play into a useful scenario – an indication that the accident was traumatic for Cody.

Joanna entered and almost threw herself onto a bench with a sigh of despair. She told the other mothers the story of Cody's accident as she had told it to me on the phone and added:

"Since the accident last week, every time Cody hears an ambulance siren, which happens often, she begins to scream uncontrollably. It lasts about 20 minutes. The only thing that stops her crying is a lollipop."

The stunned mothers mirrored Joanna's horror and feelings of helplessness as they listened silently.

The repetition and abrupt ending of Cody's play jumping the doll on the sofa, the screaming when she heard ambulance sirens, and the lollipops to soothe her were Cody's incomplete fragmented memory of the accident. The jumping had preceded the accident and a lollipop was how it ended. The entire middle of her experience including her mother's rage, terror, and crying, her father's frozen silence, the blood, the ambulance ride, being restrained, her pain, and overwhelming fear were activated each time Cody heard ambulance sirens. Her parents' anger at each other, anger at themselves, and lonely guilt were activated each time they heard Cody scream.

Cody's parents had not been able to talk with Cody about the accident, and Cody needed help to construct a useful memory narrative. In addition, her parents were too angry and guilty to talk to each other about the accident. In Joanna's words:

"It was so frightening and we still feel so guilty and angry. I feel guilty that I let Cody jump on the sofa and that I was so out of control. My husband feels guilty that he wasn't home and he was immobilized in the hospital. I am angry he wasn't home, and he is angry I let her jump on the sofa. I just hoped Cody would forget about it. I guess we need to talk about it."

The following week, Joanna brought the memory narrative book that she, Cody's father, and Cody had created about the accident, the treatment, and the recovery.

Cody and her parents read the book, played accident, and going to the hospital. Cody began to act out in her pretend play the family shared memory narrative. In a few days, Cody stopped crying when she heard ambulance sirens. Once she had a shared memory narrative with her parents to help her think about, talk about, and pretend in play many elements of the accident, she no longer screamed. Sirens now triggered the memory narrative, not the feelings of terror. The memory narrative included Mommy crying, the ambulance ride to the hospital, Daddy's silence, the treatment, and all the frightening feelings that could be talked about rather than relived; feelings of safety were restored. For a while, they continued to read the accident book, to talk about the accident, and to play going to the hospital. Within a month, the accident play had stopped, and the book remained mostly on the shelf.

Cody was no longer alone without words to describe what happened and how she felt. In addition, she now had her mother and father's comfort. While they each had different reactions to the accident, they had a meeting of minds with Cody about the memory narrative.

Dual Tracking

When Carly was 34 months old, her mother Bernadine was telling the toddler group mothers how "angry and fed-up" she was with Carly's difficult behavior. Her words were harsh and conveyed her helplessness. Carly approached her mother in a frozen stare. Bernadine's anger escalated as she continued her diatribe. I interrupted, "I wonder what Carly is feeling about what is happening right now." Bernadine gasped and said:

> "She looks very scared: she also looks like she wants something from me. Carly, you look scared. I am telling everyone how angry I sometimes feel."

Bernadine recognized that her anger was having an unintended impact on Carly. She identified Carly's feelings of fear, and modulated her anger. Carly returned to play.

The other mothers in the group recognized their own similar experiences. Daizy said, "Last night I was so angry at Gabbie. It was the fourth time she came out of bed after two stories, a goodnight song, and a gentle massage. I was exhausted. I literally threw her on her bed. I didn't hurt her, but she was scared. What was going on in her mind was totally off my radar. I was not thinking about what might be on her mind keeping her awake. Her father has been away for three days and in moments like this, I'm just angry at both of them. I felt terrible. I apologized and said that I was wrong to be rough with her. I told her that maybe it's harder to feel cozy in bed when Daddy is away. We made a calendar, designating with different colored stickers the days Daddy had been away, and when he was returning. She fell asleep holding the calendar."

Throughout the day, a mother's thoughts about her daughter, and about her daughter's thoughts and feelings move from the front of her mind to the back, and at times, as Daizy described, "off my radar." These changes in a mother's awareness of her daughter's mind can affect a mother's fluctuating feelings about being a good mother, a bad mother, and what is called a good enough mother. As noted before, the good enough mother provides sufficient amounts of sensitive maternal care so that the inevitable failures are buffered. Through tears of laughter, a mother summarized our discussion about the good enough mother:

> "Listen to us, we are a difficult group of mothers for our children. I'm grumpy until I have my morning coffee. Cynthia needs the bathroom door closed when she's using the toilet and her daughter screams. Sandra yells at her husband too much and her daughter gets frightened. Patricia can never decide what to wear so she's always late. Myla works all the time. Nicole is a perfect mother who plans to get a divorce."

A major task for all children is adaptation to the quirks and idiosyncrasies of their mothers, and the ups and downs of life. This is a gradual, lifelong process. As the mother-daughter relationship progresses, the mother that a woman wants to be and the mother that she thinks she is, become increasingly aligned. In moments, angry and frightening mother-daughter interactions are intense, but the meeting of minds and returning to affectionate interactions starts to become expected and reliable.

Summary: Meeting of Minds and Separateness of Minds

During this phase of development, mothers and daughters have increasing and deepening pleasurable moments of intersubjectivity. Although in some moments mother-daughter interactions that reflect their separateness of minds are stressful, in other moments their separateness of minds is enriching and satisfying. When behavior triggers angry interactions, a mother and her daughter can have a meeting of minds about the underlying meanings of the behavior. Co-construction of memory narratives about stressful experiences can create moments of their meeting of minds and ease the stress. Mother-daughter attachment intensifies, a little girl's identifying with and individuating from her mother progresses; more similarities with and differences from each other can be identified. While all of this is happening, a little girl discovers and begins to cultivate a mind of her own.

Play

While her little girl's imaginative, cognitive, physical, and social play are ways for a mother to understand her daughter's developing mind, she views her daughter's play through the lens of her own childhood memories. The everyday activities that capture a little girl's attention and the disturbing events that she is coping with are both important parts of her play. Rules of games begin to be introduced. Winning and losing begin to intensify. A mother's memories of play that are triggered as she watches her daughter play may be relevant even if they occurred at different ages.

Mothers' Childhood Memories and Mating Rituals

Mothers typically remember their own childhood play that contained elements of mating rituals including flirting, courting, and marriage. Attitudes that are expressed by others in the memories may be aspects of the mother's own childhood or adult feelings. During a mother-toddler group, for instance, when her daughter took her shoes off while playing with a little boy, Addison remembered:

> "When I was 6 years old, every day at school I sat next to Pete. Like all the girls, I wore penny-loafers and took one shoe off during class. The fun of penny-loafers was slipping a penny into the special slot on the top of the shoe. I can also remember the feeling of playing with my shoe with my bare foot: sliding it back and forth with the tip of my toes. One day when class was over, I reached for my shoe and it wasn't there. Pete had taken it. It was so exciting. My teacher asked where my shoe was? I told her that Pete took it. She grabbed my shoe away from him, and said that if he ever bothers me again to tell her and she will punish him. I wasn't bothered; I thought it was fun. Maybe my teacher had an old-fashioned idea that girls don't like to flirt. When I got older my mother had a rule, "No boyfriends." But I always had boyfriends."

Addison knew that she liked to flirt and rejected her teacher's attitude as "old fashioned." She also rejected her mother's rule about "No boyfriends." Mother-daughter themes: being the same and being different, attachment needs and autonomy strivings, identifying and individuating, pleasing oneself and pleasing others are prevalent in Addison's reflections. Addison giggled as she described her memory that included the fun she had slipping a penny into the slot on her shoes. This part of her memory may have been a disguised reference to genital pleasure. Some details of mothers' childhood memories include allusions to romance and to sex, and may include conflicted feelings. Addison wondered whether her daughter had any of the same feelings playing with Oscar and taking off her shoes that she had had with Pete, but refrained from imposing her memory of play on her daughter's play. Addison explained:

> "I don't like it when adults attribute romantic or sexual thoughts and feelings to little girls that they might or might not have. I especially don't like it when they tease or laugh at them. You see that on the internet all the time."

In Addison's memory, it was her teacher and her mother who were disapproving of her and Pete's play. The remnants of her mother's and teacher's disapproval may be part of her sensitivity to and protection of children from being ridiculed for having romantic or sexual feelings.

Manipulative Toys – Easy and Difficult

The pleasure of easy, and the challenge and mastery of difficult, the surrender to too difficult, and the boredom of too easy may be everyday experiences. A little girl's persistence or lack of persistence may be a temperament trait. Sometimes a lack of persistence indicates that the task is beyond a child's ability. The pleasure in the ease or meaning of a task can lead to persistent repetition. Supporting a little girl's ability to persist, even if the task is easy for her to accomplish, can generalize to persisting to learn difficult tasks.

When her daughter is struggling to achieve a task, for example, to do a puzzle, her mother decides when to help and when not to help. Many things may influence her decision including how much mess will occur and therefore more work, an assessment of her child's ability to tolerate the frustration, the mother's ability to tolerate her child's frustration, and her ideas about the value of learning from success, mistakes, and failure. Sometimes, memories of being too pushed, not pushed enough, painful failures, and embarrassing mistakes influence mothers' decisions about when to help their daughters.

Stop and Go Games

There are many things in the world and about each other that mothers and daughters cannot control. They cannot make the rain stop or always get each other to do what they want. In addition, they cannot always control themselves. Mr. Rogers' classic song, "What Do You Do With The Mad That You Feel" (1968) addresses this theme:

"What do you do with the mad that you feel, when you feel so mad you could bite ... it's great to be able to stop and think this song ... I can stop when I want to ... and know that this feeling is really mine ..."

Mother-daughter, stop and go play can provide an opportunity through play to be in control of each other and of oneself. The games Red-Light-Green-Light and Simon Says are examples. There are many ways to play these games. For example, the mother dances and when her little girl says "stop" the mother freezes. When her daughter says "Go" she starts dancing again. They then reverse roles. Being able to achieve control in play makes it easier to tolerate experiences when control is not possible, and promotes the ability to achieve control when possible.

Aggression and Play

The ability to act aggressively, that is, to behave in a way that is self-protective and hurts another, is believed to be innate for survival purposes. Aggressive impulses are normal and universal, but need to be socialized. Children are taught to process their own and others' angry hostile feelings and intentions verbally: "I know you want all the toys for yourself. But there is no hitting. The other children also want toys."

Assertiveness is socialized aggression. However, male and female aggression in both adults and children is socialized differently. The adage, "Boys will be boys" is still used to defend certain kinds of male aggressive behavior. A comparable adage for aggressive female behavior does not exist. Ideas about aggression are hotly debated and may account for the fact that the landmark Violence Against Women Act, which recognizes domestic violence as a federal crime, was not enacted until 1994.

Hitting, kicking, and biting are typical for toddlers when they are angry, frustrated, frightened, or overstimulated. They are learning how to mentally process these feelings, inhibit these impulses, and instead use words to communicate how they feel, get what they want, resolve conflicts, and defend themselves. Aggressive play provides little girls the opportunity to satisfy aggressive impulses that are otherwise unacceptable, *I am so angry I feel like hitting Mommy. I cannot hit Mommy, but I can hit the pillow.* In addition to the meanings of aggressive play, there is inherent pleasure in vigorous, assertive physical action.

Kicking a ball, punching a blow-up clown, banging pegs, bursting a bubble, and a variety of toys that squirt water are forms of aggressive play. Pretend play scenarios can have aggressive themes, for example, crashing cars and fighting animals. Sometimes toddlers become overstimulated or frightened by aggressive play. Mothers have different thresholds for their daughters' aggressive play. When aggressive play makes a mother feel uncomfortable, she may prohibit play that would benefit her daughter. Children can "say" things in play that they are unable to say in words.

Aggression and Intergenerational Transfer of Trauma

Adele thought that Rosey was "too aggressive." When Rosey attempted to hold on to a toy that was being grabbed by another child, her mother required her to relinquish it and told her, "Be nice." When Rosey wanted to play with a toy that another child wanted at the same time, Adele insisted that Rosey wait. When Rosey wanted to choose the book to be read in playgroup her mother said, "Be nice, let your friend choose." Adele described Rosey's play:

> "Rosey is too aggressive. I don't know where she gets it from. She bangs the pegs too hard with the hammer and the xylophone just as hard. She drowns her baby doll at the bottom of the bathtub. She buries toy figures in the sand. Everything she does is too aggressive. She always wants her way and never gives her friends a chance. She's too aggressive."

Adele was unaware that her reaction to Rosey's play was related to an intergenerational transfer of trauma. Adele's mother had had a baby sister who died in a neighbor's swimming pool when Adele's mother was four years old. Adele did not know any of the details. It was not something that her grandmother or mother would talk about. It had been unspeakable until Adele told her mother about Rosey's aggressive play, and her mother realized a connection to her own sister's death. Adele's mother told Adele:

> "I think I could never talk about my sister's accident because in some ways I have always blamed my mother for my sister's death. I think my mother is too aggressive."

Adele's mother had felt unsafe because she had blamed her own mother for her baby sister's drowning. In other words, she felt as if her mother had killed her sister and that she too was vulnerable to her mother's aggression. Although it was never talked about, and Adele had never known the details, she had experienced her mother's fear of aggression. Adele had viewed Rosey's efforts to protect herself and assert herself as dangerous aggression and therefore inhibited Rosey's healthy assertiveness. This left Rosey feeling unsafe and fueled her aggression. As Adele began to protect Rosey when other children were aggressive with her, to support her self-assertive efforts to choose books to read, and to applaud her strong physical play, Rosey became less aggressive. When Adele stopped viewing Rosey as dangerously aggressive, she began to see Rosie as self-assertive and strong. Feeling more protected and safer, Rosey became less aggressive. The details of the intergenerational transfer of trauma are not always visible, but the phenomenon helps to explain both Adele's and Rosey's behavior.

Rough-and-Tumble Play

Parents' rough-and-tumble play with their daughters, including various forms of wrestling, entangled bodies rolling around on the floor, tossing little girls in the air and catching them, swinging them around, may become more vigorous during this phase of development. There is implicit agreement and mutual restraint between parent and child not to hurt each other. This aspect of rough and tumble play – controlled aggression, has been credited with learning to control hostile aggression. However, fears about the aggressive components of rough and tumble play also trigger the warning, "This will end in tears." The combination of high arousal fun, vigorous physicality, and controlled aggression with the safety of a trusted adult contributes to the universality of rough and tumble play and its repetition from one generation to the next.

Mothers' childhood memories influence the rough-and-tumble play with their daughters and the ways in which they react to their daughters' rough-and-tumble play with others. Pleasurable, frightening, and exciting memories are activated. The amount, intensity, and details of rough-and-tumble play vary widely between parents and children, and among siblings. The term rough and tumble play was coined in the early 1900s to describe the fighting play among young animals that prepares them for survival when they no longer have the protection of parents (James, M. 2018). Maybe the term has persisted to describe children's play because it emphasizes the aggressive elements and de-emphasizes the erotic. A mothers' group discussion about parent-child rough and tumble play highlighted some of these themes. Mitzi recalled:

> "I haven't thought about this for years, but yesterday it popped into my head when my husband was roughhousing with Clarisa. When I was a little girl my uncle was the 'tickle monster.' He chased my cousins around the apartment, tackled them to the floor, and tickled them. His kids loved it. I didn't. It seemed, although I didn't have the word then, too intimate. I wanted to like it. Maybe I would have liked it with my own father."

Caryn added:

"Rough and tumble play always feels too dangerous to me, and my husband is not so into it. The only place we do it is in the swimming pool; it seems safer to splash and throw kids around in the water."

Other mothers in the group thought that the pool was more dangerous. They remembered being warned about heads getting bumped on the side of the pool and drowning accidents. LillyAnne remembered:

"I hated any rough and tumble play. I had two older brothers who wrestled all the time. Sometimes they hurt each other. When they tried to wrestle with me, I never liked it; but mostly they put rubber snakes in my bed. That was scary. My parents never played with us. Between work and three kids, there was no time. Both my husband and I have gentle rough and tumble play with Brigette, but she's only 2 ½. When we are walking together, she holds both of our hands and we swing her between us. She loves it. She's a good swimmer so we also swing her around in the pool. She also loves to be pushed on the swing. Nothing scary, just exciting. Maybe when she's a teenager she'll like the rollercoaster."

LillyAnne's memories of rough and tumble play with her brothers were linked to scary memories of rubber snakes in her bed and her absent parents. She chose play activities with her daughter that elicited the thrill of high arousal excitement without triggering her daughter's explicit fear or reactivating her own. She envisions the possibility in the future of an escalation of excitement for LillyAnne.

Play with Peers

Social interactions among children between two and three years of age increase and beginning friendships are formed. Both affectionate and aggressive interactions intensify; specific attractions and clashes between two children can occur. At times adults may romanticize or sexualize boy-girl or same-sex interactions. For example, "Bart, give your girlfriend Alannie a kiss. She wants to marry you." Some adults may find these kinds of comments amusing. They may seem unnoticed by some toddlers, lay a foundation for others, and for some raise anxiety. Bart corrected his mother and reassured himself and Alannie when he said, "Mommy that's silly. We are too young to get married."

As toddlers play together more, they have more conflicts. Opinions vary about the extent to which adults should intervene to resolve toddler conflicts with each other. Some mothers and professionals believe that as long as the children are not hurting each other – let them work it out; they will learn from the interaction. Others believe that adult help can teach standards of behavior and model ways to resolve conflict. In some ways, both ideas are useful. The challenge is deciding which is more useful in which specific situation, with each child, and for each mother. Childhood memories may influence mothers' decisions.

Johanna had vivid, painful memories of being bullied as a child and was angry that her mother, counselors at camp, and teachers at school allowed it to happen: "They did nothing to help me," she grieved. Maren had many guilty memories about aggressively teasing her younger sister, bunkmates, and classmates. For both mothers, understanding their own childhood memories that were reactivating intense feelings of guilt and anger, and impulses to retaliate or withdraw, helped them each decide when and what kind of adult intervention would be most helpful to their daughters.

Imitation of Peers

Sometimes toddlers imitate something that they see another child do and the imitations worry their mothers because they fear the behavior will be adopted permanently. Avery told a mothers' group about Misa's playdate with Arielle:

> "While they were playing, Arielle put her hair into her mouth and began to suck it. This is a nervous habit Arielle has. Her mother firmly tells her to stop and Arielle spits her hair out of her mouth. But in a few seconds it's back in her mouth again. I think it's pretty disgusting; her hair is always wet. I am not sure we should continue playdates. I don't want Misa to learn this nervous habit."

Sometimes, when toddlers see another child do a self-soothing behavior, such as suck their hair or their thumb, they may be curious and try it out to see what it feels like. Part of the motivation may be to imagine their friend's experience. Misa may also have had a reaction to the angry interaction between Arielle and her mother. The following week, Avery described what she said to Misa when she tried sucking her own hair:

> "I think you have seen Arielle suck her hair, I guess it feels good to her. It does not feel good to most people. Maybe she does it to feel better when she has a feeling she does not like. Her mother is trying to help her to stop. I think you are curious about what it feels like and how I would react."

Misa and Arielle continued to have playdates; Arielle continued to suck her hair, Misa did not. Misa may have been influenced by what her mother said or she may not have found sucking her hair pleasurable. A self-soothing behavior that is imitated may not have the same pleasure as one that has been originally created.

Scooters

Many little girls cherish their scooters, or other riding toys, because they have special meaning. A toddler's passionate sense of "it's mine" may be related to a scooter's connection to the early mobility of crawling and the exhilaration of walking. The speed of separating and reuniting with others is accelerated with a scooter.

A little girl independently generates the speed and direction of the scooter and embodies the power of attachment and autonomy. When zooming around on a scooter, her sense of self is invigorated. Because of this connection to her developing sense of self, in addition to a treasured toy, mothers and daughters often agree that a scooter or bicycle does not need to be shared with other children.

Pretend Play and Eating

The details of a little girl feeding a doll or toy animal can provide useful information about the meaning of meals to the toddler. Renee was two and a half years old. Her mother Chandler was horrified as she watched Renee play:

> "I could not believe what I saw. Renee was feeding pretend oatmeal to her doll, spoon after spoon, jamming it into her face and saying, 'you need to eat more! One more bite! You are a bad girl!' I always thought that I was encouraging Renee to eat. I never called her a bad girl. Maybe she feels forced and like a bad girl when she doesn't eat more."

Chandler was able to reflect on the meaning of her daughter's play. She recognized that her own behavior could have different meaning to her daughter than it had to her. Their separateness of minds was vivid. Chandler also became aware that she wanted her daughter to eat to please herself, not to please her mother. She understood the importance of her daughter using her own body sensations to begin to know when she was hungry and when she had eaten enough.

Reactivated Aggressive Themes

Pretend play scenarios led by mothers can have aggressive themes that at times may overwhelm toddlers. For example, when Tabetha was a little over two years old, she and her mother Elenore had a vast repertoire of pretend play with wild animals. Elenore led the play with her daughter as her elder brother had done with her. The play always included growling attacks and fighting. Tabetha began to hit playmates. When it was suggested to Elenore that Tabetha's hitting might be related to the play scenarios that might be frightening to her, Elenore decided to stop imitating the wild animal play and instead to take Tabetha's lead in their play. The play themes shifted to events of everyday life and Tabetha's hitting stopped. Elenore described her memory:

> "I don't remember being frightened when my brother played these games with me. It was always fun; but once I was bitten by a vicious dog and I've been terrified of dogs ever since. We were playing gently and suddenly the dog bit me on my mouth. I still have the scar. Maybe that's why I growl like a dog when we play and why Tabetha gets so scared."

Elenore's play with her daughter had elements of both play with her brother and being bitten by a dog. She remembered the play with her brother as always having been fun and the dog bite as terrifying and the cause of her fear of dogs. Although Elenore had totally separate memories of being bitten by the dog and play with her brother, her memories were merged in the play with her daughter and their play frightened her daughter. Why she merged them in their play is unclear, but maybe there were elements of the play with her brother that were frightening at the time, but that she preferred to remember as fun.

Reversal of Roles – in Play and in Actuality

When Gennie was three years old, her favorite imaginative play was being the mommy and having her mother play the baby. She tucked her mother into bed, fed her, gave medicine to her, and gently rubbed her mother's back. Silvia, Gennie's mother loved playing baby with Gennie, but wondered about it. Silvia began to notice that she frequently asked Gennie to do things for her. When she could not find her glasses, she asked Gennie to find them. When she dropped something on the floor, she asked Gennie to pick it up. She asked Gennie to pull off her socks. She especially liked Gennie's tender caresses. Gennie's favorite imaginative play scenario was for her mother to pretend to cry, and for Gennie to comfort her. Silvia realized that in everyday interactions and in pretend play, a reversal of roles was being acted out: she was being the baby and Gennie was being the mother. Silvia remembered:

> "My mother often did not take care of me. She was in and out of the hospital for much of my childhood and couldn't. She's better now and takes care of Gennie all the time. Maybe that's why I like playing the baby with Gennie."

Silvia realized that playing baby with her daughter was related to her own child-hood memories about missing her mother. With this insight, the pleasure she got from playing baby began to fade. In turn, Gennie became less interested in playing the mommy with her own mother. She started playing being the mother more with her dolls.

While mother-baby play is typical for many mothers with their daughters, usu-ally the little girl plays the baby sometimes and the mother plays the baby some-times. For Gennie and Silvia, the mother playing the baby was constant because it had been about the mother's reactivated feelings of lost maternal care that she had suffered as a child.

Screen Time

The importance of toddler play is widely agreed upon. Screen time is not traditional play, but it does have some elements that other forms of play also have. The po-tential value and potential harm of screen time for toddlers have been questioned: advice is widespread but differs. During past generations, the impact of innovations was also questioned. Worries surfaced that the telephone, television, and comic books would undermine wholesome values, family life, and sturdy development.

The irresistible appeal of new technologies, and the potential damage of "too-much" were of concern in the past as they are now about screen time. Of course, an exact measurement of "too-much" is never known, though at the extremes it may be clear. Mothers reading to toddlers is a highly valued activity; never being read to would be a loss; being read to all day would interfere with other valuable activities. Gradually, new technologies and forms of entertainment get integrated into the culture with huge individual variation.

Mothers make personal decisions for themselves about their own screen time. Their decisions are based on competing interests and responsibilities, and the impact of their own screen time on their toddlers. Mothers make decisions about their toddler's screen time; they balance the amount of screen time with what is known about the value of competing activities, especially mother-toddler play. They worry about the use of screen time as a babysitter to entertain their children or to calm their children when over-excited. There is much to consider; there are no simple answers.

When a mother is texting, emailing, or otherwise engaged with a device, her daughter loses her mother's attention as is also true when her mother is doing many other things. Daughters are interested in the things that interest their mothers. In addition, digital devices have intrinsic properties that appeal to little girls: press a button and things happen. Regulating the amount of screen time can become increasingly stressful as children develop; establishing some family routines that include no devices during meals or in bed can be useful. Establishing routines when the children are young can lay a useful foundation for creating family social time and developing interests in other activities.

Summary: Play

Play during this phase expands and is a way to understand a little girl's developing mind. Everyday activities and outstanding events are part of her pretend play. Exciting rough and tumble play intensifies. Learning occurs with manipulative toys that are easy to master and with those that are more difficult. Beginning games with rules, and winning and losing are introduced. Aggressive play and games of control provide constraints on hostile aggression that pave the way for self-assertiveness. Mothers' childhood memories of their own play are triggered as they watch their daughters play.

Codes of Behavior

Adults typically break some rules. For example, they may tell a lie to protect someone's feelings; they may cross the street when the light is red. Children need to learn which rules are acceptable to break and in what context, and which rules should never be broken. This is a long evolving process with much individual variation.

Mother-daughter interactions about learning codes of behavior may be deeply gratifying at times and painfully frustrating at others. The most effective and development-facilitating teaching-learning interactions with toddlers do not include punishment. Instead mother-daughter interactions that promote positive thoughts and feelings that motivate a little girl to adopt the codes of behavior that surround her have been emphasized. The power of a toddler's attachment to her mother is the main element of this process.

Words, Ideas, and Feelings

Most behavioral limits are learned by repeated mother-child interactions. There are few behaviors that are taught once and learned: for example, the extremely dangerous ones. The prohibition of words, ideas, or feelings as if they were dangerous may interfere with communication and emotion regulation. Strong feelings communicated in an objectionable way, for example, by kicking and screaming, can be reframed:

> "I think kicking and screaming on the floor means you are very angry at me; it's okay to be angry. You can say, 'I'm angry.'"

Some verbal communications of anger may be objectionable, but can be reformulated. For example, "I hate you!" or "You are stupid!" can be translated into, "I am very angry at you. My feelings were so hurt. I want to hurt your feelings." In these ways feelings are acknowledged and validated rather than teaching that thoughts and feelings are shameful, dangerous, or taboo. "Poopy head" or "stupid" may be terms that a toddler hears from a friend or older sibling and is trying them out. The following response can promote communication:

> "I think you heard someone say those words and you want to see what it feels like to say them and what reaction you get. There are other words you can use."

Daughters may hear their mothers curse and may imitate them. If a mother does not want her toddler to curse, a response might be:

> "Sometimes I say that word when I have a strong feeling and I am surprised, but in our family I think it is better to use other words we know. You are learning all the words in our language, and you are also learning when to say them. When we are together, I want us both to say 'Ouch, that hurts.' or 'Oops, I dropped it!'"

Words like "shut-up" may not be okay around the family dinner table, but in some contexts might be of value to be able to say, to read in books, or to hear in movies. Home can be a safe place where all experiences, ideas, and feelings can be talked about and understood.

Truth-Telling

Truth-telling is a value shared in most families. Mothers teach their daughters the importance of telling the truth and are disapproving when they have lied. However, sometimes what appears to be a toddler's lie can be understood as the expression of a wish. A question mothers know the answer to may be a perfect set-up for such a "lie."

Winona was almost three years old and liked to stand at the bathroom sink, lather her doll's hair with shampoo, and rinse it by spilling cups of water on the doll's head. It was her favorite play, as play with water is for many toddlers when they are learning to urinate in the potty. It was a little messy, but with her mother Lacey's help, it was manageable. It was dinnertime and Winona wanted to play at the sink and her mother said "No." Winona cried and Lacey went into the kitchen to prepare dinner. When she returned, Winona was naked, and there was a puddle on the bathroom floor. Lacey asked Winona, "Did you make pee-pee on the floor?" Winona said, "No Mommy." Lacey said, "You are lying? There is no lying allowed." Another way to understand Winona's answer to the disapproving accusation, however, is that she wished she had not made pee-pee on the floor because she wanted her mother's approval and was self-disapproving of peeing on the floor, but she also had been angry at her mother for saying, 'No' to water play.

A distinction between narrative truth and historical truth is useful in this situation. It was easy to verify that the historical truth was that Winona had urinated on the floor, but her narrative truth – the wish that was revealed in her "lie" – may have been more important to focus on:

> "I know you are learning to make pee-pee in the potty. Sometimes people make mistakes. I think you were angry that I did not let you play with the water, so you made pee-pee on the floor. Pee-pee goes in the potty, even when you are angry."

A mother's disapproval of peeing on the floor is important. Acknowledging and supporting a little girl's motivation to do what her mother wants and the complexity of the thoughts and feelings that motivate her behavior are also important and can promote learning the desired behavior, knowing and communicating her authentic feelings, and truth-telling.

Apologies

Toddlers are learning about apologies: accepting apologies and making them. They are learning about social conventions of apologizing and expressions of guilt. Their capacity for remorse is developing. Moments of self-consciousness and being self-critical about something that they have done are part of the process. One way little girls learn about apologies and feeling sorry about something that they have done is with their mothers.

Attitudes about apologizing have become infiltrated with gender meanings. The motto, "never apologize – never explain," is connected to being a powerful man. It has been observed that women apologize more than men. The way an apology is responded to can influence the meaning of the apology. The directive, "Stop apologizing" in response to an apology can be an assertion of dominance in response to an apology meant to be polite. An apology can be used to repair the rupture of loving feelings, be an attempt to alleviate guilt, be an expression of remorse, or to avoid punishment. Apologies can be triggered by activated childhood memories. Apologies have different meanings.

Promoting a capacity for guilt and remorse is part of development and rather than precipitous apologies, may require processing the complexity of feelings underlying interactions between toddlers. For example, when 34-month-old Sara hit her friend Patti her mother described what had triggered Sarah's hitting, identified her feelings, and suggested feelings of remorse:

"You were very angry when Patti grabbed your puzzle. You hit her so hard, she cried. You got scared. I think you felt sorry that you hit her, you did not want to hurt her."

For some mothers apologizing to their children is a frequent communication. For example, during the middle of a mother-toddler group, as she restrained her daughter, Libby said: "I'm sorry, but you cannot write on the wall." I commented:

"I noticed you apologized to Tess for telling her that she cannot write on the wall and for stopping her."

Libby explained: "I do always apologize; even when there is nothing to apologize for. I don't know why I do it." I said:

"It sounds like you are making up for all the apologies that were not made to you and all the apologies you may think you owe."

In addition to learning about apologizing by instruction, and by observing and imitating her mother, a little girl identifies with her mother's attitudes about apologizing.

Helping Mommy

Children two and three years old are highly motivated to help with everyday activities. The tasks are inherently of interest to them, but the feeling *I am helping Mommy with this important job!* is central to the experience. For example, helping to put toys away at the end of the day and washing toys can be fun. Cooking together can become a favorite mother-daughter activity. For toddlers, eating something that they have helped to cook can be especially delicious. Simple tasks, for example, peeling a hard-boiled egg, or adding several pieces of sliced banana in a special design to a bowl of yogurt or oatmeal can be fun. Helping to cook, in addition to increasing the foods that are liked, can begin to create a family atmosphere of cooperative living.

Values

A set of values is the guiding principle underlying family codes of behavior. Mother-daughter interactions are a primary way to learn values. A mother's honesty, empathy, and respect provide a model with which her daughter can identify. While at times she may break the rules, gradually a little girl acquires the values that underlie the rules that surround her.

Summary: Codes of Behavior

The power of a little girl's attachment to her mother creates the foundation for learning the dos and don'ts of everyday life and assimilating their underlying values. Home can be established as a safe place where all ideas and feelings can be talked about with the family; the challenge is finding acceptable language. The distinction between narrative truth and historical truth helps to recognize and support a little girl's efforts to express her feelings and to be truthful. Apologies that repair ruptured affectionate interactions and lead to reflections about thoughts and feelings that motivate behavior, promote emotion regulation, and learning codes of behavior.

Sense of Self

During this phase of development, a little girl's body, mind, and social sense of self begin to stabilize and consolidate. Her fundamental positive sense of self that is rooted in her relationship with her mother, and includes the accumulation of their many pleasurable intersubjective moments, becomes increasingly apparent. She asserts her likes and dislikes, many of which are bodily and include tactile sensations, tastes, scents, and sounds. Her curiosity to learn intensifies. She has been safe when frightened and comforted when distressed. Loving interactions with her mother have been ruptured by angry outbursts, but the ruptures have been repaired and loving interactions restored. From two to three years old, mother-daughter relationship themes crystallize. Tensions between being the same and being different, attachment needs and autonomy strivings, identifying with and individuating from, and the meeting of minds and the separateness of minds create more mother-daughter angry conflicts. However, at the same time, these themes simultaneously create the unique pleasures and deep satisfactions of mother-daughter relationships. These experiences are all part of a little girl's developing sense of self and a mother's expanding sense of self.

Sense of Self and Reflective Functioning

Sofia was almost three years old and had settled into pre-school after a difficult beginning. She had always enjoyed the activities, but dissolved in tears and clung to her mother when it was time to say goodbye in the classroom. Sofia's mother,

Rhonda, had vivid memories of being put on the school bus kicking and screaming every day for months when she began school. After this trauma, separations
remained difficult for Rhonda throughout her life. She wanted Sofia to have a
different first school experience than she had. Rhonda and Sofia's teacher decided
on a gradual separation process for Sofia – no kicking and screaming. They ar-
ranged three half-hour visits for Sofia to play with her teacher in the classroom.
The teacher placed a chair next to the classroom door for Sofia's mother to watch
them play. At first, Sofia frequently touched base with her mother while she and
her teacher played. This quickly decreased because her mother and her teacher
made it clear that her mother would stay on the "mommy chair" while Sofia and
her teacher were developing a trusting relationship. After the three individual visits, Rhonda brought Sofia three times to play with her teacher for 15 minutes before the other children entered the classroom. Rhonda sat on the special "mommy
chair" throughout the class to watch. When the other children arrived, Sofia remained close to her teacher. She quickly discovered that her teacher could be a
secure base in the classroom: "My teacher is the boss of all the toys." After one
week, the special "mommy chair" was moved out of the classroom into the cor-
ridor. One week later, Sofia and her mother began to kiss goodbye after hanging
Sofia's coat in her cubby when they arrived. Sofia and her teacher had developed
a secure relationship. The reunion routine with her mother at the end of the class
was securely established.

It was the middle of December and her mother and grandmother were taking
Sofia to pre-school together for the first time. They walked through the halls holding hands and approached the classroom. Sofia's teacher greeted them at the door.
Sofia said to her teacher, "This is my Grandma." Hesitating while searching for the
right words she added, "She knows myself." This was Sofia's way of saying, *My
Grandma understands me.* Sofia's statement refers to her awareness of her sense
of self being known by her grandmother and feeling understood. A tear of happiness rolled down her mother's cheek; her grandmother glowed. Sofia's statement,
"She knows myself," suggested that she could think about and reflect on her sense
of self.

Body-Care and Sense of Self

A mother's tender care of her daughter's body contributes to her little girl's positive sense of self. A mother may have things she likes and things she does not
like about her own body and about her daughter's body. A little girl may hear
her mother criticize her own body and talk about diets and surgeries to enhance
it. Adult conversations can have an impact on children even when it looks as if
they are not paying attention. Little girls are examined, weighed, and measured.
In many ways their bodies are evaluated. A main feature of a toddler's body is that
it is growing bigger, stronger, and faster. A little girl's beginning care of her own
body, which might include washing her hands, wiping her nose, and brushing her
teeth, contributes to her developing sense of self and leads to her learning to use
the potty.

Learning to Use the Potty

Although there are books and videos for mothers and for toddlers about learning to use the potty, mother-daughter interactions and their feelings about the process are the main teaching and learning tools. A mother's approach and the parts that she delegates to others may be based on professional opinion, a friend's advice, and her own experiences learning about and taking care of her own body. Learning to use the potty is a developmental achievement that contributes to a little girl's emerging sense of self. The achievement includes her autonomous body control, her recognition that the potty is the socially agreed upon place for poop and pee, her decision to use the potty and become a member of the community of older children and adults who use toilets. Her primary motivation is to please her mother. Learning to use the potty is a collaborative process that includes a mother's support and congratulations and a little girl's autonomy and pride.

Jannette, like many mothers, put her face next to Judi's bottom and inhaled the scent deeply to determine if her daughter Judi's diaper needed to be changed. This routine, intimate body interaction on the surface seemed unnoticed by them both. Though Janette seemed oblivious, her husband thought it was "weird and disgusting." On the other hand, Janette thought it was "disgusting" that Judi picked her nose. Judi was three years old and picked her nose frequently with great enthusiasm. Jannette was doing everything she could think of to get Judi to stop. Jannette was also doing everything she could to teach Judi to use the potty. They played with Judi's dolls on the potty and since Judi pooped every morning after breakfast, Jannette suggested that she sit on the potty and hear a story.

Every morning Judi happily agreed to sit on the potty for several minutes while her mother read to her. At the end of the story, she stood up and announced, "No poop coming." However, shortly after Judi got off the potty and her diaper was back on, she pooped. Janette explained, "Judi says that her poop stinks and she won't do it in the potty." Jannette's disgust with Judi's nose-picking and Judi's disgust with her own poop seemed to be connected. In an effort to understand more, I asked:

> "I wonder what the connection might be between Judi picking her nose, something you think is disgusting, and Judi thinking that her poop stinks and it is disgusting?"

Jannette was intrigued. I offered the following child development information that included an allusion to Jannette's pleasure in smelling Judi's poop in her diaper. I said:

> "Judi may need to know that her poop smells just the way it is supposed to smell. A little girl needs to know that she is giving a wonderful gift to Mommy when she poops in the potty, and that the special gift from her body is pleasurably received."

Jannette smiled, seeming pleased, excited, and a little self-conscious with the idea that Judi's poop would be given to her as a special gift and would be received with pleasure. Maybe this idea resonated, though she was unaware, with her pleasure in smelling Judi's poop when it was in her diaper. I added:

> "While poop is valued in the potty, it is also discarded – casually flushed away. It is applauded, but not touched. Contradictory attitudes about poop are held by mothers and communicated to their daughters in equal measure: poop is not overly valued or disparaged."

The following week Jannette told the mothers' group:

> "I told Judi that her poop smells just right. I dumped some poop from her diaper into the potty so she could see it there. I also told her that it is okay to pick her nose in private. I realized that it was pleasurable to her, and she was asserting her autonomy and control over her body which may be particularly important to her while she's learning to use the potty. She now tells me when she needs to poop, and she poops in the potty. I leave it there a few minutes before I dump it in the toilet and flush it. It seems important to her just to know it's there."

Judi beginning to poop in the potty may have been coincidental to her mother talking about poop smelling "just right," and to giving Judi permission to pick her nose in private, but Jannette thought that she had helped Judi to poop in the potty and to stop picking her nose. For Jannette, it was as though the personal pleasure of smelling Judi's poop in her diaper shifted to the shared pleasure of Judi's poop in the potty.

Maybe Judi's impulse to pick her nose abated as she was able to see her poop in the potty, and though, unspoken, for Judi and Jannette to smell Judi's poop together.

Reactivated Maternal Guilt

For some mothers, harsh punishments they received when they were children continue to reverberate and influence mother-daughter interactions. For example, during a mothers' group discussion about teaching toddlers to use the potty, Ryleigh described that her almost three-year-old daughter, Eloise, who had been wearing panties for a month and never wet herself during the day, was still wetting her "beautiful bed" every night:

> "I'm so angry at her, I yell at her, but it doesn't help. I don't want to yell at her. I feel like punishing her, but I don't want to do that either. I don't know what to do."

Ryleigh then shamefully confessed:

> "I just remembered when I was 11 years old I visited my cousin who lived on a farm. She had a beautiful bed with a pink satin cover and white organza canopy. It was the most beautiful bed that I had ever seen. There was

a gasoline pump on the property that the children were not allowed to touch. I filled a watering can with the gasoline and poured it on my cousin's bed. I ruined it. My mother locked me in a shed alone all night. I was terrified."

I linked Ryleigh's memory of the harsh punishment and her own guilt and terror when she was a little girl, to her current angry yelling at Eloise. I said:

"It seems as though fragments of your memory are being repeated with Eloise. There is no gasoline, no pink satin bed cover, and no shed, but there are sheets wet with urine, anger, fear, and helplessness."

This was the beginning of our exploration of Ryleigh's angry and frightening interactions with Eloise. Ryleigh's harshness in response to wet sheets lessened, she helped Eloise get to the potty in the middle of the night, and in a short while, Eloise slept through the night and her bed stayed dry.

Disapproval and a Positive Sense of Self

We can assume that when a toddler's behavior is disapproved of, feelings of self-worth may be momentarily diminished. We can also assume that mother-daughter attachment – with its ongoing security of safety, loving feelings, and expectations of loving feelings returning after disapproval and angry feelings dissolve – protects toddlers from becoming overwhelmed by disapproval.

During this phase of development, feelings of self-consciousness and embarrassment begin to emerge. These new feelings of self-consciousness and embarrassment indicate that a little girl is beginning to experience herself as seen from the outside in addition to how she feels on the inside. As she begins to sense how others see her, feeling embarrassed is linked to self-disapproval. This developmental step is important to lay a foundation for the development of a conscience – an internal guide of right and wrong. However, feelings of embarrassment also make toddlers vulnerable to being humiliated and becoming overwhelmed with shame and self-criticism. The development of a conscience is important, but harsh disapproval can become harsh self-disapproval. Excessive embarrassment, shame, or guilt can make a child feel that they are damaged or inadequate. Toddlers need to become self-critical of certain behaviors and teaching codes of behavior and skills without humiliating a little girl, requiring helpless submission, or creating excessive self-criticism is sometimes a challenge.

It has been found that boys evaluate their own performance higher than girls evaluate their performance. In addition, boys are likely to answer in class when they are uncertain about whether they are correct, and girls will not answer unless they are sure they are correct. Why this male-female difference occurs and what it means is unclear, but it may be worth thinking about in terms of a mother's early approval and disapproval of her daughter and what it means about her own sense of self. More research in this area is needed.

Dangerous Behavior

During this phase of development children may do or attempt to do dangerous things. Their ability to assess danger is limited. Sometimes, toddlers may do dangerous things to prove to themselves that they will not get hurt. Their motivation to prove they are safe may intensify when they are warned or feel threatened. For example, when Jessie was 27 months old, her mother Valencia explained:

> "Jessie does so many dangerous things. No matter what I say, she won't stop. Yesterday she kept trying to climb onto the bathroom counter and I kept telling her, it's too dangerous; you will break your neck. As I stopped her and she wrestled to get free she said, 'Don't worry Mommy I won't break my neck.' Maybe she was trying to reassure herself."

Hazel, another mother in the group said:

> "Gianna won't hold my hand when we cross the street. She fights to get away. I tell her she could get hit by a car. I think I get so scared that I frighten her to get her to hold my hand, but it seems to have the opposite effect. She struggles to get free. Maybe I should tell her, I'm keeping her safe by holding her hand."

Aubrey added:

> "When I reprimand Mara, she laughs at me. It seems like she is contemptuous of me, but maybe she laughs because I frighten her. I can't believe she is scared of me. I remember being afraid of my mother, but I was older and she was witch-like scary."

It may be difficult for a mother to imagine that her own daughter could be afraid of her. However, it is typical for children to be afraid of their mothers in some moments. Recognizing when she is afraid can be useful.

Along with feelings of security, with experience and new information a child acquires new feelings of vulnerability: *I need my blood. If I start to bleed, will I lose all my blood? If my smooth skin gets a bruise and looks so different, am I still okay? If I get a haircut, am I losing a part of my body I need to be me?* While this self-questioning of safety and vulnerability occurs in both girls and boys, there are male and female risk-taking and accident frequency differences. The ways in which feelings of vulnerability affect each child are useful to understand.

A little girl becomes aware of size and strength differences between men and women. She may first see these differences at home and quickly discover that in general men are bigger and stronger than women. Because these physical differences are reflected in laws, cultural patterns, family attitudes, and roles, it is difficult to know what determines a little girl's feelings about male-female physical differences of size and strength. Female-male differences in body size and muscle mass do not generally occur until puberty. Therefore, little girls are not comparing themselves to little boys as smaller and weaker, but they may react to the different ways girls and boys are treated in terms of their fragility and vulnerability.

A Mother's Expanding Sense of Self

As her daughter's sense of self is developing and a mother is seeing the world through her daughter's eyes, enriched by her own childhood memories, a mother's own sense of self expands and contributes to her goals for her daughter. A group of mothers described their childhood memories that they thought were related to the goals they had for their daughters. The four mother-daughter relationship themes: being the same and being different, attachment needs and autonomy strivings, identifying with and individuating from, pleasing oneself and pleasing others are core elements of their memories and goals. Anni reminisced and highlighted her hurt defiance:

> "When I was 8 years old I told my mother that when I grow up I want to be a plumber like daddy; Father and Daughter Plumbing would be very original and appealing. My mother said, that's not possible; girls can't be plumbers. So I became a urologist and a feminist. I want my daughter to know that she can have whatever career she wants."

Janie recalled:

> "When I was a little girl, there was a picture hanging in my bedroom that my grandmother had embroidered with the nursery rhyme, "Little girls are made of sugar and spice and everything nice." My mother gave it to me when I was pregnant with my daughter, but I stashed it away in the attic. I did not want it in her room. "Everything nice" is not a motto for my daughter to live by."

Lola added:

> "I was always called a tomboy. I'm not sure what that means today, or if the word still exists. Giselle is like I am, but her dad wants her to be more feminine. I think he is sensitive to gender because he just discovered that his sister is gay and while he says he is totally accepting, I think he is having a reaction. I think Giselle is fine. I think the word tomboy is a misnomer. I was doing things I liked to do, I was not acting like a boy. Giselle likes some things that mostly boys like, and some things that mostly girls like."

MaryJo commented:

> "When I was 3 years old, my grandmother asked me what I wanted to be when I grew up. My answer was, 'I want to be a nurse like Aunt Sarah, but Mommy wants me to be a doctor, like she is.' I became a Ph.D. psychologist. I'm a doctor, but not a doctor. I guess it was important to me to not be like my mother. I want my daughter to choose her career independent of me."

Camilla enthusiastically blurted out:

"A few weeks ago I decided that I'm finished being a sex-kitten for my husband. My mother thought that being a sex-kitten was the best way to get a man and to keep a man. Even though the world is still filled with sex-kittens, I don't believe it anymore. I don't want my daughter to be anyone's sex-kitten. I want more for her and more for myself."

As the women shared their memories, the four mother-daughter relationship themes emerged as key elements of their childhood memories and their goals for their daughters, which also became goals for themselves. Being the same and being different, attachment needs and autonomy strivings, identifying with and individuating from, pleasing oneself and pleasing others remain active dynamics in a woman's mind.

Summary: Sense of Self

During this phase of development, mother-daughter relationship themes crystallize and a little girl's body, mind, and social sense of self begin to stabilize and consolidate. "I am a girl" becomes part of her sense of self. Learning to use the potty contributes to her developing sense of self. Her emerging feelings of self-consciousness and embarrassment are part of the foundation for the development of a conscience. Mother-daughter interactions that include their meeting of minds and awareness of their separateness of minds contribute to a little girl's developing positive sense of self. At the same time, a mother's own expanding sense of self unfolds.

Epilogue

Central to my work with mothers, babies, and toddlers, and the books I have written are Selma Fraiberg's often cited paper, "Ghosts in the Nursery" and "Angels in the Nursery" by Alicia Lieberman. My first book, *Parenting and Childhood Memories: A Psychoanalytic Approach to Reverberating Ghosts and Magic* (2021), is about the psychological remnants of childhood experiences that are activated during parents' everyday interactions with their babies and toddlers – also a major theme throughout this book. At the beginning of *Parenting and Childhood Memories* is a quote from the Broadway musical, *The Secret Garden*: "I need a place where I can go, where I can whisper what I know." Mother-baby-toddler groups, private moments, and writing and reading books about early child development and motherhood can provide such a "place" for self-reflection and the discovery of new facets of one's own mind. *Mothers and Daughters: The First Three Years* has been an exciting book to write. I have integrated theories of early child development and motherhood with cultural changes that have empowered women.

I have identified four mother-daughter relationship themes that have an impact on both mothers and daughters, influence their interactions with each other, and continue throughout life: being the same and being different, attachment needs and autonomy strivings, identifying with and individuating from, and pleasing oneself and pleasing others. These themes provide ways to think about the pleasures and everyday stresses in mother-daughter relationships. Moments of intersubjectivity that promote the mother-daughter bond are highlighted. The centrality of emotion regulation, the discovery of the meeting of minds and the separateness of minds, the importance of play, learning codes of behavior, and the development of a sense of self are discussed by age. The mother-daughter relationship themes during the first three years are reactivated during adolescence and the early teen years. The recognition of their re-emergence can be useful.

It is my hope that this book awakens childhood memories and increases awareness about the ways in which a mother's own experiences being a little girl – the personal and the cultural – influence mother-daughter interactions. It is a further goal to recognize the ways in which a mother's interactions with her daughter from birth to three years contribute to a mother's expanding sense of self, and enrich a woman's own life.

References

Ainsworth, M. D. S., Blehard, M., Waters, E. and Wall, S. (1978). *Patterns of Attachment*. Hillsdale, NJ: Erlbaum.

Balsam, R. M. D. (2012). *Women's Bodies in Psychoanalysis*. London and New York: Routledge.

Baradon, T. (2005). *The Practice of Parent-Infant Psychoanalytic Psychotherapy: Claiming the Baby*. London and New York: Routledge Press.

Beebe, B., Cohen, P. and Lachman, F. (2016). *The Mother-Infant Interaction Picture Book*. New York: WW Norton & Company.

Beebe, B., Knoblauch, S., Rustin, J., and Sorter, D. (2020). *Forms of Intersubjectivity in Infant Research and Adult Treatment*. New York: Other Press Professional.

Bergman, A. and Fahey, M. (1999). *Ours, Yours, Mine: Mutuality and the Emergence of the Separate Self*. Northvale, NJ and London: Jason Aronson, Inc.

Bergman, A. and Lefcourt, I. (1999). Self-Other Action Play. In *Ours, Yours, Mine: Mutuality and the Emergence of the Separate Self*. Northvale, NJ and London: Jason Aronson, Inc.

Bowlby, J. (1958). "The Nature of the Child's Tie to His Mother" International Journal of Psychoanalysis, 39:360–73.

Brazelton, T. B. (1982). Joint Regulation of Neonate Parent Behavior. In E. Tronick (Ed.) *Social Interchange in Infancy*. Baltimore, MD: University Park Press.

Chodorow, N. (1978). *The Reproduction of Mothering*. Berkley, CA and Los Angeles, CA: University of California Press.

Coates, S. (1997). "Is It Time to Jettison the Concept of Developmental Lines: Commentary on de Marneffe's Paper 'Bodies and Words'" Gender and Psychoanalysis, 2(1):35–53.

Coates, S. W. (1998). "Having a Mind of One's Own and Holding the Other in Mind: Commentary on Paper by Peter Fonagy and Mary Target" Psychoanalytic Dialogues, 8(1):115–148.

Coates, S. (2016). "Can Babies Remember Trauma? Symbolic Forms of Representation in Traumatized Infants" Journal of the American Psychoanalytic Association, 8:115–148.

Coates, S., Rosenthal, J., and Schechter, D. (Ed.) (2003). *September 11 Trauma and Human Bonds*. London and New York: Routledge.

Crawford, C. (1978). *Mommie Dearest*. New York: William Morrow & Co.

Emde, R. N. (1983). "The Pre-Representational Self and Its Affective Core" The Psychoanalytic Study of the Child, 38:165–192.

Fonagy, P. and Target, M. (1991). "The Capacity for Understanding Mental States: 'The Reflective Self in Parent and Child and Its Significance for the Security of Attachment'" Infant Mental Health Journal, 12:201–218.

Fraiberg, S. (1996). *The Magic Years*. New York, NY: Scribner.

Fraiberg, S., Adelson, E. and Shapiro, V. (1975). "Ghosts in the Nursery: A Psychoanalytic Approach to the Problems of Impaired Infant-Mother Relationships" Journal of American Academy of Child Psychiatry, 14(3):387–421.

Freud, S. (1953). Screen Memories. In J. Strachey (Ed.), *The Standard Edition of the Complete Psychological Works of Sigmund Freud* (Vol. 3, pp. 299–322). Hogarth Press.

Freud, S. (1920). *Beyond the Pleasure Principle*. London and Vienna: The International Psycho-Analytical Press.

Fry, N. (2022). "How Victoria's Secret Created the American Fantasy Woman". New Yorker Magazine.

Gibson, E. and Walk, R. (1960). "The Visual Cliff" Scientific American, 202:67–71.

Gigi (1958 film), Minnelli, V. (Director). (1958). *Gigi* [Film]. Screenplay by Alan Jay Lerner, based on the novella by Colette. Metro-Goldwyn-Mayer (MGM).

Gold, C. (2020). *The Power of Discord*. New York, NY: Little Brown Spark.

James, M. (2018). *The History of Childhood*. Oxford and New York: Oxford University Press.

Klinnert, M. D., Emde, R. N., Butterfield, P., and Campos, J. J. (1986). "Social referencing: The infant's use of emotional signals from a friendly adult with mother present" Developmental Psychology, 22(4):427–432. https://doi.org/10.1037/0012-1649.22.4.427

Lefcourt, I. (2021). *Parenting and Childhood Memories: A Psychoanalytic Approach to Reverberating Ghosts and Magic*. London and New York: Routledge.

Lefcourt, I. (2023). *Mother-Baby-Toddler Group Guide: A Psychodynamic Approach*. London and New York: Routledge.

Lefcourt, I. (2024). *When Mothers Talk: Magical Moments and Everyday Challenges from Birth to Three Years*. London and New York: Routledge.

Lieberman, A. (2018). *The Emotional Life of the Toddler*. New York, NY: Simon and Schuster, Updated edition.

Lieberman, A. F., Padrón, E., Van Horn, P., & Harris, W. W. (2005). *Angels in the nursery: The intergenerational transmission of benevolent parental influences*. Infant Mental Health Journal, 26(6): 504–520. https://doi.org/10.1002/imhj.20071

Lister, E. and Schwartzman, M. (2022). *Giving Hope: Conversations with Children about Illness, Death, and Loss*. New York: Avery Press.

Mahler, M. S., Pine, F., and Bergman, A. (1955). *The Psychological Birth of the Human Infant*. New York: Basic Books.

Main, M., Kaplan, N., and Cassidy, J. (1989). Security in Infancy, Childhood, and Adulthood: A Move to the Level of Representation. In I. Bretherton and E. Waters (Ed.) *Growing Points in Attachment Theory and Research* (pp. 66–106). Monographs of the Society for Research in Child Development, 50.

Mary Poppins. Directed by Robert Stevenson. Book by P. L. Travers. Walt Disney, 1964,

Mommie Dearest (1981 film), Perry, F. (Director). (1981). *Mommie Dearest* [Film]. Produced by Frank Yablans, based on the book *Mommie Dearest* by Christina Crawford. Paramount Pictures.

Olesker, W. (1998) "Female Genital Anxieties: Views from the Nursery and the Couch" Psychoanalytic Quarterly, LXVII:276–294.

Olesker, W. and Olesker, W. (1998). "Conflict and Compromise in Gender Identity Formation: A Longitudinal" The Psychoanalytic Study of the Child, 53:212–232.

Rogers, F. (1968). Song, "What Do You Do with the Mad That You Feel" Small World Records.

Roiphe, H. and Galenson, E. (1981). *Infantile Origins of Sexual Identity*. Madison, CT: International University Press.

Schechter, D. S. (2017). "On Traumatically Skewed Intersubjectivity" Psychoanalytic Inquiry, 37(4):251–264.

Segal, D. and Hartzell, M. (2005). *Parenting from the Inside Out*. New York: Penguin.

Silverstein, S. (1964). *The Giving Tree*. New York, NY: Harper & Row.

Simon, L. (1991). *The Secret Garden*. Musical by Marsha Norman.

Spock, B. (1946). *The Common Sense Book of Baby and Child Care*. New York: Duell, Sloan and Pearce.

Stern, D. N. (1977). *The First Relationship: Mother and Infant*. Cambridge: Harvard University Press.

Stern, D. N. (1995). *The Motherhood Constellation. The Interpersonal World of the Infant*. New York: Basic Books.

Stern, D. N. and Bruschweiler-Stern, N. (1998). *The Birth of a Mother*. New York: Basic Books.

Sulloway, F. J. (1997). *Born to Rebel: Birth Order, Family Dynamics, and Creative Lives*. New York: Vintage.

That Chick Angel, Casa Di, and Steve Terrell (2023). *One Margarita (Margarita Song)* [Single]. Seven14Seven Media/House of EVO Entertainment, under exclusive license to Giant Music. Capital Nashville.

Winnicott, D. W. (1990). *The Maturational Process and The Facilitating Environment*. New Edition. London, UK: Routledge.

Index

For Product Safety Concerns and Information please contact our EU
representative GPSR@taylorandfrancis.com
Taylor & Francis Verlag GmbH, Kaufingerstraße 24, 80331 München, Germany